ARMOURED CRUSADER

The Biography of Major-General Sir Percy 'Hobo' Hobart

ARMOURED CRUSADER

THE BIOGRAPHY OF

MAJOR-GENERAL SIR PERCY 'HOBO' HOBART

KENNETH MACKSEY

GRUB STREET · LONDON

Published by
Grub Street
4 Rainham Close
London SW11 6SS

First published by Hutchinson in hardback in 1967

Copyright this edition © 2004 Grub Street, London
Text copyright © 2004 Kenneth Macksey

British Library Cataloguing in Publication Data
Macksey, Kenneth
    Armoured Crusader: the biography of Major-General
    Sir Percy 'Hobo' Hobart, one of the most influential
    military commanders of the Second World War
    1. Hobart, Percy, 1885-1957 2. Generals – Great Britain –
    Biography 3. World War, 1939-1945 – Tank warfare
    I. Title
    355.3'31'092

ISBN 1 904010 64 4

Cover design by Hugh Adams, AB3 Design

Printed and bound in Great Britain by
Biddles Ltd, King's Lynn

CONTENTS

MAPS

FOREWORD TO THE NEW EDITION

by Kenneth Macksey M.C., R.T.R.

The most welcome republishing by Grub Street of *Armoured Crusader* provides an opportunity to put straight the relationship between Hobo and Field Marshal Lord Carver with Basil Liddell Hart (B.L.H.). For, as is well known, B.L.H. deliberately persuaded some famous German generals to say that they owed their successes to him in order to claim a prescience he did not possess. Moreover B.L.H., as will be shown here, also managed to involve Hobo and Carver in his chicanery.

As I have related on page 332 of this book, in the early 1950s Hobo became passionately involved in helping to produce a two-volume History of the Royal Tank Regiment in conjunction with its author, Basil Liddell Hart. Unhappily the preparation of this ambitious study was hampered by serious disagreements with Liddell Hart. There were repeated rows over content and finance as the years passed by. At the root of the initial troubles stood the basic flaw of attempting a work governed by a Double Aim—in itself a Military Sin. To make matters worse, Liddell Hart's knowledge of the R.T.R. people, its units and the battles it had fought was quite small, and his grasp of technology extremely limited. As time went by, Hobo found himself managing a flawed project and feeling compelled to call upon several busy officers to write lengthy chapters and passages of matters that Liddell Hart could or would not cope with.

Colonel Michael Carver was one who contributed extensively to filling the gaps. Between 1950 and 1957 he and Hobo (his senior by 30 years) carried on a remarkable, erudite correspondence in which they discussed almost every subject under the sun except that of music. Besides matters to do with the History, they discussed an immense range of military matters—policy, strategy, tactics and technology—along with international and national affairs, the Arts and Literature. These letters Carver collected and edited into a book he called 'My dear General . . .' It has not been published and the manuscript, supported by the original letters and other documents, now resides in the Tank Museum Library at Bovington Camp. Within those pages can be read certain letters which not only put the future of the R.T.R. History in peril but also illustrate the diplomatic skills of both Hobo and Carver as they grappled with the prima-donna-ish behaviour of Liddell Hart (B.L.H.). For, in 1953, he threatened to withdraw from the project if Carver would not apologise for a comment he had made in an article about the 'Rommel Papers', a book which B.L.H. had edited.

Carver had commented on various other reviews that had suggested B.L.H. had attempted to prove that some German generals owed their successes by following his teaching. Hobo wrote to Carver on 30 November 1953 to try to get him to make amends, and an enlightening exchange of letters took place as follows:

Bull Lodge, Trebor Avenue,
Farnham, Surrey.

30.11.53.

My dear Mike—herewith I send B.L.H.'s letter to me. If you feel you can do anything to salve his ruffled feelings, it will be helpful and I will be glad. I don't think that you are under any obligation to do so; but I am sure you will be doing a service to the Regt. and you would put me personally under an obligation if you could see your way to putting something in the R.A.C. Journal. I think it would be sufficient , if you merely explained your meaning by quoting the German's own testimonials as quoted in B.L.H.'s penultimate para . . .?

I know you are not prima-donna-ish and will not yourself take serious notice of, or umbrage at the adjective 'graceless' in this letter.

You have given much help to B.L.H. (and to all readers of the R.A.C. Journal and The Tank) by your historical articles on W.W.II. Indeed there is no question that far the best accounts and analyses of the Desert Battles have come from your pen. And you have been most generous in all you've done to help me with the History of the R.T.R.

The delays in the completion of that book have been partly due to the Author's illnesses and dissatisfactions. I am most anxious not to have him upset again, now that we are in sight of the end.

Yours

Patrick Hobart

By the way, I had forgotten I was a Vice President of the R.A.C. Journal. That dates from the antidiluvian era when I was D.M.T. I have never been asked to a meeting or to do any sort of work to it.

2 December 1953.

O & T Division,
S.H.A.P.E.
British Forces Post Office, No.6.

My dear General,
Thank you very much for your letter enclosing B.L.H.'s which I return with this. I had not grasped that his anger was caused because I cast doubts on the fact that the successes of German generals were due to

him. I had imagined that he was annoyed at my suggesting that he did claim it!

I find it very difficult to know what to say, without either saying that I agree with this claim or adding fuel to the fire.

I enclose the draft of a letter I propose to send to the R.A.C. Journal. I doubt if it will help. If you think it will, I will send it. If not, I won't.

The only other thing I can do is to write to him, explain that my intention was to be kind to him, not the reverse, and apologize that it offended him; at the same time making it clear that I could not retract my statement altogether by saying that I accepted his claim wholeheartedly. I will do anything to help which you advise, short of admitting to views which I do not hold.

I enjoyed the dinner immensely and particularly seeing you again in such good form. I am sorry in a way not to go and command again, but glad also not to have to go down in rank again, particularly if, as Nigel Duncan suggested, it may mean the prospect of an armoured brigade again in the not far distant future.

I understood your reference to not going into business better, when David Belchem told me afterwards that he was going out at the end of the year.

Our love to you both, with a specially warm greeting for you from Susanna.

Yours ever,

Mike.

DRAFT

TO: The Editor,
        Royal Armoured Corps Journal.

Sir,

It has been brought to my notice that the final paragraph of my article "Reflections on the Rommel Papers" in the October 1953 number of your journal has given offence to the Editor of the Rommel Papers, Captain Liddell Hart. The offence apparently lies in the implication that I cast doubts on the validity of a claim by Captain Liddell Hart that the German generals owed their successes to following his teaching.

I willingly admit that Generals Guderian, Rommel and Westphal themselves acknowledged their indebtedness to the writings of Captain Liddell Hart. I cannot myself go so far as to say that I consider that they succeeded when they followed his teaching and failed when they did not. The reasons for their successes and failures were far less simple. I do admit that many of the ideas which were propounded and supported by Captain Liddell Hart before the war, were applied and developed with great success in many fields by certain German generals at certain times. I would say that the same is equally true of certain Allied generals at certain times.

My motive in including that final paragraph in my article was to counter criticism of the book on this score; criticism which had already been publicly made in the press and elsewhere. I had no intention of adding to that criticism—far from it—and I apologize to Captain Liddell Hart, if my remarks had the opposite effect to that intended.

I have the honour to be,
            Sir,
                Your obedient servant.

                            R.M.P.C.

December 28th (1953)

O & T Division,
S.H.A.P.E.
British Forces Post Office, No.6.

My dear General,

You will be pleased to hear that I have received a conciliatory reply from B.L.H. to my apologium—not giving an inch, of course, but pleasantly worded, concluding with warm seasonal wishes, even including some compliments,— and the flow of discussion over points connected with the regimental history following in full spate. So I think that we can regard that hatchet as buried. I owe you a debt of gratitude for having dealt with both myself and the incident in so felicitous and tolerant a manner. There are so few people from whom I gladly accept advice or even reproof. You have always been one and always the first among them—because your integrity has never been questioned or questionable.

Have you ever read André Maurois' "Les Nouveaux Discours du Docteur O'Grady"—published in 1950? So entertaining. If you have not, I will try to get them for you. I am now reading Carola Oman's life of Sir John Moore. Hitherto rather dull. The parallel with Paget seems rather apt! Not a patch on the dear old Duke.

I hope you enjoyed Christmas and will have a happy New Year both of you.
Meilleurs Voeux.

Yours ever,

Mike.

PREFACE

This book is about a man who became a legend in his own life-time, a man who had a profound effect on the causes of evolution in his day because he took the lead, with a few others, in shaping a type of force—armoured force—which upset whole continents.

Percy Hobart—or Hobo, as he was better known—did noth-ing personally to dispel the legend in his lifetime. He eschewed memoirs and reminiscence (generals who wrote their memoirs he considered to be committing *hara-kiri*) but fortunately he left behind the very stuff from which biography can be con-structed. Therefore to his wife, Lady Hobart, I am grateful for placing at my disposal a mass of personal documents and for giving me full access to her memories of her husband, bearing in mind her injunction that, as befitted his claim to be a descend-ant of Cromwell, he should be painted 'warts and all'. To Lady Hobart I am hopelessly in debt of gratitude for her penetrating understanding of human nature, the many personal kindnesses she has shown me and her unfaltering, critical encouragement.

Hobo's personal documents range from a number of frank, introspective, personal letters and diaries, from which shines forth the real man, to innumerable thoughtful reports and essays

produced in the course of his studies and everyday work. Hobo
is illuminated by others, first from their own written works and
second from what they have told me by correspondence and in
personal interviews. His name is to be found in the official annals
of every campaign in which he took part from 1908 until 1945,
either in respect of some outstanding deed of gallantry, or because of his dominant part in the direction or deflection of
policy.

Of those who have spoken about him, whether they were
amongst those who loved him or those who did not, I would like
to mention in particular Hobo's closest friends and collaborators
who played prominent parts in his career. To Captain Sir Basil
Liddell Hart for reminiscing, throwing open his incomparable
records to me, and for giving uninhibited advice and comment;
to Major-General Nigel Duncan, Major-General Horace Birks,
Brigadier Alan Brown and Major John Borthwick for supplying
a mass of information culled from their years of close service
with Hobo—to them my special gratitude. And to the R.A.C.
Museum for providing numerous photos.

And my deepest thanks, too, for granting interviews or main-
taining correspondence to Field Marshal the Viscount Mont-
gomery of Alamein, General Lord Ismay, General Sir Charles
Broad, General Sir Frederick Pile, General Sir Richard
O'Connor, General Sir Charles Keightley, General Sir Charles
Loyd, General Sir Alan Jolly, General Sir Michael Carver,
Lieutenant-General Sir Arthur Smith, Lieutenant-General Sir
John Evetts, Lieutenant-General Sir Archibald Nye, Lieutenant-
General Sir Denis O'Connor, Major-General J. F. C. Fuller,
Major-General F. V. B. Witts, Major-General D. Wimberley,
Major-General R. Briggs, Major- General Lord Thurlow, Major-
General E. Dorman O'Gowan, Major-General Sir Cecil Smith,
Major-General G. O. de R. Channer, Major-General Sir Francis
de Guingand, Major-General G. W. Richards, Major-General
F. W. Gordon-Hall, Major-General P. R. C. Hobart, Brigadier
J. A. L. Caunter, Brigadier R. C. Cooney, Brigadier M. R.
Roberts, Brigadier R. P. G. Anderson, Brigadier H. C. J. Yeo,
Brigadier S. Hobart, Brigadier F. A. M. Mathew, Colonel J. Dar-

lington, Major P. Martel, Major G. S. Storrar, Captain H. W. Woodland, Lord Longford, Sir Miles Thomas, Dame Irene Ward, R. P. Keigwin, Esq, E. Carmen, Esq, John Connell, Esq, and Miss Nancy Wavell.

To the following authors (or their heirs) and publishers who have given me permission to publish extracts from works in their copyright:

Major-General G. Martel: *An Outspoken Soldier* (Sifton Praed)

Field Marshal Lord Wilson: *Eight Years Overseas* (Hutchinson)

Captain Sir Basil Liddell Hart: *Memoirs*, Vol. I & II (Cassell)

Sir Winston Churchill: *The Second World War* (Cassell)

John Connell: *Auchinleck* (Cassell)

J. P. D. Stirling: *The First and the Last* (Art & Education)

Major-General Sir Francis de Guingand: *Operation Victory* (Hodder & Stoughton)

and to the Controller of Her Majesty's Stationery Office in respect of Sir Winston Churchill's official letters and minutes.

There is a detailed Bibliography and list of references at the end of the book.

Finally to Mrs. Margaret Dunn for typing the draft over and again and my wife for constant encouragement, for drawing the maps and reading proofs.

K.J.M.

Part 1

RESEARCH

Build we straight, O worthy Master!
Staunch and strong, a good vessel,
That shall laugh at all disaster,
And with wave and whirlwind wrestle!

H. W. Longfellow in
'The Building of a Ship'

I

RATHER A BOLD AIR

Grammont, writing about Mary Hobart, one of the maids of honour to Charles II's Queen, referred to her as of

> . . . a good shape, rather a bold air, and a great deal of wit which was well cultivated without having much discretion. She was likewise possessed of a great deal of vivacity, with an irregular fancy. There was a great deal of fire in her eyes, which, however, produced no effect upon the beholders; and she had a tender heart, whose sensibility some pretended was alone in favour of the fair sex.

Setting aside the difference in their sexes, that is a description which might well have fitted Percy Cleghorn Stanley Hobart. But, in fact, it is by no means certain that the subject of this book was a direct descendant of Mary Hobart, although she, the second wife of Sir John Hobart, was indubitably the daughter of the great Parliamentarian John Hampden and, thereby, the niece of Oliver Cromwell. And the indistinct connection acted, for the best part of his life, as an inspiration to Percy. Yet one more thing Mary and Percy shared beyond doubt—the experience of living in testing days, pitting their wits against elements brought to high pressure by the collision of new and old ideas. In that kind of environment wit, with or without discretion, was as often as not the key to survival in the literal or moral sense—moreover it could itself generate fresh disturbances to ruffle the composure of the traditionalists.

The Hobarts of Blickling, Mary's family by marriage, were well endowed with fortune and ambition. Percy's branch of the family had a limited supply of the former and boundless quantities of the latter. He also held fast to ideals upon whose altar he sacrificed ambition. There we find the overriding theme of his life—a ceaseless, critical search for progress, regardless of opposition, and the creation of a feeling of discomfort in the minds of those in opposition to him.

The pages of history are adorned in plenty by the names of those whose convictions have sprung from a deep understanding of matters beyond the vision of their contemporaries, and who have willingly fought the entrenched hosts of vested interests in order that their convictions might prevail. Idealists, patriots, visionaries—often martyrs—they pass before our eyes in an array of revolutionaries who motivated evolution. Men who believed themselves right, Socrates, Copernicus, Luther, Penn, Moore, Churchill and many others who endured death or considerable risk in order to voice their concern and say, unashamedly, 'I told you so!'

Percy Hobart—'Patrick' as his family called him—was a man of this kind, a soldier, educated from 1914 to 1918 in the worst-generalled and bloodiest war of all time, who, with a few others, foresaw the inevitability of yet more wars to come, believed he understood the most economical way in which they could be fought, watched a potential foe preparing the same methods, and battled tooth and nail to make the British Army adopt the new, machine warfare which dominated the Second World War.

Hardly one of the truly professional generals (or politicians) who conducted operations in the Second World War failed to become care-worn by the need to avoid the same sort of deadlock which had seized the battlefields in the First World War when, the impotent pawns in a conflict of science and material, they fell under the command of men whose military education had been fundamentally unscientific—some might say amateurish. Of course, the same was true of themselves. As was said of Hobart's prep school, Temple Grove, '. . . and science was not only never taught but not even mentioned'—but those who pondered and cared, and who survived the trenches, acquired a mass of practical, technical experience which could never be erased from their consciences. By the end of 1918 it was possible to discern a new pattern of war, dominated still by massed artillery, but moving more freely and faster at the speed of armoured, mechanical vehicles which drew extra strength from aircraft flying above and ahead of them. To the realist the day of horse warfare was fading, while, at the same time, the nostalgic romanticist sensed the urge to defend a dying era: to the taxpayer and politician there appeared the spectre of vast expense and industrial outlay to raise a new kind of mechanical force: to the armoured-vehicle enthusiast (at that time labelled tank men or maniacs) their unreliable machines offered prospects of an economy of a new sort, above all in lives.

Patrick Hobart was one of the latter—in due course a prime force amongst them, the most enthusiastic, the least compromising and one with the most influence, good and bad, over friend and foe, colleague or rival. Yet he never once fought within sight of tanks during the First World War and probably never actually saw one until it was over. A Sapper himself, he learnt his trade in India, fought in the trenches in 1915 and then spent the rest of this war on the staff of infantry formations.

The reputation of the staff fell to its lowest ebb in that war of fixed positions, as their red hat-bands and tabs became associated with a close affiliation with comfortable châteaux, deep in the safe back areas and objects of rare curiosity in the front line. To this popular conception, as to most generalisations, there were many distinguished exceptions, and Hobart, as staff captain in an infantry division in France or brigade major in Mesopotamia or Palestine, lived more in the thick of the fighting, with the leading troops, than many of the fighting men themselves. Indeed, his greatest exploits took place ahead of the leading soldiers and often above them, since, to see all the better what was going on, he took to flying regularly as an observer in rickety, string-bag air-craft, some of which were hard put to it even to get airborne. Thus, at the outset, he exploited the new mechanical devices which promised most to help ameliorate the soldier's chances and, thereby, caused many a personal adventure. And throughout he drew heavily upon an instinctive sense of the value of mobility in war and the vital importance of quick thinking as the basis of his philosophy.

Those campaigns Hobart took part in contrasted widely —at one moment the worst ever executed and even more poorly administered by unimaginative generals in conditions of appall-ing squalor and defeat—the next, textbook examples of sound judgement and meticulous, thoughtful preparation. Illuminated by startling comparison, Hobart grasped principles which were to guide him for the rest of his career, and with them an angry resentment of those he took for fools that he could never con-sistently withhold.

So it came about that Hobart felt bound to leave the Sappers after the war and join that part of the Army which seemed to him to contain the elements of the future of war—the newly created Tank Corps. From that moment his is a story of battle with the entrenched, vested interests of the Army, the disinclina-tion of his countrymen to stir in aid of their own security and a struggle within himself to overcome an exuberant impatience which denied him the leisure of a slow resolution of any prob-lem. In most events this man, who shielded his innermost thoughts from view, found it hard to refrain from outright argu-ment—in public if necessary.

In a minor key he will be observed making a hot impression on a Tank Corps which, for all its potentialities and the brill-iance of a few of its leaders, was no better endowed at that time with forward-looking, forceful men than the rest of the Army. And he will be observed bursting into the lead until he thrusts on, almost alone, when so many of the most enthusiastic protag-onists of mechanisation were officially diverted from their goal; until the time comes when he is isolated, smeared and cast out. Rich in irony, this was the prelude to reinstatement of a peculiar kind only after all his warnings had been amply justified by the German armoured subjugation of Poland and the best part of Western Europe.

It may be thought that Hobart's career was one of failure and tragedy—yet it is no such thing, since this man only rarely bent under the weight of his cares and then bowed only to straighten to yet vaster effort in getting his way. Happily, he nearly always achieved what he sought and, because he did, there may be many who read of him now only because he saw to it that machines were wrought, often against opposition, in time to land armies back in Europe in 1944 at a tithe of the price that might so easily have been paid. It may be asked why he is not better known to the public. To which reply can be made that the very violence of his advocacy taught those who dealt with him to mute their comments.

This is the story of a man who made the footnotes in the History of the Tank, eschewing the headlines as he did so—for he was an idealist who was ambitious for the idea before personal ambition. So, here is a tale of courage mixed with the essential naivety of people who do not recognise the unconquerable.

*   *   *   *   *

Robert Hobart was typical of a vigorous line. Fifth son of a large family, a member of the Indian Civil Service and acting as Inspector General of Police in the United Provinces, he conducted, at the age of forty-two, a runaway marriage with Janetta Stanley from Dungannon in County Tyrone, a small, vital person with a hooky nose and laughing eyes, who mixed a strict sense of duty with impulsive gushes of affection and fun, personality and courage. A 'black' Calvinist who habitually consulted the Bible in search of precedents for her decisions, it was she who took sole charge of the family management when, after the birth in 1881 of a first son, Charles, there followed at regular intervals two more sons, of whom the last was Patrick. In fact, it was the birth in 1885 of Patrick which convinced Robert Hobart that he must quit India to enable the boys to be educated in England. So they moved to a temporary base in Hampshire, where their first daughter, Elizabeth (Betty), was born: an important event to Patrick because she became his closest friend in the family, the one to whom he turned to pour out his deepest, innermost thoughts until the day she died.

To her the full-blooded vigour of their childhood evoked nothing but happy memories, as they lavished their talents in discussion and argument, attacking every subject that took their fancy with torrents of words and expostulation. In this environment Patrick found himself in competition from the start with forces that demanded every ounce of ingenuity, and so he strengthened his will in acquiring a tough formula in his relationship with others. Anybody whose intellect, ability or personality was the equal or superior to Patrick's, he welcomed with enduring affection, though never to the extent of subservience, and into this category entered his brother Charles, a boy of brilliant achievements, and, above all, his father, a man whose breadth of knowledge and gentle wisdom drew Patrick close for ever.

Yet in a letter to Betty many years later he wrote:

I had such a jolly dream . . . You were so cheery and I was making you laugh till you were quite helpless—you know the way you get . . . Queer thing was that the old pater was there too, in some ways, and was rotting me playfully because I refused to go to church. We were our present selves, you and I, not children and the pater at his best. Of course you know I don't agree one little bit with your theory that we had a happy childhood. *I* didn't. I wouldn't go through it again.

At the age of ten he went to Temple Grove School, one of the oldest preparatory schools in England. The games field did not repel him, but he was not a great performer there, so for one eager to read and learn the triumphs came from the classroom, to be acclaimed in 1899 by the award of a classical scholarship to Clifton, and as Charles prepared to enter the Indian Civil Service, Patrick kept close on his heels, eager to prove his own worth. But Patrick had no desire to follow Charles or his father into the Civil Service. Instinctively, it seems, he wanted to be a soldier—a choice which met with full parental approval, for however stiict she appeared, his mother entertained no desire to direct his future, although she made it clear she thought it her duty to guide him in respect of marriage, even though her views rarely coincided with Patrick's.

He became a member of the Clifton College Cadet Corps immediately, and stood in their ranks in his first term while they were inspected by Queen Victoria, the old lady driving slowly down the line of boys in a victoria, bowing gravely to them at intervals. And because games seemed to assume a place of importance in the military curriculum Patrick applied himself to them with intensity, but missed the highest honour, a place in the 1st Rugby XV. In the Cadet Corps he found himself drawn to the most highly technical activities as a leading member of the engineer squad, and in 1902, ahead of his contemporaries, passed into the Royal Military Academy at Woolwich—the 'Shop'.

This was a watershed, as many years later he tells us:

I enjoyed the Shop more than school: much more than Chatham. One was amongst chaps of ones own age, mostly busting with enthusiasm; fit, keen, and on manhood's threshold—discussing every sort of subject, falling in and out of love, unbounded mental and physical energy, some new knowledge or experience every day: windows thrown open on new views and vistas of life every day. I remember Bill Balfour giving me his Uncle's 'In defence of philosophic doubt'. I remember my bitter disappointment at just failing to get my Rugger cap: and being appointed Captain of 2nd XV. The absurd yet exhilarating grind of the riding-school. Endless evening spreads of cocoa and cakes and talk in one's room. The infinite desirability of the young women who came to the Shop dances. The long days out on survey with plane-tables in the sunshine. Somehow it always seems to have been sunny then: I don't remember rainy or dull days!

Adept at setting his thoughts on paper, quick to assimilate the contents of books, his true bent appeared in an ability to grasp practical, mechanical matters at sight, his mind acquiring the habit of short cuts to the solution of a problem, enabling his thoughts to race ahead of slower minds to reveal undreamt possibilities.

Everything that attracted his interest he liked to reduce into writing, a process designed to fix a mass of facts in a capacious and highly retentive memory upon which he could draw in detail at a moment's notice. His brain developed the power of a high-speed computer, self-taught to programme, control and question —capable of finding new solutions by rapid and, at times, unconventional channels—pushing him far apart from slower minds, and inculcating perhaps a dangerous over-confidence.

He enjoyed everything, learnt a lot and made a host of life-long friends, and while the highest honours in sport continued to pass him by, he excelled as a shot with a distinguished pass out of the School of Musketry at Hythe, and his final report out of Chatham showed that his career pointed straight in the direction of a distinguished future. Graded not less than very good or above average in any subject, it was noted that he was fond of society, zealous, smart and punctual, with the commandant of the School of Military Engineering pleased to add: 'As good a type of young officer as one could wish to have in the Corps. I cannot speak too highly of him.'

*   *   *   *   *

In the autumn of 1906, at the age of twenty-one, Patrick Hobart set sail for an India that had slipped into the Kipling dream of Empire. The intimate, mutual understanding between the British and Indians was in the process of being replaced by a tendency amongst many of the former to treat the latter as an inferior species. The two races were drifting apart under the influence of those more concerned with protecting the British position instead of improving that of the Indians.

Yet, in the Indian Army, the relationship between the British officers and non-commissioned officers and their Indian counter-parts remained close and was tried and tested, at irregular but frequent intervals, in skirmishes across the frontier. Few distractions or pursuits were permitted beyond the orbit of the Service. The officers, when not training with their men, were expected to occupy their time with activities that contributed to a Spartan militarism. Sports on horseback or with a gun in hand took precedence over others, and if leave was spent travelling and hunting in the more inaccessible quarters of the vast sub-continent where danger intervened, so much the better.

This was the life Patrick Hobart longed to lead as soon as he arrived in India, but an attack of diphtheria, within a few weeks of landing, added to the frustration of work in the Nilgiris on a power project. He found the work 'amusing enough' and the attack of diphtheria tickled him because it remained undisclosed until the worst was over, but his thoughts roved elsewhere until, by unhappy fortune, he was posted north to replace an officer who had been drowned fishing in the Ganges.

His train drew into Roorkee on Christmas Eve, 1906, and he joined the 1st Bengal Sappers and Miners. As he wrote:

They were very much a Corps d'élite as the C in C India had re-cently called them. Picked from a long waiting list—one had to resign if one got engaged to be married . . . of the establishment of 18 officers, nine became Generals, three Brigadiers and four were killed.
We all played polo: we all pigsticked: we all shot big game both in the Plains and in the Himalayas . . . We got our whisky out in casks and it was the subalterns duty to bottle it—the fumes made one quite intoxicated.

Responsibility was given to young officers at once, since it was intended to mop up their surplus energy by application to military virtues alone. Within six months Hobart found him-self despatched, with two companies, two hundred miles into the Himalayas to cut a specified number of deodar trees, each of a size anything up to twelve inches in diameter and fifty feet in length. He learnt fast and well in this hard school, mixing delight at the quality of his posting with a long-standing sense of his own inadequacy. His first company commander, a Kentish squire named Tylden Patterson, by his excellence assumed for Patrick the ultimate essential authority. He was:

. . . a magnificent shot and great fisherman, and a first class field engineer, but quite ready to leave the men to me—which I loved. He was a hard man, and very good for me. I never had a word of praise from him for three years. He told me then—after I had been alone with the Company in Peshawar for eight months whilst he was in UK on leave, and the Company in that time had built most of its own lines, won an Open Rifle-shooting competition and been publicly commended by the GOC for the smartest guard in the Division—that it wasn't too bad : but he was sorry he had felt bound in conscience to enter an adverse remark on my annual Confidential Report : 'This officer is addicted to the reading of poetry.'

In 1907 he took the first of the annual leaves and in the Tehri Garhwal Hills, while hunting, put his foot amongst a nest of wild black bees, whose venom and persistence in rage have not infrequently killed those who have disturbed them. But by good fortune there was a stream at the bottom of a slope, and Hobart, throwing himself into the torrent below, escaped the wrath of the bees—the first of many narrow escapes in a lifetime—many on expeditions such as that, most at war.

*   *   *   *   *

The Afridis from the Bazar Valley had started raiding in 1907 and caused enough damage to warrant a punitive expedition being sent against them in February of 1908 from Peshawar, but it had scarcely returned after three weeks away when trouble broke out afresh amongst the Mohmands, aided and abetted by Afghans. The country grew exceedingly wild, rugged and desolate, the hills practically waterless at that time of the year, causing the inhabitants to depend on artificial tanks to contain a water supply. Even the beds of the valleys ran dry, so the maintenance of a punitive force in these regions relied to no little extent on the efforts of the Sappers and Miners to open up routes, to find and pump water, and blow up enemy buildings.

After permission was received to cross the Mohmand border, two brigades thrust deep into the dissidents' territory without meeting a strongly held defensive position at any point, for the tribesmen on the North West Frontier, equipped with only rudimentary firearms, could only hang on the flanks of a powerful, disciplined force, inflicting as many casualties as possible by raids against exposed posts and, from the heights, a desultory fire against the columns forging slowly ahead below.

At night, in the valley camps of the main column, lights could not be shown, while further back along the routes leading to the frontier toiled a third brigade, to which Hobart's section of sappers were attached, repairing the rugged valley road amid incessant nightly disturbances from sniping which for a week made it impossible to light cooking fires.

But being denied the glory of man-to-man combat did not prevent Hobart studying frontier warfare objectively and receiving his baptism of fire. He recognised the slowness and wastefulness of the mandatory picqueting of heights, and deprecated the use of soldiers as a kind of police force, although at this stage his objections were only mistily conceived. He learnt first-hand how essential are the processes of good supply and administrative arrangements in undeveloped territories. Not least, he was able to study the pyschological effects of hostile small-arms fire on his own courage and that of other men—to learn how the crack of bullets and the fear of death can inject a speedy reaction in some, throw a cautious cloak of care over others and leave none totally unmoved by the experience.

Now he stepped up the rungs of the 1st Sappers and Miners at the prescribed rate, thoroughly content that it should be so, with time to study a widening range of subjects, reaching from the history of his own country and India through an appreciation of philosophy, religion, art and poetry. He revelled in intense inquiry, finding loosest rein for imaginative descriptions. While stalking alone in the Salt Range of North Punjab he wrote in his diary:

This Nala . . . has a certain fascination of its own. The sides are very steep—no rock: hard earth that crumbles into little round balls—impassable mostly; and the bottom is filled with a tangled criss-cross of weird pink and white peaks and ridges, tortured and writhen into a fantastic, impossible, meaningless jungle. It's rather reminiscent of Watts, 'Chaos' . . . one felt that the only appropriate denizen would be the Dragon of one's nursery—the scaly crawling monster whose breath had destroyed every trace of vegetation . . . And indeed to this day men pick up hereabouts great fossilised

A.C.—C

teeth the size of my fist, which they tell one are veritable dragons molars—the sort of thing he used to whet on the fascinating golden-locked morsel of delicate female humanity. . . . What stupid old dunderheads those dragons were to be sure, with their opportunities.

Devastating as a conversationalist, he inclined to dominate, and never more so than when in the company of his brother Charles. A brother officer remembers dining with the pair and 'not being able to get a word in edgeways' himself, but perhaps it was not entirely unkindly meant that at this time Charles, in the Indian Civil Service, was known as 'The Civil' and his brother Patrick 'The Uncivil'. Yet there was in Patrick a rough exterior and manner that required polish, though he deliberately cultivated strictly non-military activities to counterbalance his professional duties, and in so doing widened his horizons and flung open his mind to new thoughts and ideas. Enthusiastic as he was concerning his profession, he instinctively shied from becoming a narrow-minded warrior.

Sometimes there were other digressions, as for instance when one night six members of the 21st Indian Cavalry Regiment drove into Nowshera in their four-in-hand to dine in the gunners' mess where Hobart happened to be living at that moment, and after dinner they all decided to go to the railway station to see if any friends were passing through on the Peshawar express. It was a wild party! The two four-in-hands that set out were driven at full gallop, the Jehus blowing their coach horns as they approached the station. To quote Lieutenant Hastings Ismay,[1] one of those present :

The station staff thought all the devils were after them and abandoned the station altogether. Some idiot got into the booking office and started issuing first class tickets to all the Indians on the platform, and when the express came in, some other idiot, marched up and down shouting, 'all change'. In the end we had to induce the station staff to come back again and get the train on its journey, but the delay had been a full half hour and heaven alone knows how many first class tickets were missing.

1. Later General Lord Ismay—head of the Military Wing of Winston Churchill's War Cabinet.

Returning to England on leave in 1910 in a leisurely journey via Venice, Padua, Lugano and Paris, Hobart allowed a spate of thoughts pent up after three years in India to roll forth from his notes. On Venice:

St. Marks. Two Hours. [In matters concerning art and architecture he never permitted himself to be unduly rushed.] Stands alone: colour galore—the mosaics the last word in permanent decoration of colour. But no feeling of solemnity . . . Some of the lamps most beautiful, but, for me, the floor: exquisite little panels of perfectly blended marble and the great marble slabs of the walls. Absolutely unornamented, save for its own glorious veining. K grieved by my inability to refrain from criticism! It seems to me that the difference between this and our great gaunt Northern Gothic is the difference between the most beautiful flower-filled valley in the world, and the gaunt grey crag and snowfield of the hills.

Yet all he wanted, once finished with the rounds in England, was to be back with his beloved sappers and miners, and found his reward in frustration by a call to public service and an introduction to ceremonial in a unique manner. The newly crowned King, George V, had mounted the throne of England with the earnest desire that he should be crowned a second time before his Indian subjects at a Great Durbar. Protesting volubly, Hobart left for Delhi in February 1910 to carry out a complete re-survey prior to designing the layout for the whole camp—a formidable project, from which followed his translation to the appointment of staff captain on the Durbar military staff.

From here he could watch the evolution of a great project and detect the devious influences working in the background. The Durbar Committee fretted. As each ripple of consternation spread outwards, the staff captain and minor deities such as he were put to it to amend and reconstruct. And the staff captain more than most was inclined to resent what appeared to him to be panic, counter-orders, and for the first time in the Service found himself at loggerheads with authority.

The organisation to deal with fire was his most elaborate creation, founded on watch-towers erected to enable guards to detect the location of an outbreak in the maze of tents no sooner had it started. Fire picquets were practised repeatedly, and no less than five times before the royal party arrived came into action in earnest. Moreover, when it became known that Queen Mary entertained a particular horror of fire it evoked an authority for Hobart to enter the Queen's apartment in the event of fire, seize her bodily and carry her off to safety.

Never again was there to be a spectacle such as the Durbar to colour the Indian scene, the mass of richly dressed dignitaries passing in a brilliant cavalcade through the ranks of sailors and soldiers in a seemingly endless series of reviews, pageants and tournaments. But when the time came for the King to pay thanks to those who had welcomed him by presenting awards at an investiture, and over three thousand high-ranking personages packed the reception tent, there came, half-way through the proceedings, a smell of burning and from outside the sound of the fire alarm. The Queen sat motionless. The King continued, unconcernedly, dropping orders over heads and pinning stars to breasts. Outside a tent blazed in the still night.

Right on hand stood Hobart, directing the fire-fighters to the outbreak, positioning other men round the reception tent ready to cut down the sides if the flames spread, and girding himself for his supreme act in aid of the Queen. The organisation came to life with gratifying smoothness, complete success crowning the many rehearsals that had gone before, and his own reward came next morning: a call to the King and the presentation of a gold tie-pin in gratitude. But best of all to Hobart was the stern bearing and rebuke from Queen Mary, 'Young man, we might all have been killed!'—a moment he cherished for ever.

*   *   *   *   *

At this time Hobart is revealed as being increasingly introspective, measuring his failings and mourning the depressions which sometimes overcame him. Hunting in 1913 and left on his own for a while:

. . . the blackness of the Pit descended on my soul. God knows why. I've never felt so bad before: without hope: the horror of utter darkness upon me—looking longingly at the water slopping over into the pot . . .

Depressions such as these plagued him and cannot be associated with the normal ups and downs of success or failure. He inclined to the maudlin, favouring the philosophic arguments of Kant (one of the few pessimistic philosophers) and Schopenhaur. From this thoroughly practical person of fathomless energies could emerge enormous swings in emotion, completely in tune with his Irish ancestry. While pig-sticking one day on Sikandar, 'the best pony I ever had', and at full gallop, a hoof entered a hole and the pony did a Catherine-wheel, rolling over her rider's legs and belly. By a miracle Hobart was thrown clear only blown and bruised, but Sikandar lay done, with a broken leg. He wrote:

Poor old devil in awful pain, but so quiet, gentle and plucky. When the vet came in response to a wire he said, 'Hopeless'. I asked him to shoot . . . May we meet again in Valhalla. Gallant, glorious beast.

And he could be caustic. A small collection of caricatures of friends and acquaintances in Roorkee, accompanied by short verses lampooning their frailties (including his own), might well have given pain to those who did not appreciate his wit. They also highlight a vanity close-linked with his overriding self-confidence. Of enormous significance, in the light of their subsequent association, appears the remark: 'Winston Churchill, spiritual kinship with Hobart.'
Writing to Betty in 1916 he recalled:

I've always been afraid right down inside. Afraid of being a coward. I had to do a long course of forcing myself to take shooting risks in India: all those bad climbing places in the Hills where a slip means 2,000 feet to the first bump: and ones stomach was in ones mouth all the time. It is to my Regiment—to the 1st Sappers and Miners—that I owe the inspiration and training that gave me a control on myself, a grip on my feelings.

But a photograph taken in 1914, compared with one from 1907, graphically illustrates the changes that had been wrought. Whereas in 1907 there is shown the slightly puzzled, shy, image of the newly joined subaltern sitting cross-legged at the feet of his seniors, now, seven years later, glowers an image of set jaw, piercing eyes looking straight into the lens of the camera from beneath the topee. In a minor key the shyness remains, but the total effect is gaunt, powerful and dominating. Not an ounce of spare flesh appears—just the impression of a controlled spring waiting to be released upon some task as yet undefined.

2

SHOCK

A full-scale war was being fought in France and Belgium and an Indian Expeditionary Force fitted out to fight there. But it looked as if that force would not arrive until late in the autumn of 1914 and by then Hobart (on leave in England), was persuaded, together with many others, the war would be over and the fleeting chance of glory lost. When told in August to return at once to India the black depression descended upon him, to be followed, as so often, by a raging, ruthless determination to have the order countermanded.

Nothing could alter the mind of the authorities. As far as they were concerned the adjutant of the 1st Sappers and Miners had to play his part training them for war and could only do it in India. At every port on the way back Hobart went ashore to badger the staff, always in the hope that a telegram would be there telling him to return to England. And once he had arrived at Bombay, instead of reporting back directly to Roorkee, he rushed to Simla to harry Army Headquarters to let him go at once to Karachi to join his old company which, as part of the Indian Corps, was about to embark for France—all to no avail.

The Indian Corps joined the European battle at the end of a

war of movement just in time to enter into a state of semi-siege. After the Germans' initial plunge through Belgium into France had been followed by the outflanking race to the Channel coast, the series of offensives broke irrevocably on the newly cut trenches in Artois and Flanders. The reversion to trench warfare had been quick but perceptible to the men who witnessed the creeping paralysis brought about by the unchallenged growth of firepower: the transition for them had been by stages and not an outright shock. But to the Indians, with experience only of the gentle drizzle of tribesmen's rifle-fire from the Frontier peaks, sudden immersion in the downpour of metal that imprisoned them from the start in sodden holes in the ground was shattering because there was no transitional period.

On the 5th November, as Britain and France declared war on Turkey after a series of hostile Turkish acts against the Russians, a brigade of Indian troops went ashore near Basra, starting the greatest side-show of all—the Mesopotamian campaign. Concurrently the war spread to the waste lands between the Suez Canal, Arabia and Palestine as the Turks tried to cut the Suez Canal, the vital link between Europe and the East. So, while the Indian Army lay in the filth of the trenches in France, the territories most vital to India came to the boil. And not long afterwards a Finance Member of the Viceroy's Council proposed cuts in military expenditure of half a million pounds.

When in November there came the news that Hobart was to accompany the first draft of reinforcements from India to France, his relief was enormous. On New Year's Day, with forty-four other members of the Sappers and Miners, he landed at Marseilles to receive, a week later, the longed-for order to go to the front. 'Glorious,' he wrote. 'Go on the 9th'—and promptly collapsed with a fever. It was so typical of his experience of life. Repeatedly, by ill fortune, he fell just short of the goal as it opened before him, driving him to place further demands on his enormous energy to help himself across the last few yards to his objective. His failure to reach the zenith at school, the hesitant path to the 1st Sappers and Miners via the Nilgiri Hills in 1906, the task at Delhi in 1911 instead of remaining with the sappers, all were to him typical of the barriers erected in his path by

Fate. It is intriguing to speculate that these interventions were part and parcel of a strange providence that shaped his resistance to frustration. Because he so frequently overcame obstruction by redoubled efforts he began to believe that nothing could defeat him. Empirically he became indefatigable.

Convalescence amongst fellow sufferers at a home run by aristocratic British ladies at Nice he bore with patient enjoyment, revelling in picnics and the pleasure of feminine company, on condition that they stimulated his intellect by being themselves intelligent and brimful of character. He rejoiced in the company of mature women, who, in return, rarely declined his immense charms. Moreover, there was awakening in him a feeling, provoked possibly by the marriage of his sister Betty in 1912, that he should find a wife, but he was held back chiefly by the celibate creed of his regiment and the responsibility of war, although not by a shortage of candidates for the job.

On the 24th February he was pronounced fit and 'got leave to go forward tomorrow after some juggrah with stonewall stupidity of the staff'. The rumble of the guns was in his ears on 2nd March 1915, and for the next three and a half years rarely absent from them, blotting out nearly every thought other than those of war.

Arriving to join the Indian Corps in the front line, close to Neuve Chapelle, Hobart was in time to take part in the final preparations for a British attack to capture Aubers Ridge. In those days, early in 1915, there was a disinclination on the part of the French and the Germans to credit the British Army with the ability to conduct successful offensive operations on its own. The British record in defence had been impressive, but in attack quite the reverse, a notion Sir John French, the British Commander-in-Chief, was determined to dispel. Chiefly for this reason he ordered General Sir Douglas Haig, Commander of the 1st British Army, to proceed with the plans to break the German lines at Neuve Chapelle on the 10th and then advance to occupy Aubers Ridge. It had to be done quickly, for, although the weight of artillery available was the greatest ever assembled by a British Army, its supply of ammunition was barely sufficient to sustain three or four days' intense fighting. Thus Hobart's battle

inoculation on the Western Front occurred in connection with
a prestige plan with no strategic aim—for a French offensive, to
which the British attack acted as support, had already been can-
celled.

The trenches at Neuve Chapelle lay wet, and in many places
flooded, in the valley of the Layes Brook, making it necessary
to raise breastworks on both sides of the line above ground level.
The British concentrated fifteen battalions here for the attack
against only one and a half German battalions in the line opposite
them, a situation due largely to the secrecy of the British preparations, but enhanced by the disbelief of the Germans that the
British were fit for offensive operations.

It was Hobart's good fortune, in his first major action, to
witness the first planned British offensive aimed at breaching
a consolidated trench line, and to see the initiation of a whole
series of embryonic ideas that in a year's time were to become
commonplace. The early stages of meticulous planning, preparation of stores, jumping-off places, deception and the organisation
of the artillery fire support went on all round him.

In the artillery plan for the Neuve Chapelle battle was to be
found the key to surprise, but the least resemblance to techniques
of the next two and a half years. To destroy the barbed-wire
entanglements guarding the enemy entrenchments, as well as
the trenches themselves, the shooting was to be of short duration and immediately prior to the attack. Not only would surprise be achieved by this method, but, a most compelling reason,
ammunition would be saved as well. Nevertheless, to achieve
the maximum effect, the most careful registration of each gun
on to its target was required without arousing the suspicions
of the enemy that it was going on. The lesson was never lost
on Hobart. Gropingly, but soon with a crisp clarity, he came
to value surprise always above what he called 'porridge-making'
by artillery.

The day before the attack, Hobart worked with his sappers
in and around an exposed strong point called 'Port Arthur' where
his inherent inquisitiveness at once led to an adventure. Writing
in his diary on the 5th March:

Got hold of Holt and one Scout and over parapet into old muddy, deep trench. Along for 30 yards. Left Holt and crawled out with Scout southwards. After 50 yards found ourselves close to chevaux de frise. Scouts, 'We are forestalled', and were fired on by two sentries less than 15 yards. Saw their heads against the sky.

He was extraordinarily lucky and still unscathed in readiness for the 10th when he was to advance with the infantry of the Jullunder Brigade and continue the attack towards Aubers Ridge. The sappers, because they were specialists and rated more valuable than the infantry they were to follow and assist, had to be shielded from excess casualties and employed only on the objective on special engineer tasks, and Major E. R. P. Boileau, commanding the 2nd/2nd Gurkhas, to whom Hobart was attached, made it clear from the outset that he was not prepared to relax these rules in the slightest degree. These were not the sort of restrictions that were likely to appeal to Hobart, but if he resented them they were swept from his mind by the awesome panorama that now opened before him. Shortly after action he pencilled into his diary words that are as plain and as firm now as the day they were written :

Arrived at breastwork 3.30 a.m. Boileau went on to Port Arthur. Dossed down without our blankets. Very comfy . . . Guns started punctual 7.30 a.m. Absolutely indescribable. . . . The swinging swish of the shrapnel alone—apart from all noise of explosions or discharges, and replies of German guns would drown ones voice. We must have had best view of all—within 200 yards of the German breastwork on which the majority of the guns were concentrated.

He saw the infantry go over the top, hardly opposed, the guns lengthening their range as the men dashed in on the surprised enemy, the prisoners coming back in dejected disconsolation. An hour later, following Boileau, he set off with his men to 'Port Arthur' and thence across ground that had just been taken, but still swept by heavy fire. Sappers fell close behind him and suddenly he found himself alone with five soldiers of the Leicesters in a trench that had 'a beastly stink', in time to see the 3rd Londons lose fifty men in a gallant attack close by. He noted:

One officer got up to the wire. Couldn't get through so fired standing at loopholes. Hit in head, took his cap off and knocked him back. But he up and fired again. Bolt jammed, bent down to wrestle with it. Hit plumb in top of head. Even then lying dying tried to get in another shot. A very brave man. This is all 40 yards from us.

Assisted by his five Leicesters, he had been shooting at the enemy himself:

. . . where I could see their bayonets over the top. Next to me was a Leicester who was shooting hard and said to me, 'There he is, sir, can't you see the red band on his hat?' 'Where?' I said. He just replied, 'There . . .' and laid his head slowly on his arms like a tired child. His neck went purple and a slow trickle of blood fell from under his cap.

Around him men were dying or being wounded; the sappers were passing bombs up to the Leicesters, who did not seem to know how to use them, and Boileau would not allow Hobart to go forward to show them. The '1st Army Order was very strict', but he simply could not remain inactive. Going back on his own initiative to Lieutenant-Colonel H. Gordon, commanding the 2nd Leicesters, 'a good man', he persuaded him to send a company to outflank the German position. At the same time, 'Gordon pointed out to me that I'd got a bullet through the left side of my kurta and one of my stars knocked cock-eye by another', but at once he was on his way back to the scene of action to see the Leicesters assail the breastwork with bomb and rifle. Then, perhaps as he had schemed it would, came a call from the Leicesters for sapper assistance.

Boileau actually tried to stop me going. However, I was on firm ground here as C.O. Sappers. Out along ditch. Found a pretty little hand-grenade dog-fight going on. We couldn't get any further. Went up with subaltern to the end, leaving the men. Decided to build a barricade about 15 yards beyond the furthest point the Leicesters had been able to reach. . . . Helped by Leicesters pulled sandbags out of German breastwork and passed on to men who built up the breastwork. The Germans got some men out into the ruins just behind and made things rather hot, as the parados was very low and we couldn't charge across as there was a morass in between. But they're rotten shots and didn't hit one of us.

For the remainder of the battle, for three days on end, he moved restlessly about the sodden field, seemingly tireless and taking the minimum sleep. The first British attack had broken clean through the German front line and nearly breached the second, rearward, position, but then the men who were meant to exploit the initial success became jammed into the trenches amongst the wounded coming back from the front, all at the mercy of the searching shells and threatening counter-attacks. The ability to move became stifled in a half-blind maze below ground level as, on the surface, men wilted before the torrent of fire sweeping it.

Ammunition was running out and with it the means to motivate the attack.

The men were exhausted, although Hobart's diary reflects the rosy mood of the 13th March—the last day of hope, until the reaction sets in after a visit to H.Q. on to the 14th where he discovered 'everyone awfully pleased. Surprising to us mere regimentallers who think we ought to have got much further', and it is from this moment that the sour note, product of shock disillusionment, the fore-runner of his growing discontent with the higher direction of the battle, began to disturb his writing— faintly at first but louder and louder as battle followed battle and the abortive slaughter increased:

Sir D. Haig congratulatory order with Sir J. French's congratulatory message. Says enemy lost 16,000 and 2,000 prisoners. Doubt the 16,000. A touch of the ingenious John Charteris.[1]

In the days that followed he continued to work at high pressure although his diary illustrates a conscious effort to turn his mind to lazier ways as, on St. Patrick's Day, he wrote:

1. Charteris was Haig's senior intelligence staff officer.

Such a wealth of snowdrops in Churchyard amid the debris of broken glass and tiles. And in the little walled garden of the priests brown-brick, red-tiled house opposite the first primroses I've seen among torn box-hedges and on the edge of a shell crater. So much Nature cares for our tantrums. . . . It was so wonderfully peaceful in that little garden, with the twisted iron-work railings above the low wall—and a shell hole in the middle of the path.

*   *   *   *   *

For the rest of 1915 he remained at the front in various capacities and with very few breaks. He took his first wound with good cheer, his venom reserved for the reports of friends from Ypres, mixed with a stream of criticism of the generals, their staff, the division of work and the tactics employed; and saw the next failure to take Aubers Ridge on the 9th May from the gun lines when Haig, persuaded that the enemy positions had become too strong to be taken by a rush, decided to send his men across no-man's-land in the dark after prolonged bombardment for two days on a narrow front left the Germans in no doubt of what was to come.

Hobart was with the Jullunder Brigade on the extreme left of the next assault on the 15th, once again with the Leicesters, and delighted by the greeting of their C.O., Gordon, with 'I *am* pleased it's *you* who are going to be with us'. He liked to be liked, although equally prepared to be disliked if necessary. The Jullunder Brigade had only to line the parapet and fire volleys of small arms fire as the infantry on their right advanced, but :

That might have been the signal for the Germans too, for, on the very tick, up went so many flares that it was like day, and such a crash of musketry as I have never heard before. Only one machine gun at first, apparently, but there must have been nearly a German a yard rapid firing. And one doesn't keep men standing up on the parapet under shell fire usually. Looks like extraordinarily good German information. But just at the time one was overwhelmed by the revulsion, the chill at one's heart : physical fear : and the horror that men should have to face such fire. It seemed impossible that anyone could pass 5 seconds unscathed. A quarter of an hour passed: and more machine guns began to join in. Germans sending up flares always and some red ones: and always the tornado of bullets. Then started pipsqueaks on our parapet. Good shooting at midnight.'

Hobart began to find it difficult to visualise morale remaining high if no substantial advance could be made. To a professional mind it was a crass waste of trained men: to a compassionate soul heart-breaking. In his diary, reflecting on Aubers and Festubert:

All that courage and endurance. All that forethought, effort and organisation. All those gallant lives, given—to crack the shell of the German line. And didn't. And then we *sit still* for a whole week and let 'em build up a new shell again which will take all that effort to break again. Every advance of 1,000 yards cost 15,000 lives and to be followed by 2 months footling?

With more time to spare came an opportunity for reflection. Ambitious regular soldiers, naturally enough, saw the war as a ride to rapid advancement on the back of glory—for those who survived. Hobart's mental approach to the war, that strange mixture of ambition and intense patriotism overlain by heroic, sometimes quixotic, gallantry, made him an uncertain candidate for promotion. Still, he was thirty, well aware of his own ability and increasingly conscious that, as a staff officer, he might make a greater contribution than if he remained a mere sapper officer in the front line.

War is a young man's game, but older men had to be sent to the front because in 1915 there was nobody else with their knowledge, and so many of the best of the younger regulars were killed before they could acquire experience; and in Kitchener's, as well as the Territorial Army, could be found all too many potential officers serving, and dying, in the ranks, where they felt happier amongst their pals from civilian life. It was a shocking waste of good material and Hobart hated waste. This squandered talent was what he wished to see advanced rapidly over the heads of the less-adaptable older men.

Seniority to him looked a haven of experience and not necessarily of efficiency. If a man proved wanting then in Hobart's
view he ought not to be retained: if a man had talent he should
be pushed ahead regardless of age or seniority. Yet, at the heart
of the whirlwind of his disgust and protest, he kept sight of the
essential values of life, relating the past to the future without
being swamped by the present. It seems he went deliberately
to the Ypres salient on the 18th June to be as close as he could
to the field of Waterloo on the 100th Anniversary of the battle.

Glad at heart to have been in Belgium this day: that great determined courage that met its reward 100 years ago. And the moderation that followed victory.

There is astonishing maturity here in the midst of popular
hate, for there can have been few in France that day who, remembering the event of 1815, also gave thought to magnanimity.
And when, a week later, news came of the award of the Military
Cross for his exploits at Neuve Chapelle, his immediate reaction
was one of humbleness. Instinctively he shrank from the limelight by emphasising the awards made to others, or complaining of decorations that had been misdirected or wrongly withheld.

Shamefully few rewards for Sepoys. Especially considering what
they did at Neuve Chapelle. Great indignation over 3 ADC's all
getting Military Cross.

From Gallipoli shortly before had come sad news of the death
of Betty's husband, Waldo. His thoughts flew to her, but his
actions went beyond sympathy; from now on he took her under
his care, making her the recipient of a constant stream of entertaining, discursive letters designed to advise, distract and help
in any and every way. His re-entry into her life became an affec-
tionate domination that was to remain quite unbroken until she
chose to marry again over ten years later.

On leave in England in July, Hobart spent much time laying
the foundations of a circle of friends, an exotic group of people

whose interests lay far outside the narrow confines of the Army, amongst whom were to be found politicians, artists, authors, spiritualists—above all, people with strong personal views and the ability to express themselves with force and clarity. With them he could not dominate to the same degree as he did so often with his contemporaries in the Army, and they, impressed by his striking character, enthusiasms, bubbling staccato conversation and reception to new ideas, made him welcome. But as his own knowledge and intellectual powers were being stimulated, several of the flaws in his character were exposed; for an explosive power in debate, urged on by the desire to be provocative led to clumsiness and indiscretions that, on reflection, gave him and others acute pain.

It was the contradictory effect of this brilliant circle of non-military friends that, on the one hand, fostered his inquisitive, freely expressed enquiries and, on the other, smoothed away the more vulgar aspects inherent in his presentations without destroying his deepest entrenched convictions. By conviction a thinker, at heart, even at this relatively early stage, Hobart was a man of action who would, in a phrase he used about this time, '. . . find his own particular way to Hell.'

When in feminine company he failed to throw off his masculine preoccupations, as he had commented in reply to Betty:

I think you are probably right in what you say about women. I've fought long and strenuously against the idea. I've wanted to believe they had all man's qualities really : only latent.

But—you say 'she is essentially the sensitive transparent globe into which man pours the riches of his originality. And there it is—visible. And often she so absorbs and reproduces as if she had created it herself. But she never has.' Yes. I think that's true—physically and mentally. But spiritually? Our old Romance (or was it Sentimentality) having come down in ruins, we must build anew the True Romance.

*   *   *   *   *

Back at the waiting game of siege warfare repeated hazards were sketched on almost every page of the diary. But the days

A.C.—D

with the 1st Sappers and Miners were numbered, ending when, at the prompting of friends, he was sent to Headquarters 3rd (Lahore) Division as a Grade 3 staff officer. A letter to Betty finds him puzzled:

One's hard put to it now. There's far too much office work to suit my taste. It seems to be endless: and inevitable. And somehow I don't feel it ought to be . . .[he was working more than 16 hours a day] . . . When I've got hold of things it may not take so long. But for the present it's beastly—one's insides resent it!

The Battle of Loos was being planned, letting Hobart see for the first time the staff problems connected with the launching of a complex attack, and it is hardly likely that the depressing failure of this battle to achieve a breakthrough, after a superb beginning, was lost on him. So it is unfortunate that during this battle the volume of work seems to have prevented him keeping up his diary or maintaining a coherent correspondence with those at home. Yet it matters little because when next the diary opens it is to describe his activities as a staff officer on another front, where his loathing of the rank stupidities in war can no longer be contained.

3

FRUSTRATION AND KUT AL AMARA

When five thousand Indian troops landed at the mouth of the Shatt al Arab on the 5th November 1914, and began preparations to advance on Basra, the Turks were taken completely by surprise, for they had not expected anything like that on the very outbreak of war. Mesopotamia was largely desert, flat and featureless, treeless except where palm trees sprouted close to the rivers, stoneless and, in the dry season, firm underfoot. But when the rains came, as they do in abundance between December and April, vast expanses of the countryside became covered by expanses of water, making cross-country movement over the greasy mud virtually impossible. Then what little could be carried went in flat-bottomed boats along only two reliable routes—the great Tigris and Euphrates rivers.

The two rivers, flowing from the north-west to Basra and the Shatt al Arab in the south-east, passed through a country that was, in winter, cold, wet and miserable and, in summer, choked with dust and stickily hot, with temperatures as high as 140° Fahrenheit in the shade. Disease lurked in every nook and cranny: there seemed no end to the list of destructive plagues; and overall there hung the flies—not a swarm but a myriad of swarms

that turned the sides of tents black and crowded in on everything
rotten—the carrion and the filth of the country made more hideous by war's waste produce.

Within three weeks of the first British landing, the Persian
oilfields and Basra were securely held and the inadequate Turkish
garrison in flight, leaving the local Arabs mightily impressed by
so prompt a demonstration of British power. The aim of the
invasion had been achieved: from then on it was only necessary
to hold a defensive ring around the approaches to Basra and the
oilfields. Nevertheless it seemed prudent, at the time, to push
further up the two great rivers to add depth to the defensive
arc in front of Basra; and so, step by step, the British Army
paced up the Tigris. Each successful local engagement under
their commander, General Sir John Nixon, played enticingly
upon the ambitious susceptibilities of the Government of India,
so that, with every local victory and each advance, the confidence
of the troops grew to a feeling of invincibility, no matter the odds
against them: even the paucity and dire shortage of administrative resources in an undeveloped country were no deterrent.
The lines of communication lengthened until, by 30th September 1915, maintenance of the leading elements at Kut al
Amara, four hundred miles up the Tigris from Basra, hung on a
shoe-string. But ahead lay a goal which General Nixon could
not resist—Baghdad—its mystical name and historical associations, linked with the urgent desire for an Allied victory to offset
the disasters of 1915 in France and Gallipoli, driving into him
like a spur.

In August General Nixon's suggestion that, if he was to
advance on Baghdad, he ought to be reinforced by an Indian
division, coincided with a submission by Mr. Austen Chamberlain, the Secretary of State for India, that the Indian Corps
should be spared another winter in France. Both prevailed, but
the instructions to withdraw the Indian Corps did not reach
France until the 31st October, only fourteen days prior to Nixon
sending General Townshend from Kut, with his tired little division, on the last hundred miles of the adventure to Baghdad;
and by the time the first Indian troops embarked at Marseilles,
Townshend had been repulsed at Ctesiphon, twenty miles from

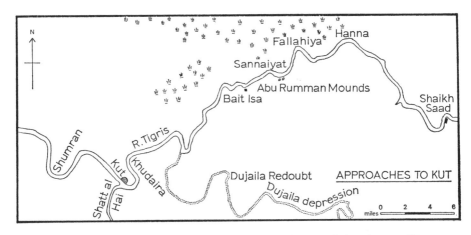

Baghdad, and was struggling back to the bend of the river at Kut that sheltered his advanced base.

Nixon's decision to let Townshend stay at Kut rested on his understanding that there were five months' supplies there, but he wrongly overestimated the strength of the reinforcements on their way to him, just as he wrongly underestimated the strength and skill of the Turkish force which came to besiege Kut, and then dig itself in on either side of the Tigris thirty miles downstream. Nixon's disillusionment soon became total. First, Townshend, hoping to hasten the relief operations by injecting a sense of urgency, falsely announced that he had only a month's supplies; next the Turks demonstrated that they were not going to be easily dislodged from their siege lines or covering positions; finally the newly arrived reinforcements from France did not come up to expectations.

Originally the Indian Corps was intended to stage in Egypt to reorganise, re-equip and re-train, with the result that the divisions did not embark to a tactical plan to allow them to land in fighting order. Now it was projected, pell-mell and grossly disorganised, up country to the front on the Tigris. Fighting units came ahead of their staffs, administrative components arrived any old how and in no condition to support the fighting units. The Corps was flung into a campaign managed on Crimean lines.

Hobart, still G.S.O. 3 of 3rd Division, landed on 5th January with the headquarters. The best part of 7th Division, with part of the 3rd, was already ashore: indeed, 7th Division, with an assortment of other units under the new commander of the Indian Corps, Lieutenant-General Sir Fenton Aylmer, vc, with an improvised staff, was on the eve of its first attempt to drive the Turks out of Shaikh Saad. Of this Hobart was not aware: all he knew was what people told him as he travelled upriver, and what he saw for himself.

He heard of local Arabs who preyed on Turks and British alike, to the extent that the Turks had suggested a temporary halt in the main war to enable them to stage joint punitive action with the British: he was depressed to find practically no reception arrangements for the reinforcements, a matter of insignificance compared with the treatment given the wounded. It was snowing(!) when:

Passed two large barges towed by river steamer. All full of wounded. No beds. No bedding. Lying on hard deck. Even officers. Only one Medical Officer to 600 wounded.

And two days later, as he arrived at Ali-al-Gharbi, not far from the front, he saw:

2,000 wounded on two tows. One doctor on each. No dressings. First field dressings had to remain. Little food. Water from river.

As each boat-load sailed down stream it carried with it a stench that defied description— a pollution of gangrene, excreta and decay hanging overall in a deathly pall which, to a certain extent, numbed the minds of men who were powerless to overcome the sheer lack of materials in a barren land. But it woke Hobart to a fury which hardly left him from then on:

No stores: no assistance! A good man, Fagg, said we from France expected too much when I asked for a sheet of paper for Cavalry Sketch Board. That is the attitude. Wounded still coming in. Saw Lewis (O.C. Leicesters), wounded in shoulder 48 hours ago, not yet dressed. Crowds of wounded. Many said to have shot themselves.

The datum line for every operation was the Tigris, up which nearly all the supplies had to be floated. Therefore a lengthy march round the desert flank of the Turks holding the river bank became dependent on a tenuous overland supply route guided by good navigation across a featureless desert, but if the Turks dug their defensive positions with one flank on the river and the other on a nearby salt marsh it became nearly impossible to outflank them.

This was what confronted 7th Division on the left bank of the Tigris at Hanna, where the Turks had established their right flank on the river bank and their left on the Suwaikiya Marsh. But on the right bank, where the 3rd Division was to operate, there was an open flank, the Turks being content to defend the river here fourteen miles to the west of their main right bank position, and only ten miles from Kut. There they stood on a dried-up river bed called the Dujaila Depression, with their left on the river and their right in a strongly constructed works called 'The Dujaila Redoubt'.

On the 21st January an attempt to storm Hanna failed miserably in a torrent of rain and a sea of mud. The artillery support proved quite inadequate due to lack of guns and ammunition. Men actually died from exposure and a truce had to be arranged to collect the wounded. General Townshend now reported he could hold out until 17th February 'or by taking certain measures, much longer', and a new commander, General Sir Percy Lake, arrived to take over from Nixon. A few days later Townshend announced he could last until 27th April—the truth at last. At any rate, there were now two months, time enough to make more thorough arrangements for the next attempt to relieve Kut by a full-scale advance via Dujaila with a view to extracting the garrison across the river.

The next two months provided Hobart with a unique opportunity to study the desert and its effects on the art of war at close quarters. He learnt that very few Westerners are at home in the desert, that loneliness attacks their equilibrium by making them panic and lose their sense of direction so that, as often as not, when lost, they move in the opposite direction to safety. He found that it takes time and training to accustom men to the desert and that, having achieved confidence, there is still no guarantee that they will fight effectively.

Then he contemplated the utter confusion imposed by muddled thinking amongst commanders and staff through inaccurate instructions. In his diary on the 26th and 27th January, referring to ill-thought-out moves from bank to bank on the Tigris, he enters a furious tirade:

28th Brigade ordered to move back at 4 a.m. after already moving from front line to Reserve and having to dig in wet. Brigade reduced to 1,000 and very few British officers—General Kemble very rightly flatly refused. Corps in a hopeless panic and orders for crossing anticipate ferrying twice as many as is conceivably possible. . . . Hardly one order issued by them so far not counter-ordered. Order, counter-order, disorder.

The bungled moves heralded the transfer of strength to the right bank prior to the attack on Dujaila, in accordance with a plan rich in minute detail prepared by the improvised Tigris Corps Staff, under General Aylmer.

It was intended to advance by night on the 7th March in three groups, attack the enemy trenches at Dujaila with one group, moving round its right flank with the second, leaving the third group in reserve.

Keary's 3rd Division formed the bulk of the third group in reserve, largely because Keary did not like Aylmer's plan and had preferred Hobart's proposal (rejected by Aylmer) for bridging the river in rear of the Hanna position. In essence, Hobart thought it best to wait for the bridges—but time, in Aylmer's view, was not on their side and no bridging material had arrived. Now Hobart found himself acting as G.S.O.2 to Keary, responsible for ensuring that his group kept station at the rear of the main body, behind Aylmer's headquarters.

The night was fine, clear and starlit and, despite the advance being delayed by late arrival of the artillery, the approach of the leading troops was accomplished without undue delay, bringing them to their deployment area only a few hundred yards short of the appointed place as dawn was breaking. Keary's column wandered twice:

Owing [Hobart thought] to lack of experience and having a man with a rifle close alongside the compass. Had to gallop off into darkness twice to get column back behind Corps. . . . Extraordinary sight at dawn, flat plain, manœuvre movements going on all over. Not a shot from the Turks. Long time taken by the guns reconnoitring etc. Believe if we'd pushed in straight without waiting for artillery preparation we might have rushed it.

This was all too true. The leading British officers were certain the Turks were unaware of their presence, a view confirmed later by the Turks themselves. But General Kemble, commanding the first group, who had seen before how well the Turks concealed themselves until the last moment before unleashing their fire, could not believe he had achieved the surprise Aylmer sought, and would not depart from the rigid plan even though part of the columns had been delayed. He waited for them to catch up. But then General Aylmer decided that the Turks must know what was going on and ordered the artillery to open fire two hours after dawn, regardless of the fact that the delayed columns were still not fully ready. Folly piled on stupidity. Again the men at the front pleaded to be allowed to go on, for now the enemy was certainly alive to their peril and his infantry could be seen hurrying into the empty trenches. But the orders laid down that the main attack was to be nearly four hours after dawn and nobody was prepared to go against them.

So it was that men who caught the enemy unawares after a superlative night march were not allowed across three thousand yards of open desert until the enemy had been given ample time to recover from his surprise. The casualties mounted and the waves of attackers began, gradually, to wilt before a heavy fire. By the middle of the afternoon it could be seen that the first two groups could go no further, Turkish reinforcements in large numbers were crossing the Tigris from the left bank, and only Keary's group, which so far had not been employed, was left fit to carry on the attack.

Keary went in person to the 8th Jullunder Brigade to impress on them the need to press their attack fully home, and like the Old Guard at Waterloo they responded with a steadiness and sense of purpose which impressed all who saw it. Then, like the

Old Guard, after beating against the enemy redoubt, they fell
back exhausted. Starting 2,300 strong, they returned with not
half that number. In a valedictory letter to Betty, Hobart wrote
a few weeks later :

Dujaila—which we know as the impregnable redoubt that wrecked
our plans, that barred our way and held us, that stopped the relief
of Kut. And yet our men, after that long and unique night march
and a hot day in the sun, assaulted across 3,000 yard of open flat
against this tripled ringed redoubt and actually got into it. Had
there been any troops left to back them up we might have got through
when Arbuthnot of the Sappers reached the crest. That's what
Dujaila is to us.

The fate of Kut was sealed on this day, although for nearly two
months more it was to eke out its existence in the hope of one
last blow that might hack a way through. Again there was a
change in command, General Aylmer being replaced at the
head of the Tigris Corps by Lieutenant-General Gorringe, a
new leader with an old plan—another direct advance along both
banks of the river—frontal assaults on entrenched positions.

The last attempts to reach Kut depended on the arrival of
more fresh troops, the 13th Division, and the weather. But 13th
Division could not attack Hanna until 5th April and when they
did so it was to discover that the Turks had forestalled them and
slipped back to Fallahiya, which then turned out to be only an
outpost of the main position at Sannaiyat. In twenty-four hours
the 13th and 7th Divisions pushed forward from Hanna to
Sannaiyat, attacked the grim Turkish defence and foundered in
the way of subsequent attacks there.

On the right bank Keary's 3rd Division was to advance towards Bait Isa before taking possession of enemy trenches at
Abu Rumman, an operation which impelled Hobart to a frenzy
of activity, for when an assault was not in progress it was he
who organised and personally took part in many a reconnaissance
and whenever there was fighting on the grand scale he was usually to be found at the front at the side of General Keary.

He began to share some of the perils of the Royal Flying

Corps. Their aircraft were types such as the old Henri Farman, the Voisin and, at best, the BE 2c—machines that had become obsolete on the Western Front a year before. Maintenance facilities were practically non-existent, and when the temperature rose above 100 degrees the old biplanes would not climb through the layer of rarified air that had been super-heated from the ground. Not surprisingly, the enemy had air superiority. Pilots were few and far between, their efforts restricted by the total absence of trained observers. This was where Hobart made himself useful by going in the observer's seat and sketching the enemy positions from the air, for, of course, there were no aerial cameras in Mesopotamia at that time. Soon he acquired an unrivalled mastery of the art of interpreting what he saw while acquiring an insight into the problems and potential of the flying men and their machines, at first suggesting that they were 'rather an unenthusiastic crowd', a judgement he happily reversed with experience. He seems to have flown over Sannaiyat for the first time on 18th February, but not again until the middle of March. Thereafter he was frequently aloft, the entry for 31st March typical of his experiences:

Up in BE with Petre. Very bumpy. Lightning, rain and heavy clouds. Henri Farman landed just as we started, crashed. Total wreck. Observed Abu Rumman OK.'

Just before the battle reopened on the 5th April he became G.S.O. 2 again, noticing that day, of Keary, 'The old man has cut off the perky ends of his moustache.'

The right and left bank divisions advanced and 3rd Lahore Division moved swiftly into Abu Rumman to the accompaniment of shrewd comments by Hobart on the performance of his colleagues.

Casson doing GSO 1 well (in absence of GSO 1, Stewart, sick). Quick, energetic, capable. Puts people's backs up. Self alone with GOC most of day. Directly counter attack (at *most* 2,000 men with 1 battery on south) developed, Egerton (the Bde Cmdr) yelped (before losing single man, or fire opened) 'might be able to hang on if

reinforced by 2 battalions'. Implored General to order all fire to be
withheld till enemy close, or if round behind us use Reserve Brigade
(9th) to bottle 'em in. Unique opportunity. Not a bit of it. 9th frittered in supporting Egerton. Fire opened by every battery in the
place of extreme range. Enemy naturally never within rifle range.
Our casualties all day 12 wounded.

The incident is significant; not only did it sour his future
relationship with Keary, but it represents a classic example of
Hobart's uninhibited submission of his personal views to senior
officers, not every one of whom was prepared to appreciate his
rapid comprehension of a situation at the expense of their own
feelings. Here can be seen the lightning rapidity of his thoughts,
and his manner of assembling them into a plan aimed aggress-
ively at the total annihilation of the enemy in diametric opposition to straightforward caution. But the tactics he had called for
were not of his day. Whereas the use of the divisional reserve
to envelop the enemy had been commonplace generations before
1914, it seems to have been relegated to history by trench warfare.

The destruction of his confidence in Keary becomes apparent
on the 7th when some 150 Buddus (Arab marauders) advanced
towards Divisional Headquarters:

General saddling up horses, mad with excitement, sending officers
galloping in all directions to turn out troops and order all guns to
fire: telephones red hot 'Casson—save the maps'. Guns opened fire
at 4,000 yards as Buddus cleared off. If we'd let 'em come on
quietly, 100 rifles might have bagged the whole lot. Makes one
damn rude.

Almost feverishly he was alternately pressing his views on
Keary, reconnoitring the Bait Isa position and flying in appalling conditions, often low enough to draw rifle-fire, as he
assembled a picture of the state of the trenches comprising the
Turkish defence. His thoroughness drove him into extraordinary
peril—to be his companion in itself was an act of faith. For
instance, when information was wanted about the Turkish
trenches stretching south from Bait Isa, Hobart, with three

Indian troopers, cantering in advance of an escorting squadron of cavalry, came across an empty trench and immediately drew rifle-fire from more trenches concealed in grass only a hundred yards off. Two of the troopers were killed at once, and the horse of the third dropped as it swung to escape, throwing the man clear. In a moment Hobart, on his pony Sheila, had reached him, swung him up behind, and started off. But already a bullet had entered the trooper's heart and it was a corpse as well as her master that Sheila galloped out of action, twisting and bending to disconcert the Turkish fire that followed them for a thousand yards. And still later he was back there on foot to see if anything could be done for the fallen men even though the enemy were far too close.

Next morning he was 'outed' at last, by a leg wound, as he calmly sat in the front line sketching the enemy positions, but even then he managed to keep it to himself for the rest of the day, for, as he later wrote:

I had a lot of work to get done and couldn't spare time to go to hospital till it was finished. Which was just as well because the doctors, of course, seized on to me and put me into bed. But, thanks to clean living forefathers and the good constitution we've inherited, there were no complications. There might well have been and it was about as narrow a shave of bone, artery and tendon as could well be. However, now it remains merely a small scar to show—in confidence—to my more intimate lady friends!

His remarks were for the eyes of his sister alone—they are not those of a boastful man, and in the years that followed he was rarely given to talking much about his personal achievements in battle, although he was vociferous in criticising or extolling the performance of others. But undoubtedly he relieved tension by describing his actions on paper, and getting the matter off his chest.

* * * * *

Townshend was negotiating his surrender on the 27th April;

there was an armistice to allow boats, by the chivalry of the
Turks, to sail upriver to Kut and bring out the wounded, and it
was time to count the cost—5,651 casualties from 3rd Lahore
Division alone in three months—and reflect on the rewards and
promotions. Hobart could hope for none. He had seen that his
G.S.O. 1 had put him in for a decoration, and that Keary had
crossed it out; nevertheless, on the 11th May came the news
that he had been given an immediate award of the Distinguished
Service Order. The campaign in Mesopotamia was pausing to
draw breath. It was time for Hobart to do the same.

If errors are the best of teachers, those who learnt from the
art of war in Mesopotamia were taught enough to last a lifetime.
Hobart missed nothing, but undoubtedly was most deeply impressed by the vital need to establish a sound administration
before fighting in a hostile, underdeveloped country. The sufferings of the wounded and the drudgery of working in squalid
surroundings, on a meagre diet, left indelible marks in his
memory; just as did the futility of expecting unacclimatised and
ill-trained troops to retain their bearings in a featureless waste.
He grasped the value of employing every possible mechanical
aid to enhance mobility and associated it with his exhaustive use
of aircraft for reconnaissance. Then, commenting on a staff
officer's opinion that 'machine guns are more use against aircraft
than anti-aircraft guns', and of General Lake's remark to
General Keary, 'Men are much safer from bombardment in the
open than in trenches'; 'These are the sort of men, utterly ignorant of modern conditions, to whom this campaign is entrusted.'

Criticism such as this simply preceded a scathing denounce-
ment in the Press and has been, largely, upheld by the Official
History when it appeared after the war. From General Nixon,
whose infectious, unreasoned optimism guided the campaign into an appalling situation, to Generals Lake and Aylmer, with
their impossibly detailed plans that were incapable of breaking
the deadlock, and General Townshend, whose fine tactical victories spurred on Nixon, but whose misrepresentation of the state
of his supplies had fatally hastened the relief operations, there
ran a thread of incompetence that at times belied credulity. We
can sympathise with them from the horizon of time, for they

were ordinary men, lacking in brilliance, immersed in events that could only be overcome by brilliance.

But the fact that ordinary men had been picked was the burden of Hobart's complaint. He yearned for leaders who were 'brilliant' (his word). They had to be prompt and energetic even if, as it occurred to him, they were liable to 'Put people's backs up'. Already the man to solve the Mesopotamian problem was in the country. Major-General Stanley Maude had arrived in command of the 13th Division and on 28th August assumed command of the Mesopotamian Expeditionary Force in place of General Lake.

Maude possessed the essential qualities that Hobart most admired in a professional soldier. He was a Staff College graduate (they were comparatively few and far between before 1916), enthusiastic and well read. His powers of concentration, grasp of detail and capacity for hard work were quite abnormal and sorely needed in Mesopotamia where such virtues were distinctly in short supply. Furthermore, Maude was the youngest of the Generals in the theatre and his appointment reflected the insistence of the War Office that their own nomination should take precedence over the heads of older men from India. This use of talent, regardless of seniority, tallied with Hobart's notions just as it accorded with Maude's tendency to overcentralise control and training. Here was a man he could emulate, if from afar, in the hierarchy.

4

MOBILITY

Everywhere the battle fronts were stationary and nowhere did it appear possible to restore mobility for a sufficient length of time to strike a blow that would end the war. So far massed artillery, pulverising the ground ahead of assaulting infantry, had done as much to seal the front as open a gap through which the cavalry could ride, and even on the rare occasions when horsemen found room to manœuvre they were chopped down by a few machine guns. Only on the open flanks of the desert wastes, such as in Mesopotamia and Palestine, was it possible to launch cavalry wide of the trenches deep into the enemy rear. There it was that success became more dependent on the ability of commanders at all levels to seize fleeting opportunities and to squeeze the utmost from their tenuous administrative resources. Here was bred a nimble mental attitude, the reverse of the moribund psychology, associated with static trench warfare where every move was meticulously prepared and the routine of relief and supply a dull routine—'trenchiness', as Hobart described it.

Nevertheless it was in the last quarter of 1916 that the weapon appeared which, as no other was to do, changed the balance of power on the battlefield and began to sweep away the suffocating trench web. Tanks, only thirty-six of them, went into action for the first time on 15th September 1916. On 20th November 1917, 378 tanks took part in one operation at Cambrai and broke one of the strongest sectors of the German Western Front in a single blow at a comparatively small cost in lives. No tanks were sent to Mesopotamia and so Hobart was not to see them until after the war, yet the début in France on 15th September 1916 shaped his future as did no other single event. His reaction to the new machines, even from a distance, was characteristically inquisitive, although one has to base one's imagination of it on an interpretation of two short entries in his diary. That for 28th November reads: 'Wilmer and Buston (of *Mantis*) rolled up. Former described "tanks".'

Now *Mantis* was a gunboat, and her officers were sure to have technological leanings, so it is not difficult to conjure up a picture of Hobart shooting forth a volley of short sharp questions concerning the machinery Wilmer had seen. Obviously his engineering ability and curiosity were temptingly whetted, for on 9th December he wrote: 'Walked to 7th Brigade camp with Hickman and saw Caterpillers of 6 inch Susans.'

Even if there were no actual tanks to be seen, the next-best thing, a tracked vehicle for towing six-inch guns, would help fix the principle in his mind and set it racing ahead with fresh ideas.

*   *   *   *   *

Not quite the whole of 1916 had been devoted to war, for in August Hobart had enjoyed four nostalgic weeks' leave in India, indulging in a potted version of a year's pre-war pastimes—a whirl of riding, shooting, walking and social intercourse. Not that it was really possible to indulge in India with the same attitude as before. Far too much had happened since 1914: even the code of the Sappers and Miners was slipping, permitting him to become engrossed in a short, intense liaison which all but swept him out of bachelorhood. The diary note, 'Tonight we climbed the heights of Valhalla', leaves little to the imagination of the intensity of his feelings.

But leave had to end and Mesopotamia reclaimed a somewhat

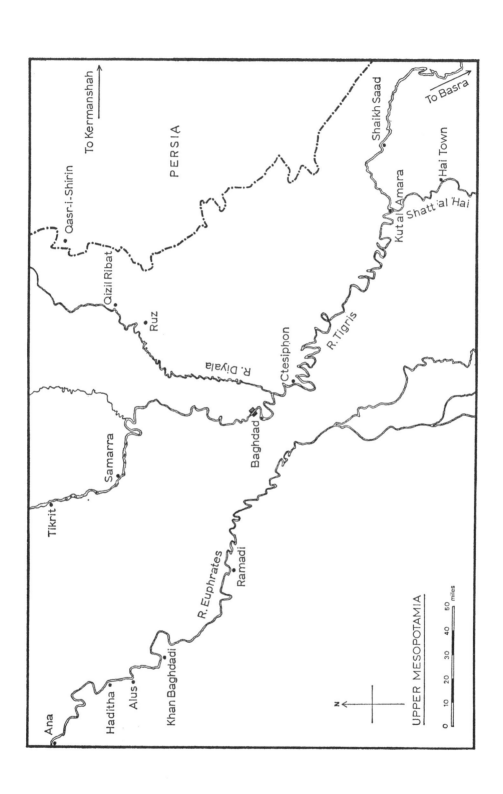

UPPER MESOPOTAMIA

N

0   10   20   30   40   50 miles

To Kermanshah

PERSIA

Qasr-i-Shirin

Qizil Ribat

Ruz

R. Diyala

Ctesiphon

R. Tigris

Shaikh Saad

To Basra

Hai Town

Kut al Amara

Shatt al 'Hai

Baghdad

Samarra

Tikrit

R. Euphrates

Ramadi

Khan Baghdadi

Alus

Haditha

Ana

disturbed personality—but to a fresh task. For the best part of November Hobart worked as temporary brigade major of 8th Brigade, and was supremely happy in his association with the 1st Manchesters, 2nd Rajputs, 47th Sikhs and 59th Rifles, who comprised that highly experienced formation—the 'Fighting, Starving 8th Brigade', as it came to be known. It was a trial appointment, made permanent by Keary just two days before a new man was due to arrive, and, indeed, only two days before Maude's offensive was to begin.

The appointment was more than opportune, for it introduced him at once to a fascinating mixture of General Maude's wary enterprises, in a war of limited aims, designed to defeat the Turks and then take Baghdad. They began on the 13th December, restricted on the one hand by the imposition of a 25 per cent limit to casualties and encouraged on the other by Maude's ability to apply superior resources to successive Turkish positions on the right bank of the Tigris, prior to crossing the river in the rear of the strong left-bank positions.

A process of tentative sidesteps gradually carried the British Army past Dujaila to the Hai River and against the various fortified positions constructed by the enemy at strategic points along the right bank. It was at Khudaira that 8th Brigade, along with 9th Brigade, found itself, having got there with a deal of caution, a minimum of casualties and a new B.M. learning about his new post, making a few inexpensive mistakes in the process. Quotation from diary:

'. . . Worked the Brigadier up about scuppering Turk picquet at K11. On return found that last night's patrol found it empty.' (He had not been fully aware of all the facts.) 'Damn!'

But now he had to help forge a highly modern adaptation of ancient siege methods to throw the Turks of Khudaira into the river behind. There was to be no march across an open desert expanse here, but instead the systematic excavation of twenty-five thousand yards of trenches in the direction of the enemy, protected by outlying picquets. The operation, in the design of which Hobart had a big part, relied upon the ability of the diggers to maintain their bearings at night and for the picquets to forestall Turkish sorties: Hobart, who was in no doubt that there would be heavy casualties no matter how well he arranged matters, was mightily relieved to count only 350 after a fortnight of digging and see the assault start well on a narrow front on the 9th January 1917.

Then he was caught in the usual fog of war, communications from Brigade H.Q. to the leading infantry, the Manchesters, broke just as a violent Turkish counter-attack came in, followed by confused fighting. At Brigade Headquarters in the front line only snatches of pessimistic information arrived, each seemingly designed to prompt his brigadier to cry for help, but each in its turn put carefully to one side until the situation clarified in the afternoon. There was little or no order and counter-order—a sign of cool staff work—and prudence supervened on the side of a systematic renewal of a carefully prepared fresh attack. The British losses had been heavy: those of the Turks probably heavier, but the defeat inflicted on the Turks was the first they had suffered after a deliberate assault for some time. Next day patrols found the Turkish trenches empty except where they held a small enclave on the tip of the river bend, and this fell on the 19th, with 8th Brigade only participating in a watching role.

Gradually Maude edged along the right bank, amidst mounting confidence that soon the river could be crossed and an eager volley of suggestions as to where it might be done. Patrols seeking crossing places all along the river bank helped distract the enemy's attention and during one of these, in the Hai bend, Hobart, making full use of Sheila's speed and the cover afforded by patches of dwarf tamarisk, got right up to the bank unseen. But then, the mission completed, a long range sniper got Sheila in the off-forehoof as she raced for safety, bowling her over like a rabbit on top of her rider. The horse was hardly scratched, but her rider was badly concussed and knew nothing of the next twenty-four hours. Yet such was the habit of discipline that he remounted, rode back to camp, his topee bashed in and his nose streaming blood, and sat down to write orders before his clerk could get hold of the doctor to put him to bed. But his comment 'no one noticed that these orders were any worse or more muddled than those he usually wrote', turned to a more serious vein to Betty, later that year:

Of course there is no doubt that concussion affects temper, and memory. Even that rotten little dunt I got . . . has made my temper even worse (yes!) and quicker than ever. Perhaps I'll be able to take a pull and I think it is improving slightly : my shoulder is still a bit stiff—perhaps they'll both recover together.

Baghdad fell on the 11th March—the routed Turkish Army falling back before a tardy pursuit. It was for 8th Brigade to follow the cavalry, and for Hobart to register the need for a substitute for the horse on mobile operations in views crystallised in 1923 for a tour of the Mesopotamian battlefield:

The outstanding feature [of the pursuit] is the timidity of the Cavalry, and their remarkable reluctance to leave the infantry or to use mounted action. They had in front of them a tired, beaten enemy . . . The country was admirable for cavalry work . . . The only reason alleged is that they were held up for rations. Compare the cavalry in Allenby's pursuit in Palestine. General McAndrew [then] got his rations from the Turk.

It was not as if this judgement, delivered six years after the event, was made in the absence of personal experience. After Baghdad had fallen on the 11th March, Maude had to chase the broken enemy away to the north in the direction of Qasr-i-Shirin in the Persian foothills to link with the Russians closing in from Kermanshah.

Only a small force could be allotted to the task, since the desolate country, through which it had to advance, barely supported its small indigenous population and, consequently, was no place for a large army. Keary's 3rd Division, to the best of its ability, had to become a fast-moving mobile force and advance eighty miles at high speed, clearing opposition on the way. Indeed, speed was the keynote. By the 16th March 8th Brigade had arrived at Baquba, thirty miles north of Baghdad, and forty-eight hours later Brigadier Edwards, its commander, was able to report that the town was clear and the river bridged.

For a force to advance on its feet at this rate proclaimed its physical fitness, the high state of its training, and the excellence of the staff work. During the planning and execution of a long advance to contact, followed by an opposed river crossing, a brigade looked to its brigade major, Hobart, for accurate orders reflecting a sound tactical plan based on efficient supply arrangements. All of these were forthcoming from the brigade major of 8th Brigade and throughout the ensuing operations, carrying 3rd Division over fifty miles against opposition in a fortnight, there was no let-up. Ahead the Russians were getting close to the Pai Taq Pass, the hump between the valley from Kermanshah and the route from Qasr-i-Shirin, bringing with them, as it happened, the British liaison officer in the Caucasus, one Lieutenant-Colonel A. P. Wavell, who twenty-two years later became Commander-in-Chief in the Middle East when Hobart was a divisional commander there.

Lacking the strength to hold tightly even where the ground was in their favour, the Turks could only fight a rearguard action and delay the advancing British at natural obstacles. The task of the cavalry attached to 3rd Division was to seek and report on the delaying positions in time to prepare the rest of the division in order that it could assault with the minimum waste of time. But, Hobart, by acting as observer in an aeroplane flying in the van of the cavalry, did the work of cavalry and planned more quickly and efficiently than could the cavalry on their own. By seeing for himself the way the Turks were working, he was able to make his orders reflect a personal knowledge of the ground and issued them well ahead of events.

It was from an aerial reconnaissance by Hobart that the nature and strength of the enemy position between the Ruz Canal and the Jabal Hamrin became apparent, and brought about the circumvention of a premature attack that might have been abortive and costly. That he was even believed speaks volumes for the confidence everyone had in his reports, for it is still not uncommon for airmen's observations to be rejected when they tell unpalatable truths. This fight at Jabal Hamrin was almost as grim as that at Khudaira Bend, with the 8th Brigade in the thick of it and coming at least once (to Hobart's ill-concealed satisfaction) to the aid of the 9th Brigade when it was worsted in a Turkish counter-attack. But inevitably the Jabal Hamrin was taken, opening the way for the cavalry to ride through Qizil Ribat on the 1st April and meet the Russians at Qasr-i-Shirin. For the first time direct contact was made between the eastern and western battle fronts, but too late to affect the larger issues. The Cossack cavalry Hobart saw that day were not yet infected by the Revolution that had already broken out behind their backs, and the celebrations that marked the junction of the two forces were between soldiers. In any case, it was the stomach that predominated, for although the British column was on short rations, the Russians were starving. Yet these were fine men, ill-equipped and poorly mounted, but full of the spirit of mobility which impelled them on long advances supported by next to no adequate supplies.

Hobart's comments on a fortnight of mobile war, written at the time, show how he had penetrated to its heart.

Indeed I have been very hard put to it. It is not like trench warfare, you see, where all factors are known and can be provided against. This is open warfare against modern weapons and in a country infested with Arabs ready to pounce upon wounded or small parties, in addition to the regular enemy. Where questions of supply, even of water, are acute, and where one's work is never done. There are so many courses open to the enemy (and to ourselves) so many little accidents which must be guarded against—any one of which might mean disaster.

And all of this in a country which is, practically speaking, unknown and, of which, no reliable maps exist. It is only possible to march at night and it is so hot in the sun by day that it is impossible for men to sleep—we have no tents or shade.

＊　　＊　　＊　　＊　　＊

The war in Mesopotamia began to shuffle off-stage. 8th Brigade fought a war of outposts, repeatedly called to put down Arab raiders or disperse some fresh concentration of Turkish troops gathering on the upper reaches of the Rivers Adhaim, Tigris or Euphrates, often on the edge of battle, but only once

more, at Tikrit, asked to grapple with the same desperation as at
Dujaila, Khudaira or Hamrin.

During the hot summer of 1917, when more often without
his brigade commander than with him, Hobart turned to training
the brigade as it had never been trained before. Left to his own
devices, he experimented and enthused whilst developing his
own methods. He was already a firm believer in centralised
instruction and in the value of competition between units and
individuals, and whenever possible would group students in
brigade classes under expert instructors. There was no waste.
Gatherings, in which competitions abounded, brought the
various units of the brigade to know each other almost as well
as they knew themselves.

He understood other people so well too. Of his great friend,
Ginger Chase, killed in March 1917, whom he compared with
his father:

But the pater had been 'through' more. Ginger was made of that
fine stuff upon which the grosser temptations have little effect. The
pater one felt had been through it all and worn out. The fire of
passion had purified, not burnt and soiled his soul. . . . And then his
glorious deep-rooted fundamental love of beauty in man, woman
or child, body or spirit: tree or flower, view, smell or sound. . . . And
I—a rolling tangle of all.

Revelling in his own failings, he contrasts this with incisive
advice to Betty:

If you decide you can't really do more than you are doing, close
the subject: till circumstances alter. If you decide you can—make
up your mind on the other points, and then you won't find it difficult
to get what you want—more or less. . . . This sounds harsh? Dear
heart, I always speak gruffly and hard and straight. It's a fault which
has been punished pretty severely not only professionally. Though
my plain speech is the cause of my still wearing three stars. But—
you see a little deeper, don't you?

Tenderness lights up the man of battle. The multifarious

facets of his complex character sparkle around the greyer central figure.

      *   *   *   *   *

By stages the British Army advanced up the Tigris, engaging in mobile actions (of the sort to be fought in the next war in the Western Desert against Rommel) wherein fast-moving cavalry columns with armoured cars operated deep in the desert flank, while slower, less mobile, infantry forces slogged it out amongst fortified positions. Here for the first time armoured motor vehicles proved able to outmatch cavalry both in fighting capacity and duration in the waterless wastes.

On the 5th November 1917, partly by chance, battle was joined at Tikrit, the birthplace of Saladin. Leading 7th Division, the 8th Brigade cleared the enemy outposts as the cavalry division circled the enemy flank. Ahead, the walls of Tikrit rose above an eighty-foot bluff overlooking the Tigris and the surrounding desert, and from trenches and the artillery behind, an accurate fire fell upon the British infantry, by then only eight hundred yards off. This was the first proper sight the men of the 8th Brigade had of their objective; no plan of attack existed because no detailed reconnaissance had been made beforehand for a battle which had developed haphazardly.

One can visualise the Brigadier and Hobart spurring on the leading patrols, and from their reports, constructing a patchwork picture of the enemy positions when they became revealed; and imagine Hobart dashing forward in person to observe and confirm, racing back to write orders and organise the artillery support. The ground was hard, time was short and the slow, methodical sapping technique used at Khudaira quite inappropriate. Frequently the telephone lines were cut by enemy artillery fire, slowing preparations for the attack until fresh lines could be laid. Nevertheless, everything was ready in two hours, a remarkable feat of staff work if aided by aerial photographs and wireless, but well-nigh fantastic with the sparse equipment of 1917.

Now the arduous training of the summer paid its final dividend. The men, fit and confident, advanced with an invincible steadiness, hardly pausing as the casualties mounted from the

fire poured down from the enemy above them. Behind them the
19th Brigade fired in support and prepared to pass through once
the 8th Brigade had broken into the enemy trenches. That was
the plan, but unfortunately the 19th Brigade became as heavily
involved in the Turkish fire as the 8th it was supporting, and
lost three-quarters of its strength before beginning its main task.
So 8th Brigade, as it triumphantly broke right through the enemy
trenches, found itself beset in isolation by a furious Turkish
counter-attack—and barely held to what it had won. The brigade had played the preponderant part, as Hobart claimed, and
drawn the major portion of the Turkish defence upon itself at
a cost of 999 casualties out of a total of 1,801 for the entire
force. The brigade major's reward was a brevet majority—a
fitting finale, he thought, to his part in the Mesopotamian campaign.

For in March, with 3rd Lahore Division, 8th Brigade went
to follow the 7th Division to Palestine, though Hobart very
nearly did not go with it, as once again his curiosity got the
better of him.

Amongst the many friends Hobart had made in the Royal
Flying Corps in Mesopotamia there was the strongest mutual
bond with Lieutenant-Colonel J. E. Tennant, the Flying Corps
commander, based on their profitable co-operation. Above all,
they shared the kind of individual courage that seems to per-
meate men who fight in machines. Hobart's farewell visit to
dine with Tennant happened to coincide with the planning phase
of a surprise attack scheduled to take place against a Turkish
division occupying the banks of the River Euphrates near Khan
Baghdadi, on or about the 26th March. In connection with this
Tennant intended to fly next day, the 25th, to Hit to ensure
that the squadron there was fully prepared for the coming
attack. Now Hobart had still not seen the Euphrates and eagerly
pressed Tennant to take him along, regardless of the fact that
it was a breach of the rules to take an unauthorised passenger
to the front, particularly on the eve of a surprise action. But
the risk looked negligible, particularly since they had no intention of crossing the lines, and so with light hearts they took off
together next morning.

To the Turkish officer in command of anti-aircraft machine guns at Khan Baghdadi the appearance out of the clouds of a British DH9 aeroplane low over his guns presented a target that could hardly be missed! To Tennant the rattle of machine-gun fire indicated not only that he was lost but had also inadvertently disobeyed orders! To his observer, Hobart, there was merely the excitement of the Turkish trenches coming suddenly into view as they broke through the base of the clouds that had enshrouded them throughout most of the flight. Above the roar of the engine he could neither speak to the pilot nor hear the crack of the bullets about them, and it was not until the engine cut dead that he suspected they were in trouble.

A bullet had holed the radiator, the engine was boiling and a forced landing unavoidable. With bullets crashing into the machine, Tennant picked a broad nullah and somehow made a perfect landing not far from some Turkish infantry, who, leaving their trenches, rushed towards the aeroplane. Thereupon there occurred a slight altercation amongst the aircrew, Hobart crouching over the machine gun and shouting, 'Shall I let 'em have it?' and Tennant, leaping out to disconnect a petrol pipe, snapping back, 'No, give me your matches!' Escape was out of the question, the machine had to be destroyed, for the Turks were firing and a bullet grazed Hobart's leg as he fumbled in his pockets. But at last the petrol flowed, and the aeroplane burnt fiercely.

At once, as the firing stopped, a triumphant Turkish officer ran up, seized them by the hands and cried, 'Don't be frightened; put yourself at ease; you are quite safe now!'—an introduction to captivity that was just the first of a number of novel insights into the mentality of their enemy. At that moment, on the Western Front, the German spring offensive was carrying all before it, and so the Turks jumped to the conclusion that they had done the airmen a service by speeding their exit from a war which in their eyes was about to end. Nevertheless, the Turks made no secret of their dislike for their advisers, announcing the arrival of a German interrogator with, 'Here comes the Sausage, but pay no attention to him!'

In fact the Sausage was a man to be handled with care, for

while every Turkish officer treated them with an old-fashioned chivalry and hardly attempted to question them, the German was hoping for promotion and eager to extract information from the prisoners. If he had guessed the storm that was about to break at the front he might have pressed even harder to discover more than the statutory 'name, rank and number' of his captives, but this was all he found out.

In the event, the Turkish general told the captives more than they told him, quite the most alarming item being the news that they were to be moved to Aleppo as soon as possible. Now, on the one hand, they wished to avoid interrogation with its attendant danger of accidentally letting slip the news of the coming British attack, but on the other the longer they delayed their departure to the rear, the easier it would become for the attackers to recapture them. They could only guess at the exact date of the attack, but it must undoubtedly fall in the next two or three days, and so playing for time was well worth while.

A policy founded on evasion of Germans, delay of all attempts to move them, allied to constant watchfulness for an opportunity to escape, was adopted. They struck up a hopeful friendship with some Turkish guard dogs with a view to being accepted in silence by at least one element in the enemy camp, and on their first night in captivity went to sleep with the longings that there might be '. . . a heavy storm that night: a murrain on all Turk transport: or a plague of profound slumber on all our guards'. But the storm did not materialise, there was no murrain and sleep was cut short by the entrance of the Turkish general's A.D.C. with curt orders to get up and prepare to travel at once.

The barrage of cajolery, argument and expostulation this provoked was to no avail: the order came from on high and must be obeyed, so out into the cold comfortless night they went to find, wrote Hobart:

A small springless waggon, closed in all round with canvas flaps, surrounded by about a dozen men. We found next morning that these were Tartars. They were looked upon by the Turkish authorities as very trustworthy and quite unbribable—in any case they could not understand our best-intentioned attempts at bribing them in any known language. Strong, cheery, hearty fellows, but absolute barbarians.

Next morning, tired, stiff, sore and hungry, they arrived at Haditha, thirty miles as the crow flies from Khan Baghdadi, and not one glimmer of a chance to escape. Here they were well cared for by the two Armenian doctors who ran the local hospital, and who displayed the customary Armenian preference for the English instead of the Turks. There resulted an invitation to visit the hospital and with it the opportunity to reconnoitre Haditha. Away to the south-east Tennant thought he once heard the rumble of guns, and with it a redoubled urge to escape that night before they were moved further on. Timing was critical. Apparently their escort never relaxed, so for the moment they must pin their hopes on a break-out from their lodgings and dash for the open desert. Hobart stole a quart water-bottle from the hospital: they knew the lie of the land: they also knew of the presence of Germans, seen by Hobart in an upstairs window as they promenaded with the doctors through the streets. A shock this discovery, the more so since Tennant was talking rather loudly and earnestly in French to an Armenian and could barely be silenced in time by a hoarse growl from Hobart.

A thorough examination of their prison revealed various escape routes, while its flat roof provided a point of vantage from which they could study the village. Apart from this nothing happened until, within half an hour of sunset, an Arab horseman galloped up the street, dashed up to the local Turkish commandant and babbled forth a torrent of words. In a flash the basking village was convulsed, and Hobart, who had seen the Arab appear, jumped down from the roof, shouting, 'Wake up, old bird—Bob the Thruster is getting a move on.'

That morning infantry and artillery had closed on Khan Baghdadi, while cavalry and armoured cars swung round the flank to set up a blocking position in the Turkish rear. Heavy fighting went on in the trenches, left unresolved in the British favour until the next day, but the mobile troops under Brigadier Robert Cassels, in co-operation with aircraft, had established their blocks just after midday and, in addition, pushed patrols in Ford vans towards Haditha. It was these patrols which had precipitated the Arab messenger with his tale of disaster.

But it came at the wrong time for the prisoners, as, in next to no time, they were bundled into their waggon and sent at a gallop into the gathering dusk with their fierce escorts. Alongside flowed the flotsam and jetsam of panic, men driving animals in wild confusion to the west, even though the pursuit was still more than twenty miles off. Through the night they careered until the weary horses could barely lumber. Next day they reached Ana, still only another twenty miles on, but now nearly fifty from the front. Pleas for delay still seemed worth while, but the need to make a direct escape became more urgent with every turn of the waggon's wheels. Moreover, as the Tartar escort showed increasing signs of boredom with every hour that passed, it became obvious that no guarantee could be given that they would not resort to murder at the slightest provocation.

At Ana the horses drawing the waggon expired: there, too, Hobart's effort to feign sickness convinced nobody and in a short while they were on their way again—a ludicrous spectacle of two British officers mounted on camels without nose cords, driven onwards by its Tartar escort on foot. These were the kind of camels used only to being driven in herds: they were certainly not trained for riding and registered their disgust by lashing out at all and sundry, refusing to obey the guards and generally doing far more to hinder progress than their riders' blandishments. Unfortunately, each act of aggression by the camels served also to increase the sulky dangerous mood of the Tartars.

Breaking point came when two British aeroplanes passed overhead, their attention attracted by Hobart desperately waving his topee. With a roar the aeroplanes turned to dive, and as they did so a furious Tartar fired point-blank at Hobart's back.

By the law of averages when a man points a rifle at the back of another at close range and pulls the trigger without warning the bullet strikes home and the outcome, more often than not, is fatal. In days gone by it was not uncommon for cartridges to misfire, but the small-arms ammunition of 1918 had reached a high state of reliability and failures were few and far between.

So by all the odds this story should have ended here—but in the case of Patrick Hobart it seems that the Deity had decided there was a special case in favour of his survival.

The firing hammer only gave vent to a 'click': an outsize chance had produced a misfire! But the target did not even know what had taken place, so busy was he waving at the aeroplanes, and ironically his life was then saved by the very man who had tried to kill him a moment before, for a blow from the defective rifle across the buttocks sent him spinning into the ditch just as one of the aeroplanes opened fire. The peril had not departed, as next the pilots seemed to recognise the seniority of their target and proceeded to concentrate on them instead of the escort.

Yet somehow all remained unscathed, although rescue seemed more remote than ever, and as darkness fell a clammy depression came upon them. Then, suddenly, there came a sign, simply a natural phenomenon connected with the rising of the full moon— but to Tennant in particular a spiritually re-energising symbol. There, to quote Hobart:

Standing upon the horizon was a single pillar of silver fire—a thing unique—so that for a moment we had no thought of moon-rises. Extraordinarily impressive and most wonderfully beautiful. In the whole sky there was no other cloud. After that there was silence.

They spent the night in a filthy mud fort. Round and about seethed the dispirited, half-starved survivors of the routed army, Armenians, Turks and Germans, each with his own thoughts but none still arrogantly confident of final victory. However, the single-mindedness of the Tartar guides appeared not in the least affected by the disarray and next morning they set out again, but now alone, with their prisoners. Survival hung by a thread, for this was barren country they were entering, even more barren than that they had already crossed, and the guards became ever more sullen and menacing.

In the middle of the morning (three days after the crash) the party halted by the banks of the Euphrates and had a wash— their first since capture. Two guards went with them to the water's edge, one amusing himself by firing his rifle into the water close by. Four aeroplanes flew overhead and sent a few idle shots in their direction. The Tartars stirred to start off, but the camels were their normal aggressive selves, rounding savagely as they were mounted, and at that moment a horseman dashed up shouting 'Auto'. Already the Tartars were distracted and once again they got alarmed and very threatening.

A long burst of machine-gun fire from nearby again settled the matter by making the Tartars bolt for cover while Hobart searched the sky for an aeroplane. It was Tennant who first saw the Rolls-Royce armoured car only a hundred yards away and howled the news, and as one they leapt from their camels and ran madly to where the car was pumping bullets at the Tartars amongst the rocks. The doors were open and the commander already dismounting, ready to fling the fugitives into the turret.

Inside the crew were yelling with excitement, delighted with their success, for they had come a long way for just this moment. But at that instant—as the fugitives regained their breath and the taste of whisky and bully-beef told them they were free— it was all too good to be true.

At Khan Baghdadi nearly the entire Turkish force had been rounded up, and Brigadier Bob Cassels then decided to try to recapture the two officers along with the rest of the defeated enemy. The armoured cars were despatched with orders to operate out to a range of a hundred miles and save Hobart and Tennant if they could. If necessary petrol was to be dropped from the air, so Captain Tod, the commander of the cars, simply drove straight through the Turkish remnants, scattering them with fire and the sheer momentum and daring of his speed. At each stop to refuel or secure captives he investigated clues which might lead him to his quarry, but as the trail got hotter Tod came to realise that he might well overshoot the Tartar party if they had warning of his approach and hid to let him pass. It was distinctly fortunate that he noticed the party far off from a hill, was able to stalk them unseen, and time his final attack to perfection. It was a great moment and a triumph for the endurance and silence of his machinery.

At the court of inquiry both officers were invited to explain their absence of three days with the enemy, but the verdict reflected the chances of war and Hobart was allowed to go post haste to Basra in time to sail for Palestine.

*   *   *   *   *

General Allenby launched his last offensive using an army whose organisation and training had been disrupted by the need to syphon off elements to bolster the shaken front in France. Nevertheless, the units that stood ready for action in September were of high quality. The wartime British Army was fast learning to adopt new techniques, to make professional use of the ideas of amateurs and to centralise its training organisation so that the experience of a few experts could be used for the benefit of the majority and not frittered away in an unco-ordinated manner. Mass production in training was beginning to override the freedom of individuality traditionally enjoyed by the commanding officers of regiments. Whereas, in the past, the regiment and its commander had been sacrosanct, the backbone of the spirit of the British Army (and still to a large extent remained so), some of its internal functions were being superseded by direct control from above.

In the coming battle it was Allenby's intention to break the Turkish front near the coast, north of Jaffa, wheel the infantry on a hinge ten miles inland, and then pass the cavalry rapidly through the ten-mile gap deep into the enemy rear, to Nazareth and the enemy General Headquarters. It was the essence of Allenby's plan that the gap should be made quickly with the pursuit aimed at the enemy's nerve centres, not directly at his army.

There is nothing in Hobart's documents indicating that he was overworked by preparations for the coming battle. For a start, Allenby's plan was cloaked in profound secrecy, the 3rd Indian Division required a minimum of reorganisation and retraining, and 8th Brigade through Hobart was fully attuned to centralised training programmes. But a letter written shortly before Megiddo tells us much about the man.

A.C.—F

I've spent a whole crowded lifetime. Three campaigns : failure, retreat, victory, pursuit : cold and want and misery : heat and torment
and disease, wounds, sickness and injury. Captured and escaped.
Lost my three best friends, and broken my heart (like one's arm or
leg I suppose it mends up again in time : but it isn't ever the same
again) lost most of my illusions, the hair from the top of my head,
and the small remnants of my temper; but not my delight in good
food and drink : flowers and hills and running water : women and
speed and litheness.

Buston lent me *Les Liaisons Dangereuses*. The only thoroughly
revolting book I've ever read. It's very bad for one, a book like that :
makes one feel so damnably self-righteous !

I've read *Sinister Street* also. Not bad. But he's not a master of
English. Nor does he ever succeed in making his point perfectly.
However, he feels. Anatole France's *L'ile des Penguins* is delightful.
But—after a single reading only, I admit—I don't feel he is either
as great or as deep as Samuel Butler. His satire is more superficial
than the satire of Erewhon.

The short, sharp construction of his written sentences dupli-
cate the rattle of his questioning conversation and pour uncor-
rected from his pen as they did from his tongue. In the midst
of a serious declamation he might toss out a caustic provocation
to make the listener wince and doubt the wisdom that had gone
before or, worse, become convinced of the false truth of a half-
sincere aside. In this way, as time went on, he became sadly
misunderstood, for his mind moved fast and far ahead of the
great majority of his contemporaries, taking rapid short cuts and
leaving all but the quickest behind.

With a solid trust in its training 8th Brigade took its post
in the battle. The History of the 47th Sikhs' records how they
fared on the 17th September.

That night and the next, troops were on the move to and from
all directions and the Staff work that enabled us all to get into our
positions without a hitch was excellent.

The sense of purpose inculcated by Allenby's personal touch
was infectious, his objectives boundless and his answer to a
battalion commander who asked what line he should consolidate

—an abrupt 'Aleppo'—could be heard and felt far beyond the small circle to which it was given. By a few extravagant utterances the Commander imbued his troops with a sense of confidence and ambition. He may not have inspired devotion, but he did give an immense sense of purpose. So Hobart, before action :

Now, when I'm still fresh, not thirsty, full fed and know that all my plans are made : and ready. At least one never *knows* that : with human beings there's always the element of misunderstanding possible. But everyone has been seen finally and all understood their job.

When, at 4.30 a.m. on the 19th September, as the rain of shells fell on the Turks and thousands of flares rose skywards from the targets under bombardment, it was borne on those who saw it that victory was assured. For the flares confirmed that the enemy were still there and therefore certain to be destroyed by the massive blow. 8th Brigade on its wide, thinly held front had merely to conform to the movements of the two other concentrated brigades in 3rd Division as they burst through on the left, then advance to the north, prior to swinging rhythmically to the northeast and east, sweeping the Turks out of the corridor through which the cavalry were jostling to ride.

Soon, along the coast, deep in the enemy rear, the cavalry were loose, practically unimpeded by any form of resistance. And to their front the Turkish Army recoiled, driven off its main lines of communications towards the River Jordan and the Arabs waiting in the desert beyond.

Both Indian divisions continued to the east on the 20th against isolated pockets of the enemy, notably German troops. Where the sharp folds and ridges of the hills afforded cover the Germans took full advantage of the defensive nature of the ground and fought to the death, and it was against them that 8th Brigade were pitted throughout the 20th, mostly without artillery support and often when cut off from telephone communication with other formations. Again the units of the brigade record their appreciation of brigade headquarters always being close behind them, directing the battle and squeezing every drop from opportunity. The penalty that this frequently led to a break-down in communications to the rear drew from Hobart the retort that it was for those in rear to supply a better service. The advantages of having a headquarters in the forefront of an advance far outweighed the perils of loss of communication with the rear and, in any case, he was never one to refuse the blind-eye technique if it was advantageous.

Indeed, there is an unconfirmed story[1] that at one vital moment, when his brigadier wished to make a last-minute change of plan before an attack, Hobart refused to pass the order and made doubly sure it would not be sent by seizing possession of the telephone until the attack had gone successfully ahead to the original plan. It is said that this incident brought his association with 8th Brigade to an end, and the purists will agree, with justification, that for a staff officer to defy his commander is poison to the roots of discipline and confidence.

The choice of conscience when men's lives are at stake is one which has tested soldiers from the beginning of time. Must a soldier bow to what he believes to be wrong? When does he refuse to obey? And if he decides to disobey how does he go about it? Hobart, his habitual critical faculty ever near the surface, found it natural to disagree and on these occasions had a distinct inclination to throw moderation to the winds; for when it came to the well-being of an organisation he cherished and the men he had trained he knew not how to compromise; these, to a man who loved beauty, were beautiful and to be protected. Deep inside an instinctive anger at the stupidity of others surged up; if time was short it burst forth—as it was to do more than once throughout his tempestuous career.

Two days later orders came for him to join 53rd Division as G.S.O. 2 and move with it to Jerusalem to prepare for a fresh task. His despondency was complete. The new job held no prospects, and even had he known that 53rd Division was earmarked for an invasion into the Balkans it is unlikely he would have been appeased. The division was on the move, the general ill, there was no G.S.O. 3 and the rest of the staff were split up all

1. *Dictionary of National Biography.*

over the place. Worst of all, there was no work to do, allowing his mind to wander into dangerous channels.

In Jerusalem he faced a daunting problem—should he go on in the Army? It was a time for deep thought, initiated by loneliness and the place wherein he stayed:

I've just walked down this evening in Gethsemane and out to the garden with the little, gentle brown garbed Franciscan monk. I was meditative and wished to think on immortality, and sufferings, the great mystery of sacrifice, and the unconquerable spirit of man. But, in that garden, already in shadow, . . . I did not think at all. Only the peace that is of gardens fell upon me like the comradeship of a wise friend.

You speak of immortality. And so there is for you my dear [Betty] and the likes of you. Maybe not only in your sons. Nothing is destroyed by Nature. It is changed. I would like you to read a very wonderful and inspiring book called *The Origin of Life*. It has been an illumination to me. You will find it hard reading, taking all your attention two and three times. But well worth it, indeed.

These are not the thoughts of a deeply religious man, nor those of a soft, gentle person—but they are the expressions of an emotional person torn with doubts and forbiddings who is looking for help and sees no clear future. He could not write with much hope.

But I have no money and no influence. I can see, therefore, little or no chance of finding an opening in any business or factory at home. Remains that refuge of all failures—the Colonies. When I thought of it before the war I had two great assets in my two prospective partners, Ginger [Chase] and Geoff Maxwell. Neither of those will be with me now. . . . I must . . . leave the Army altogether and make a fresh start elsewhere from the bottom.

Part 2

DEVELOPMENT

If you don't stake your claims
high, no one will listen to you.

Attributed to
Major-General J. F. C. Fuller

5

THE WATERSHED

In the minds of many surviving regular officers it would be true to say that the signing of the Armistice in 1918 was more than a relief; for a majority the instinctive reaction was an unvarnished desire for time to withdraw to leisure. With several there was the spoken wish that the end of hostilities should signal a reversion to the more formal, half-pace, soldiering as it had been before 1914. To many there could be no relaxation at all, since, at once, they found themselves involved in duties in the occupied enemy territories, or wrapped in the struggles between English and Irish, or Whites and Reds in Russia, or fiercely engaged in a frontier war with Afghanistan. To a very few, peace heralded the beginning of a struggle to modernise the Army. Whereas it was in the nature of many to wallow in backwaters if they could, a vital minority could not accept a reduction in tempo because, they would argue, the upsurge of technical knowledge which had revolutionised the Army during four years of war could not be forgotten; world wide, the art of war was in galloping revolution.

Converting the wartime army into a peacetime version was bound to absorb a high proportion of time. The reduction of a huge conscripted, citizen army to a small volunteer, regular force capable of carrying out its various world-wide commitments in many more territories than had required its presence in 1914 was a tall order. To expect men to enthuse over the risks of active service when 'the war to end all wars' had only just stopped demanded a staunch belief in causes at a time when causes were in decline. On top of this, an invitation to a serious debate, coupled with expensive research and development, on the way the next major war might be fought was, to the vast majority, ludicrous —and the British people as a whole were bound to agree.

Taking their cue from the electorate, the British politicians pursued the same high-pitched aims as the League of Nations, with careful reference to the aspirations of the Covenant of the League where it dealt with disarmament; and closest to the desires of the industrialists dwelt the demands for conscripts to be demobilised and the need for a rapid change-over from a war to a peacetime economy. The manufacture of war material had to give place to something else, while the Armed Services set about retrenchment in line with the decision of the War Cabinet, in 1919, that 'the British Empire will not be engaged in any great war during the next ten years, and that no Expeditionary Force will be required'. In any case, the French Army retained immense strength and France in the twenties was united in one aim if no other—Germany must not again become a threat. Hence, disarmament for France became surrounded by distinct, nationalistic, self-preservative qualifications.

In 1919 the Army and Air Force became subject to an arbitrary Budget of £75 million per annum and entered a decade or more of declining interest in the public eye. For the next dozen years the occasions for their emergence into prominence could more likely be ascribed to a minor social scandal than to a major disclosure of inherent weakness. According to the Secretary of State for War, in 1920, Mr. Winston Churchill, the closest attention would have to be paid to every penny spent and the general approach in the future would be in the direction of experiments to try out new tactics to solve those problems left unsolved by the upsurge of mechanisation in the last year of the war. But progress became mighty slow, even in the publication of new training manuals.

It is easy to generalise and well-nigh impossible to pin-point the root causes of the malaise which ate its way into the creative cells in the brains of the Army after 1918. The spur of sheer necessity is not infrequently the motivation of creation and progress, and history shows how often the most fundamental innovations have sprung from impatient men who, as often as not, were living in conditions of semi-privation or under great stress. It could not be said that army officers, as a tribe, lived in privation. A large number supplemented their pay from private income and looked on their military careers as a pleasant occupation, about which, to say the least, they could become detached. So, to the majority, the spur to innovation was absent when technology was leaping ahead. Indeed, officers with technical leanings were despised as part of the self-protective habit amongst orthodox officers to decry technical advances in case the *status quo* was threatened. At the bottom of it all lay the traditional schism between country and town—gentlemen and industrialists. Gradually a minor tactic in defence of leisure in the Army, part of the backwash from four years' struggle, began to develop into a binding habit—the strategy of 'no-progress-in-our-time-if-we-can-help-it'. In this environment, when a majority were not sympathetic to progress, new ideas withered on the branch.

Yet, to a vital few, the study of the future of war became an absorbing passion. Scattered about the world, sitting in offices in the War Office or studying outside the curriculum in the staff colleges, dedicated officers with enquiring minds began to lay the foundations of an army that retained the mystique of discipline and comradeship of 1914, absorbed the lessons of the war and projected its developments along the lines suggested by the campaigns of the last year of war. Of their number the name of Colonel J. F. C. Fuller was pre-eminent.

Three shortened courses were held at the Staff College, Camberley, after the war for officers whose immersion in active service during the war had prevented them graduating with the symbol *psc*. Gathered together were men whose talents and experience set them apart from their contemporaries: the list of students makes fascinating reading. On the first course, to which Patrick Hobart was nominated, were two holders of the Victoria Cross, Lieutenant-Colonel Bernard Freyberg and Major Lord Gort; there too was Major Alan Brooke amidst a host of others who were to find fame with him as he rose to the pinnacle of his profession after 1939. Standing next to Hobart in the formal course photograph is Major Maitland Wilson, later to become a Field Marshal and a central figure in the Middle East; seated in the front row is Colonel Charles Broad, a senior instructor but destined to be the man to command the first all-tank brigade in the world, a man who, as a gunner, when he looked on the tank battlefield of Cambrai, remarked how un-usual it was to see so few bodies! At the next course there was to be Major Bernard Montgomery with a fellow student, Patrick's younger brother Stanley. Not to be the holder of a D.S.O. on these courses was to be in a distinct minority: to fail to reach the rank of brigadier, at least, in the years to come was tantamount to being labelled an eccentric.

The course itself did not entirely appeal to the students. Their wide practical experience, often only a little short of that of their instructors, led to a high standard of debate (provided the out-look was not circumscribed and not old-fashioned): their high spirits, natural from men rejoicing in a release from a night-mare, provoked wild races across country on horseback, after studying the ground for some theoretical exercise, as only one of several ways of expressing the joy of being alive—and in England.

Yet the course could hardly offer immediate advantages when the Army was being drastically reduced and outlets for promo-tion becoming as rare as new posts to fill. Brooke, the future Chief of the Imperial General Staff, found himself a G.S.O. 2 in a Territorial division. Hobart became a G.S.O. 2 in the War Office, dealing with Intelligence problems. Others were not so lucky.

In fact the translation to his first appointment in the War Office was not entirely unwelcome. To be incarcerated in the offices of Whitehall was repugnant; to live in London was not, because there he could reassemble his circle of friends and for two years bask in an exciting society and found life-long friendships. Of the latter, without doubt, the most important and closest to him were those with Alan Patrick Herbert and Eric Kennington.

In Herbert, Hobart detected the brilliance that in 1919 was still revealed only to a few. They shared much in common and were part owners of the barge *Water Gypsy*. To Hobart, the genius of the young author was to be found less in the gay, sophisticated prose, than in his deep inner comprehension of humanity and of all Herbert's works he admired most *The Silent Battle* wherein a great-hearted man is worn, broken and finally destroyed by the machinery of military discipline. Herbert, in Hobart's view, never wrote a better book than that—it seemed to penetrate the soul of fighting men and expose the weaknesses that must inevitably be exposed in the heat and pressure of unrelieved fear: it tallied too with his sympathy for the private soldiers and an oft expressed desire to improve their lot. The trials of Topsy were just frivolities—fun, but no more than that.

And then there was Kennington, whose sculptures and portraits saw either into the innermost recesses of their subject or barely tinted the skin. Here was a boisterous, full-blooded, dedicated man who rode high on the rough and tumble of life—and moulded material into the most exquisite shapes with a simple, direct and unique skill. Amongst people such as these, well informed and deeply perceptive, he projected and sharpened his wits to a high pitch, and in this company rejected the mediocre and the traditional. Contact with a radical environment redoubled his own taste for the radical solution to problems when the direction of common thought was either backward or, at best, aimed at stability, or in the 'Bloomsbury Circle', in his opinion, cynically indifferent.

The time had come yet again for Patrick Hobart to reconsider his position. By sending him to Camberley the Army forgave his misdemeanours and deflected him from resignation: at the same time it encouraged him to study the lessons of the last war by conventional analysis, and arrive at thoroughly unconventional conclusions, based, as often as not, on his own experiences.

He had found in 1915, in France, that movement above

ground was prohibitive in the face of machine-gun and artillery fire, but that although these weapons magnified the power of defence they only marginally assisted in attack. In Mesopotamia he had taken part in movement round a permanently open desert flank, but seen that, even there, it became desperately slow if lives were to be preserved. The slow siege methods of Khudaira had been cheaper than the quick assault at Tikrit, but neither employed surprise any more than did the long-prepared attacks in France.

Repeatedly in Mesopotamia and Palestine he had seen horsed cavalry ride deep into the enemy rear, but only after the enemy had been totally disrupted; and even amongst the fluid conditions of pursuit to Baghdad and beyond, Hobart had seen horsemen repulsed time and again by only light-machine-gun opposition. But he had seen armoured cars exploit far more effectively because they could operate faster, at a greater distance from their base, bring fire to bear from behind armoured protection and do all this using far fewer men. If it had not been so he would not have escaped from the Turks.

In coming to an independent conclusion that mechanical, armoured vehicles would be the key to the future of war by disrupting and then exploiting the confusion of the enemy, Hobart agreed with the band of Tank Corps officers whose practical work in France had actually broken the trench deadlock and disrupted the Germans. The publication in the R.U.S.I. Journal of May 1920 of an essay by Colonel J. F. C. Fuller set fire to controversy, for Fuller did more than win the Gold Medal for the first post-war military essay—he crystallised the case for the tank and suggested that its place in future armies would be at the gradual expense of the older, traditional arms—notably the infantry and, above all, the horsed cavalry. Succinctly, Fuller drew attention to what had been inherent in the plans to defeat Germany had the war lasted into 1919—a future battle revolving round armoured vehicles. But now the heat generated by his proposals was converted by its opponents into accusations that Fuller wanted an all-tank army—and so the resistance to what was, in fact, a rational case for an armoured, mechanised army (with infantry and gunners in mechanical vehicles as adjuncts to the horsed element) became centred on a campaign to denigrate the future prospects of the tank. It mattered not that the fighting tank was a specialist vehicle dependent on the other arms for its survival—almost anything with armour, an engine and tracks was, to the pundits, a tank and Fuller himself did little to discourage the thought.

Hobart's sympathy was with Fuller, linked with a deep knowledge of the way all arms should be employed on the battlefield. From the moment his career as a Sapper had virtually ended in September 1915, his attention had focussed on the combined use of infantry, artillery, reconnaissance, communications and the technique of command. Close analysis told him that infantry and artillery succeeded only as the product of mutual assistance, meticulous plans based on correct information and the personal exercise of command from the forefront of the battle. If the existing channels of communication by telephone, messenger and pigeon broke down when applied to this system, then a better method, probably wireless, would have to be developed in its place. But nothing worked unless armoured vehicles could disrupt the front and exploit—and by so doing introduce a new element to the battlefield.

Further than this Hobart does not seem to have gone at this stage although undoubtedly he visualised, in accord with Fuller, that armoured formations would impose their will by striking at the brain of the enemy as Allenby had struck at Nazareth after Megiddo. But there had to be a pause for war again— war of the old sort with not a tank in sight—as at the end of 1921 he left the War Office and returned to India.

*   *   *   *   *

Waziristan is a barren, rocky and extremely hilly country perched across the routes connecting the western fringe of India with Afghanistan. Its inhabitants are nomads, steeped in poverty and a passion for tribal feuding, their unruly spirit making them the friend neither of India nor Afghanistan because, whenever there was the prospect of plunder, the Waziris were happy to seize it regardless whence it came. In 1893 the signing of the

Durand Agreement had marked the renunciation of Afghan claims to Waziristan, and British acceptance of a Wazir offer to control the routes through the country from a post at Wana.

Transport through the valleys at the turn of the century and in 1921 was still by pack animal, yet the pacification of the country depended on the construction of roads along which forces could be rushed to combat dissident tribesmen but, above all, the need was for education related to long periods of peace and a minimum of fighting. Therefore, where action had to be swift, decisive and economic, the use of regular military forces for what was, basically, police work became inherently uneconomic. Only when the tribesmen took to guerilla warfare was military action justified and then it was more logical for the forces concerned to seek a military objective, the destruction of the enemy fighting men and their leaders, rather than the enforcement of economic sanctions that only put a further brake on progress. In theory, this was a highly satisfactory aim except when it happened, all too often, that the locally raised militias later became the core of a hostile guerilla army armed with an increased fighting ability.

The vigour of tribal warfare had multiplied since 1917 and culminated in the outbreak of the Third Afghan War in May 1919. Waziristan went aflame and for the first time the tribesmen found themselves pitted against aeroplanes and armoured cars. Even after the formal war, the frontier seethed, so that by the end of 1920 it appeared essential to re-establish the British post in Wana and form a new militia to control the turbulent tribes. On 11th November 1920 a foot-and-animal-borne force, called the Wana Column, set out under the command of Colonel O. C. Borrett, supported overhead by Bristol fighters of the R.A.F.

The main route to Wana, dominated by the hills that rose on either side, provided the perfect setting for ambushes, and in the Shahur Tangi, a narrow gorge four miles in length overlooked by steep creviced crags, there lay the most threatening spot of all. To seize the peaks against opposition would be costly, to fail to do so suicidal.

Oswald Borrett was a remarkable man, with a wealth of

active service to his credit since the Boer War. A thinking soldier, to whom a conventional solution was anathema, his career was almost unique in that he never passed a promotion exam, except to captain, and had never attended Staff College, because, as he claimed, he 'had been too busy fighting'. Idleness would hit him hard with the same cruel despondency as that suffered by Hobart.

The Wana Column reached its destination practically unmolested for the good reason that Borrett did not adhere to the accepted gambits of frontier fighting. By moving to the Shahur Tangi by night and occupying the peaks before the tribesmen were ready, he routed them, morally and physically, from the outset.

On 5th April 1921 Borrett was joined by his new brigade major, Patrick Hobart. They were kindred spirits, men with minds of their own, open to new ideas and imbued with an innate sense of the unexpected, the original and the dramatic. Together, with a two-pronged policy, they set about the domination of the Wana countryside in a manner reminiscent of present day anti-guerilla operations.

On the one hand they sought to deny the enemy the use of their homes and cultivated areas by subjecting them to bombing and shell-fire. On the other they carried the war to the guerilla bands, first by locating and then by ambushing them in their own territory.

In a land where secrets are the gossip of the bazaars, Borrett and Hobart strove hardest of all for deception and surprise. A successful raid on the village of Spin Warsak, known to contain a number of hostile tribesmen, illustrates their methods. Beforehand a feint was made at dusk in the direction of another village, with the intention of lulling the dissidents in Spin Warsak into a false sense of security. Concurrently a force was placed across the line of retreat from the village. Complete surprise was achieved. Only at the last moment were the villagers aware of their danger as cavalry and infantry dashed in to catch forty-eight wanted men, including their leader.

In retaliation the tribesmen tried to close the Shahur Tangi, the jugular vein of the Wana Column, one of the few places

A.C.—G

kept permanently picquetted in the old wasteful manner because of its importance. Often the tribesmen crawled under the noses of the picquets, opened fire on convoys and had to be driven off by the reserves rushing in from either end of the gorge. On balance it was Borrett's men who held the upper hand, largely as a result of his seizing the initiative and rarely enacting the same plan twice.

With the decision to withdraw and leave the newly formed Militia in charge at the end of 1921 came the Wana Column's most difficult test. The preparations for the move could not be cloaked in secrecy, for not only had the Militia to be warned of the date they were to start their duties, but the stores accumulated in Wana and the subsidiary bases along the lines of communication back to Jandoal had to be removed. Thus the convoy had to pass in the face of a forewarned enemy eager to settle old scores. Withdrawal in face of the enemy is the most difficult operation in war and one which, until then, Hobart had never experienced. The withdrawal of the last stores had to match accurately with the time the fighting troops gave up each position: the enemy had to be deceived, over and over again, of the exact moment when each piece of ground was to be given up: each advanced detachment had to be provided with the fair chance of a clean break to the rear unhindered by the enemy: every element had to be ready to strike hard at a moment's notice at any of the enemy who threatened to disturb the even pulse of the other arrangements.

The journey of fifty miles took three weeks and for the last three days was harassed by heavy rains and floods. Yet there were only three casualties in this period, no stores were lost to the enemy, and even the signal cables were wound up and brought back whole.

*   *   *   *   *

Hobart's reputation was established and although his next appointment as G.S.O. 2 at the headquarters of the Eastern Command in Naini Tal lacked glamour, the awards that followed were overwhelmingly gratifying. In quick succession came the appointment as an Officer of the Order of the British Empire, promotion to the rank of brevet lieutenant-colonel and the share with Borrett of a personal commendation in General Rawlinson's Wana Despatch, 'a capable and resourceful staff officer, well above the average'. He later looked on the experience as 'a useful corrective to preoccupation with mechanisation', but it is much more likely that it acted as an inspiration. The praise and public recognition were of the kind that had evaded him for the whole of the Great War.

His assistant in Naini Tal, Michael Roberts, recalls the morning Hobart opened an envelope lying on his desk, seeing him sit back reflectively for a moment with the unfolded paper in his hands, and then say softly, 'My God! At last.' He was posted as an instructor to the Staff College at Quetta. Roberts, now engaged in the writing of Official Histories of the Second World War, has many clear recollections of his dynamic master. He remembers Hobart remarking, in surprise, 'You are the first man I have worked with for six months without a row'—and the explosive argument that broke out between them next day. Above all there was the declaration that the 'future lay with the tank', followed by Hobart's application to transfer from the Royal Engineers to the Tank Corps next day. The idea had taken root long before in Hobart's mind, but only when the decision had been made did he impart it to his colleague.

On the 1st April 1923 Hobart became a tank officer. Six weeks later, wearing his new badges, he took up his duties at Quetta, responsible, in addition to his instructional duties, as the tank representative at the Staff College. Thus an extraordinary situation arose, because the new instructor was, by experience, a practical expert on almost every aspect of war except tank warfare. Moreover there was no reason to suppose that the older members of the newly established Tank Corps would welcome a flood of newcomers from outside to spoil their already tenuous promotion prospects, and not for them to know that Hobart had lost seniority himself by making a transfer.

Horace Birks, an officer in the 1st Armoured Car Company in Quetta, who had served in the Tank Corps from its early days, was highly suspicious of the new man, and recalls being thoroughly taken aback when the subject of his mistrust 'warned into' the mess as a normal member instead of waiting for a formal invitation. But seduced by the complete range of Hobart's charm, Birks and the others wilted, their surrender aided and abetted by Hobart's pony winning several point-to-point races to the financial benefit of them all. Nevertheless, they were not displeased that two miles separated their mess from the Staff College, where the students complained that 'Hobart had the answer to the questions before they were asked'. None denied that he was a brilliant teacher in very close touch with his students, guiding and encouraging their studies in and out of class with meticulous care, commenting on their written work with crisp questions, followed by his own penetrating exposition. It was mightily invigorating to be pummelled by his restless demands for new ideas, his single-minded search for the truth based on the lessons of history, and the example he set by the superlative quality of his own work. Moreover, in no time he was more than master of tanks. Birks was astonished to find that in 1925 he knew more about the mechanical details of armoured cars and the handling of them than he did himself.

Hobart's students and the younger members of the Royal Tank Corps came to accept him with the reservation that he was 'dangerous' and a 'go-getter'. They were moving into an era of change, he said, when the machines would reduce the manpower bill in guerilla warfare as well as in conventional battles, and summarised the nub of the debate in a lecture saying:

The enthusiast is apt to visualise possibilities as actualities: he dreams dreams.

The conservative soldier (and soldiers are apt to be conservatives) on the other hand sees the danger of his beloved arm, with its glorious records and proven powers, being replaced by a crude monster, an upstart with only three years of war experience and known to have many limitations. He is hurt, annoyed, outraged—and consequently obstinate.

His fault is that instead of ensuring that the Army takes over the tanks, he is waiting—hopelessly—for the tanks to take over the Army.

Part of his new knowledge came from correspondence with Colonel George Lindsay, an ex-member of the Rifle Brigade, who, like Hobart, had transferred to the Tank Corps in 1923 and was chief instructor at the Tank Corps Central Schools at Bovington in England. It was Lindsay's task to organise instruction in the schools, and expound the views of the new corps outside its own boundaries; but to do so in a manner least likely to encroach upon the traditional functions of the cavalry, infantry and artillery, and mitigate, to some extent, Colonel Fuller's frightening suggestions that the tank would become predominant. While Fuller aimed chiefly to inject urgency into 'mechanicalisation', as it was then called, he probably did more to create opposition to the tank idea than help its progress.

And so, writing to Hobart in India, Lindsay could only suggest:

My present policy as regards Mechanicalisation would be to:
(a) Develop gradually, and with due experiment, a True Mechanical Force.
(b) Provide in addition, a sufficient number of Tanks for assault work with the Infantry.
(c) Make the Cavalry really Mobile by Mechanicalising their transport—and lightening the load on the horse.

and then go on to discuss the new Vickers tank. Here was a revolutionary machine, the forerunner in shape and layout of those that were to predominate for the next forty years, with a speed and range cross country that made the tanks of the First World War appear elephantine. Designed at first as a so-called light tank, it had come to be the main battle tank of the British Army when no money was allotted for the construction of a heavy, expensive machine. It was the test bed for all the great experiments to come.

From these exchanges, and as a result of intensive study, Hobart evolved a doctrine that was to guide him for the next two decades, and which was at the heart of his future career.

The foundation of the charges and the acrimony surrounding Hobart's leading part in the struggle for the tanks are interwoven with the misconception that he was wedded to the evolution of an all-tank army that excluded the cavalry, the artillery and the infantry. Nothing could have been further from the truth. What can be demonstrated is Hobart's unbending determination to develop the tank idea as the prime element in a mechanical, armoured army that moved and fought at the speed of the tank. Certainly this tolled the knell of the horse; inevitably the artillery needed to be mounted on mechanical vehicles; undoubtedly the infantry would need to travel in vehicles to keep pace with the battle; essentially this fast-moving, hard-hitting force would have to be controlled by wireless by commanders who led from the forefront of the battle: but this was not a pernicious scheme aimed at placing the Army under the control of the tankmen.

Complementary letters between Hobart and Lindsay in 1925 etch their materialising vision of a mobile force:

Hobart:

Until we have the means of commanding and controlling tanks on the move, we cannot be a formation or force, but only an unco-ordinated crowd of units in action. . . . The other paramount need, I take it, is Accompanying Artillery. The Royal Tank Artillery. Extreme mobility—go for nerve centres. Live on the country. You'll only need petrol, oil and very little food, all of which are endemic in any (even semi-civilised) country these days. . . . We always preach the necessity of infantry following up to take over, *at once*, what tanks have captured. Is that the idea of war that Alexander, Hannibal, even Ziethen or Napoleon had? We were reduced to that by inadequate mobility . . . Why limit ourselves to a 3,000–4,000 yards advance? The distance gunners can reach without moving. This artillery obsession. Given (a) efficient, fast tanks with good means of control; (b) accompanying artillery (i.e. The Royal Tank Artillery, designed for the support of tanks just as RHA was for the support of Cav) (c) suitable air force. Why piddle about with porridge-making of the Third Ypres type? When one is possessed of modern weapons one shoots a tiger in the brain, heart, or spine. One doesn't painfully hack off a foot at a time 'consolidating' as one goes.

Lindsay:

Why fight for positions? If centres of command and supply, and communications, are overcome by the Mobile Force, the enemy cannot remain in their positions. . . . No, the war will be won, or lost, as far as military operations go, by the Mechanical Force, in the air and on the ground, working in co-operation. The ground troops, present infantry and cavalry, will occupy, administer, and police, the areas conquered by the Mechanical Force.

Hobart's lectures in 1926, his last full year at Quetta, crystallise the concept of the mobile force of the future and reach maturity in a long paper proposing an organisation for a mechanised force. The arguments are beautifully balanced in that they consider every side of the problem, arising from a study of the lessons of history concerning the old mobile armies, linked with recent experience of mobile war, and then interwoven to form a tapestry of striking originality.

From the ancient days of bow and arrow against armour, Hobart demonstrated how the varying relationships between fire power, protection and mobility impinged upon organisation, tactics and strategy. Applying these thoughts to recent events, he foresaw a quickening of the race between gun and armour on the tank—a race which had started with the very first tank action, when it was discovered that the Germans already possessed, by chance, a bullet that would penetrate the armour of the early machines. He sought to circumvent the gun/armour race by means of speed, concentration of effort joined with surprise, and the co-operation of all arms.

Thus at an early stage Hobart spoke of the need for other arms to work in co-operation with tanks, 'the infantry to hold gains' and 'artillery to protect by fire and smoke. Tanks cannot cover themselves with smoke. Great increase in tank casualties when beyond support of artillery.' But he was convinced that, unless the infantry stayed relatively close to the tanks in action, they would fail in their task, and that the artillery had to be capable of keeping up with the tanks to ensure the guns could maintain continuous fire support no matter how far the tanks travelled. Here was the point at which vested interests came into contest, the cause of a host of misunderstandings and of bitterness in the years to come. With the old, slow-moving tanks it had been comparatively simple for the infantry and artillery to keep up with the speed of advance. Now, said Hobart, 'the pace of the modern tank [the Vickers Medium] has rendered this method obsolete'.

He agreed, with General Eric Ludendorff, 'the fact that the *"light"*[1] machine gun was now the true "infantryman" had not yet sunk deep into the army', and that being so, the infantryman with his light machine gun needed to travel in a light armoured vehicle. He enquired of the progress in artillery mechanisation, of the 'Birch' gun, which was a field gun mounted on the chassis of a Vickers tank. Only a few of these machines were ever produced and held no attraction for horsed gunners—not least, one suspects, because they bore a strong resemblance to a tank.

Today it is taken for granted that infantry travel, if possible, in their own lightly armoured vehicles, and that artillery has to be self-propelled on tracked vehicles when fighting alongside tanks and mechanised infantry. Moreover, one of the original staff of the Tank Corps, Major G. le Q. Martel, was at that moment designing and manufacturing a thinly armoured, one-man track-cum-wheeled vehicle in collaboration with the motor manufacturer William Morris, from which was to descend the generations of light carriers that became the first armoured infantry carrier. In 1926 this was a dream, but clearly visible to Hobart in his search for a technical solution to his demand for armoured mobility. He went even further, suggesting that the time might come when the general advent of cross-country vehicles would lead to the disappearance of the Tank Corps as a separate entity. But in the meantime he applied only what was immediately obtainable to his short-term proposals.

The tank was the only armoured vehicle available : it would dominate and therefore its destruction would be a matter of overriding importance. In Hobart's view, mines could impede tanks and field guns be a menace in the close battle, but once action became mobile, the tank with a three-pounder or six-pounder gun

1. Author's italics.

became the only viable anti-tank weapon. The naval battle concept was popular in this respect, but Hobart remembered, 'sea is
a uniform plane surface: it is in the *use of ground* that the
great genius of commanders on land is shown', and went on to
extol the advantages of the control of fire power from within
tank formations by instructions over the wireless, seizing upon
the advantages enjoyed by the tank over horsed units in that
the former could shoot on the move and the latter could not.
Yet there stirred in the back of his mind the realisation that a
tank need not be the only sort of threat to another, for anti-tank
guns might, in time, do to the tank what the machine gun had
done to infantry and cavalry.

To overcome the growing power of the defence, he lectured
on the necessity to increase endurance, pace, fire power, the
use of ground and cover, and for the need to employ accompanying artillery, listing machines for the task as:

> A fast light tank for reconnaissance.
> A medium tank for general purpose.
> Artillery carriers.
> Tanks to act as Communication Centres.
> Infantry transporters.
> Heavy tanks.
> Mine-layers.
> Mine-sweepers.
> Gas and Smoke Producers.

The final stage in the development of his ideas centred upon
organisation. Here he found himself imbued with the ideas expressed by Captain Liddell Hart when, in the early twenties, he
had written about the 'Expanding Torrent' of exploitation once a
hole had been made in the enemy front. In a long paper setting
out his own ideas for a 'Light Division of the Future' can be
found passages such as these:

> The object is to destroy the enemy's will to resist . . . If blow
> reaches the heart or brain combat would be over . . . Thus a *supreme
> effort* and heavy casualties are worth while if campaign's duration
> can be shortened. . . .

Pace is Protection, Rapidity means Surprise . . . Increased mobility and range entails great calls not only on endurance . . . but on intelligence and initiative in all ranks . . . A new sort of discipline is required. The 'You're not paid to think' variety is obsolete.

The demand was for a *corps d'elite* and one whose organisation was based on five fundamental elements which he called:

A Reconnaissance Group comprising armoured cars, light tanks, motor cyclists and anti-tank guns.
A Fire Group comprising light tanks, mechanised artillery, infantry heavily armed with machine guns and anti-tank guns.
A Tank Group comprising medium tanks, scout tanks and tracked artillery.
A Div Troops Group to include three squadrons of aircraft, engineers and bridging and communications elements.
A Maintenance Group which cared for the administration of the whole division.

An elastic interchange between groups to suit different situations would be vital in a flexible arrangement.

This was, in essence, the armoured division of the future and shows more clearly than any other document the way Hobart thought in terms of the essential co-operation between all arms. The paper leaves us in no doubt that the implementation of this force would be initially expensive and could only come to pass over a period of time. But then it had perforce to come into collision with vested interests, since not only a change in attitude to soldiering was being demanded but the wholesale sacrifice of the traditional tasks of the older arms.

Basically the British Army through most of its history had been a police force—its excursions on a large scale into Grand European Wars a phenomenon of the past quarter century and its return to policing made as rapidly as possible. The kinds of force for both kinds of war are in many ways incompatible and, therefore, to a considerable extent, the creation of the new light divisions would be dependent on the Army being relieved of many police duties and converting itself to a European state of mind and organisation. High on his list of the arms which might have to be severely reduced were the horsed cavalry.

Here for the moment Hobart stopped—restrained no doubt by the discipline of the Staff College that he should not range too far beyond the bounds of official policy. Restricted too by the distance separating him from England where most of the new ideas were being matured by debate and acrimony. So it is all the more significant (and a pointer to his own partially isolated attack on the problem) that Hobart constructed his views on the future of the Army while away from its main stream. But we are left in no doubt that he foresaw a protracted struggle ahead, when he quoted to his students a passage from Mahan's *The Influence of Sea Power*.

The Student will observe that changes in Tactics have not only taken place after changes in weapons, which necessarily is the case, but that the interval between such changes has been unduly long.

This doubtless arises from the fact that an improvement of weapons is due to the energy of one or two men, while changes in tactics have to overcome the inertia of a conservative class; but it is a great evil.

Then, wistfully, in his paper on the Light Division, relating Von der Goltz in 1883 to his own day:

Looking forward into the future we seem to feel the coming of the time when the armed millions of the present will have played their part. A new Alexander will arise who, with a small body of *well-equipped and skilled*[2] warriors, will drive the impotent hordes before him.

*   *   *   *   *

The year of 1927 was one of revolution for the armies of the world led by Britain. It was also a year of revolution for Hobart himself, personally, as well as militarily, for then there came the moves that led to his marriage the following year. Unorthodox in his solution of so many problems, he now shaped a thoroughly

2. Hobart's italics.

unconventional course to matrimony. For Dorothea, whom he decided to marry, was already the wife of a brother officer he had known since first they met at Naini Tal in 1912.

Quite by chance their postings coincided and repeatedly threw them into each other's company. Fatally, inexorably, like homing magnets, Patrick and Dorothea found themselves forming an attachment of enduring strength and, by the beginning of 1927, their emotions had practically overcome the resistance of conscience. On the brink they delayed and then finally decided that divorce for Dorothea followed by marriage was, for them, the only course open. It was a decision that neither ever regretted, their union becoming an unqualified success, bringing to the dynamic soldier a woman of character and immense charm who would assuage his fiercest dispositions.

Yet it could have gone so ill for them. The destructive power of the divorce court with the awful pressure that legal proceedings exerted upon them, was one thing: the recriminations of the everyday moral attitudes of the outside world and elements in their own families another. But their future happiness depended to an enormous extent on whether or not Patrick could remain on in the Army in defiance of society and a few rather sketchily written rules.

The latter were sketchy indeed. Officers had divorced and married the wives of other officers before and it was not unknown for the event to involve close brother officers and for the offending party to remain in the Service. But Hobart's involvement caused a stir and seems to have provoked the War Office into issuing a letter indicating that if an officer were to disrupt the marriage of a brother officer in his own regiment he would be expected to resign his commission. The letter caused more amusement than distress at the time, since it was flippantly assumed by some that it was, by omission, permissive to take off the wife of any other officer provided he belonged to any regiment other than his own. In any event, it left Patrick free to remain in the Service. He was in the Royal Tank Corps and Dorothea's husband was a Royal Engineer: they were not in the same regiment, although it was true that the relationship between instructor and student introduced a confusing factor.

In a frank letter to Dorothea, Patrick gave the reasons for his determination to fight convention :

. . . and you know all the facts which it is impossible to ignore . . . the cruel slights and social outrages to which a divorcee is exposed even more in the Army, and the misery that can be caused thereby : my dependence for a livelihood on my profession : the useless loose-ended dreary sort of creature I would be if I had not this work and the illusion at least that I was some good at it and wasn't an entirely useless member of the British Commonwealth.

If you ask me to give up . . . [the Army] . . . as the only way to get what I desire most and the companionship which I know to be the chief prize in life, I might well do so . . . I should be deterred to some extent by knowledge of my own nature : by the bitter certainty of my own egoism which would make me fret at the bars . . . and would in time change my nature. . . . That is the only consideration in inevitableness of ones own nature—that makes it endurable for me to let this whole burden of decision and of action fall on you. My whole nature revolts at standing by whilst anyone else does my job. Everything in me is up in arms against such inaction.

The decision was taken, a divorce took place in mid-1928 and in November that year they were married. The effects of their action cannot be ignored in relation to the subsequent development of Hobart's story. Mostly their friends closed in tightly in support, and loved them as dearly as ever. Accompanying them on a delayed honeymoon to Switzerland went Arthur Wauchope, a life-long friend who was later to be High Commissioner in Palestine, and Nancy Wavell with her brother Archie. There were others who reacted as Hobart expected. Against them he bridled—but in the long term his already throbbing ambition to achieve something for himself, for the Service, above all for the tanks, was given a savage boost by his ruthless determination to justify himself to the woman he had married. Inescapably, one is driven to the conclusion that, in the coming years when he erupted like a volcano in the face of opposition, or when his career or ideas suffered from set-backs, the prime motivating force behind his violence was a fierce, protective shielding of Dorothea.

She arrived at absolutely the right moment in Patrick's life, because in the summer of 1927 Betty had married again and could no longer be monopolised by her brother's help and protection. To relinquish so overwhelming and long standing an influence bore down hard on Patrick: for a while there were disagreements between brothers-in-law, the more so since the man Betty married was not the sort readily to share his authority. His name was Bernard Law Montgomery—at that time a lieutenant-colonel in the Warwickshire Regiment and an Instructor at the Staff College, Camberley. Thus through the link of marriage there met two of the outstanding military brains of the Second World War, and if at first they did not agree, professionally as well as socially, it was also because each was seeking the way by the light of new ideas along separate routes towards a revolution in the art of war, the paths of their researches still apart, sometimes crossing but not yet merged. In any case Hobart's enquiries and experience were in advance of Montgomery's, for while both were possessed of a profound knowledge of infantry, Montgomery was not yet fully aware of the potential of the tank, so engrossed was he in his study of the broad issues of war and the part the traditional arms must play. In Montgomery's own words—'militarily I had not yet grown up.'

Not that Hobart was himself yet a master of the tank. He grasped its philosophy well enough, but several essential elements associated with technical intricacies had still to be learnt, since so far he had not served in a battalion alongside the men who manned the machines. He went to the Tank Corps Centre, Bovington, in 1927 to attend tank courses and learn the foundations of the tank trade. Here he began to meet those who were to work closest with him in the future, and shock them with his questions.

Lieutenant Nigel Duncan, as adjutant, was putting a squad through foot drill on the square when he was rudely interrupted by an irate colonel demanding to know why tank soldiers were wasting their time on infantry-type drill when it was their task to acquire the modern techniques needed to fight in machines. It was an uncomfortable question because, as Duncan says, 'They only drilled on the square because that was the way it had always

been done in the past.' Nobody had bothered to question it
before, but many years later Hobart came to write:

I dislike all this dressing up. This emotional intoxication produced by bagpipes and bearskins, and the hypnotism of rhythmical
movement and mechanical drills. The glorification of the false side
of war. It's not the gay flaunting of danger that I greatly admire.
It is the deliberate inebriation to avoid seeing things as they are.

In the 4th Battalion of the R.T.C., then at Catterick, there was
in 1927, when Hobart was sent to join them as second-in-command, a similar acceptance of well-worn routine. Not that the
4th was a badly run unit. The commanding officer, Lieutenant-
Colonel M. C. Festing, was just about as strong in character as
his new deputy, and was capable of being equally rude to all
and sundry when the occasion demanded it.

Now a ludicrous situation arose because, as second-in-command, Hobart, who had been given the brevet rank of full colonel
on the 1st January 1928, was senior to his C.O., who was only
a lieutenant-colonel. The situation facing the adjutant, 'Ricky'
Richards, was thus one of extreme delicacy, and made no easier
by Hobart's attempt to reorganise the battalion during Festing's
absence on leave. A state of armed neutrality grew as each tested
the belligerence of the other, ripening into conflict when the
local staff elected Hobart as chief umpire on their exercises and
gave him the task of criticising his own C.O. Then the cudgels
were drawn, but then too the ingrained imagination of Hobart's
tactical and dramatic ability overcame all petty differences and
clashes of personality. His exercises achieved a bite and a realism
that few had discovered before.

Richards and the other officers of the 4th suffered from their
second-in-command's burning desire to teach and says:

We learnt a tremendous amount from him, but he nearly drove
us beyond the brink.
Once, in Catterick in February we were out on the moors with
two feet of snow on the ground and an icy wind. After an exhausting
day we assembled for what was the last session at about 3 p.m. But
not a bit of it! We finished up fighting a rearguard into Camp about

6 p.m. in the dark. He expected everyone to be as enthusiastic on
military matters as he was. Well, we were not, especially from
about 3 p.m. onwards on the Catterick moors!

Their teacher's winter enthusiasm remained hot from the heat
of that summer's trials of the first Experimental Armoured
Force—the parent of all the armoured divisions of the future.

It is extraordinary that the experiment took place at all, for
the Continental Powers were happily immersed in the second
year of post-Locarno contentment. The Treaty, signed in 1925,
which guaranteed mutual assistance between the Powers, had
opened the way to widespread negotiations, the fundamental intentions of which were the belated execution of the spirit of
the Covenant of the League and disarmament. Top of the list
for abolition were offensive weapons, and tanks, with bombers,
came uppermost in that category.

Not for the first or last time, the Army showed its disrespect
for the politicians. On the one hand its leaders were staking
claims for all types of weapons as a bargaining counter should
more large-scale reductions be suggested, on the other hand tentatively joining a number of offensive weapons into a combination of potentially unheralded power. At a stroke was demonstrated a glorious mixture of shrewd, short-term trading and
naive miscalculation of the political climate. Perhaps the unwillingness of the politicians to enthuse can be well understood.

The story of the manner in which this trial came about and
the method of its prosecution has been given in detail by Captain
Liddell Hart in the history of the Royal Tank Regiment, *The
Tanks*. It is a tale of delays that put the date of the trial back
one year while the matter was discussed at length in the War
Office; of a series of failings in personal communication leading
the designated force commander, Colonel Fuller, to decline the
appointment because it seemed to him that he would not be
able to give the trial the whole of his attention and the guidance
it deserved; of the appointment of a force commander, Colonel
R. J. Collins, who lacked the knowledge and experience of fast-
moving armoured troops which alone could ensure a realistic
experiment.

Yet it is a tale of success despite the deficiencies of the commander and the inequalities of the motley collection of vehicles
that comprised the force. Where several categories of vehicles
each with widely differing performances cross country, or on
the road, are brought together and invited to move like a phalanx there will be chaos, a concertina in speed and space as each
differing element shuffles to adjust its movements to the speed
of the other. In this force, fast-moving armoured cars and light
tanks found themselves out of step when integrated with slower-
moving medium tanks, and neither were matched with tractor-
drawn artillery or infantry transported in six-wheeled lorries and
half-tracked carriers. And even if the machines had been more
equal in performance there was as yet no comprehensive system
of radio communications to enable them to talk amongst themselves and co-ordinate their actions. The whole could be compared to a promising middle-weight boxer out of training, all
muscle but lacking in brains.

Mistakes were made in plenty, partly caused by the heterogeneous composition of the force, partly as a result of sheer inex-
perience. The fundamental lessons that were taught confirmed
the opinions of the armoured experts : the mistakes led to improved training and a rapid speed-up in reactions within the
force staff. In any case, sufficient had been demonstrated to provoke the C.I.G.S., Field Marshal Sir George Milne, into giving
forth a striking address on the glowing future of mechanised
forces.

Buoyed up by recognition from above, the Experimental Force
was last pitted against the conventional 3rd Infantry Division,
plus a cavalry element. This division was to advance and seize
vital ground thirty miles ahead of its starting point, while, from
eighty miles away, the Experimental Force was to frustrate it as
much as it could.

Thus one battalion of armoured cars and light weapon-
carriers, one battalion of medium tanks, a battalion of infantry,
a regiment of artillery and a company of engineers were invited
to engage a homogeneous formation five times their size. To the
minds of conventional soldiers, the prospects seemed hopeless,
though less forbidding when the calibre of the men commanding

the mechanised units is recalled. The one commanding the armoured cars was Lieutenant-Colonel F. A. Pile, later the wartime
commander in the Second World War of A.A. Command: another commanding the Engineer Squadron was Major G. le Q.
Martel, a brilliant inventive engineer and Commander of the
Royal Armoured Corps in the Second World War. And at the
invitation of Colonel Collins an extra staff officer joined his
H.Q.—Patrick Hobart.

Now, it could be a coincidence that his presence tallied with
the momentous events that followed, but that final exercise embraced a verve and sweep that had been absent from its predecessors. Undoubtedly the unmatched elements of the force were
becoming used to combining their cross-bred virtues; unmistak-
ably the genius of Pile's leadership and sense of mobility with
his armoured cars blazed a trail that could not be mistaken by the
remainder of the force and set the tone of the whole exercise; but
in addition there was an aggressive willingness to grasp every
fleeting opportunity that hinted at a new, fast-thinking brain,
urging the whole force to emulate Pile's example. It is inconceivable that Hobart did not egg on all and sundry to the manœuvres that baffled, outfought and finally paralysed the crawling, vulnerable conventional infantry division: and the suppo-
sition is confirmed by Collins's invitation immediately after for
Hobart to join his staff permanently. But Hobart had other ideas.
He truly wished to have the experience of serving with the
4th Battalion before going back to the staff, but he declined the
invitation because, as he wrote much later:

> I was certain that the organisation, conception of manœuvre and
> handling of this brigade were on completely wrong lines and that
> I should not be able to effect the fundamental changes that I felt
> essential.

In any event, by the end of 1928 he had made his mark in-
delibly on the minds of the 4th and the rest of those in the Tank
Corps with whom he had come in contact. His brevet rank labelled him as one picked for advanced promotion, provided a
vacancy appeared: but this was the difficulty. Vacancies for pro-

motion were still few and far between and need not be of the most attractive kind when offered. An ambitious officer could forget his aspirations if he did not command a Regular battalion, and at that time there were only four Regular R.T.C. battalions, plus two nebulous commands in India under the title of Armoured Car Groups—amorphous organisations which gave no scope for talent because each of the four companies in the group were, to all intents and purposes, autonomous, thereby inclining to cloak the lieutenant-colonel, set above them at group headquarters, in the guise of an unwelcome intruder.

Command of one of these groups Hobart feared above all else. Not only would it take him back to India, where his new wife, now expecting a child, could hardly go with him, it would take him away from the centre of the debate on the development of armour and separate him from access to the rippling currents of new ideas. Yet it was so typical of his earlier experiences that this was the very thing to happen. He was ordered to take command of the Southern Group in India early in 1930.

Spending their last few weeks together in London before he set sail, alone, for India, the Hobarts passed their time wrapped in the tingling sociability of Chelsea, fatalistically awaiting the parting. The rage in his mind blotted out the finer shades of his character and darkly clouded his whole demeanour. Gripped by a furious, intolerant resentment of the injustice of it all, he sat for Eric Kennington, and the artist, who had sketched him before and was to paint him again and again, caught his mood with rare, uncompromising intuition. The blue-grey eyes glare at the onlooker with a fierce intensity that is raw and frightening. The muscles are taut, the lips tense, and the moustache, thrust out above those lips, dominates with a brusque intimidating ferocity.

Here in stark relief he is Hobo—the soldier who in course of time was to overshadow his contemporaries as a man who irresistibly accomplished all he set out to do. A ruthless man, self-centred, perhaps vindictive: above all a leader, a soldier with a mind set pre-eminently on his profession. Not one glimmer is there in this picture of the kinder thoughts beneath, the devoted husband, the lover of beautiful things, the emotional being whose kindness and tolerance could soften and mould, the man who loved children (of his own family) and could charm them as he charmed all who were close to him.

Few there were who could call him Hobo to his face. The name had been acquired before the First World War, but only in later years had come to be used more than infrequently, and as a mark of respect mixed with awe. In the near future it was to become synonymous with the ruthless propagation of the Armoured Idea, with strict discipline and a standard of excellence that surpassed all.

6

THE FIRST TANK BRIGADE

Returning to England in the spring of 1931, Hobo discovered that in his absence little of substance had changed in the world of armour, but much else had turned to his personal advantage. To begin with he had become a father, and there was his six-month-old daughter Grizell to meet for the first time: next, the reason for his early return was his appointment to command a Regular unit—the 2nd Battalion Royal Tank Corps, the appointment to the group in India having turned out to be the customary false start that seemed to precede each of his important steps forward: finally there was the thrill of progress and innovation inseparable from a vital stage in the evolution of the armoured idea.

The economic structure of the world lay frozen by the financial blizzard of 1929, refrigerating men's minds against expansion and progress. Instead of injecting new life into a decaying monetary system, the British Treasury sought refuge in retrenchment, cut Services pay by 10 per cent in 1931 and thereby further discouraged the unemployed to join the Army at a time when it was eight thousand men understrength. The Ten Year Rule of 1919 reigned supreme, its original meanings slightly modified in

1928 by the Chancellor of the Exchequer, Winston Churchill, announcing that '. . . there would be no major war for a period of ten years, and that this basis should advance from day to day, but that this assumption should be reviewed every year by the Committee of Imperial Defence'.

France still looked overwhelmingly strong, Italy under Mussolini could not be considered a serious threat, Hitler was only just in sight on the political horizon and Japan's Manchurian venture only in the planning stage. Britain instinctively regarded her navy as the shield, and her air force, because it held the public attention by romantic deeds and propaganda, as its umbrella. Anything associated with the Army smacked of mud and the trenches and was abhorred.

In a climate such as this it was to the credit of the generals whenever they achieved anything at all in the way of progress. The bulk of the Army served abroad to keep Imperial Policing Forces up to strength, the workings of the Cardwell System ensuring that home units acted, first, as draft finders, employing what remained for experiments. In consequence, the units engaged upon experiments suffered from a constant turnover of soldiers, many of whom had newly joined and lacked experience. It is generally understood that the generals dragged their feet over innovations and those who made the greatest display of their conservatism had been heavily, and often justly, criticised. But the frustration and despair of leaders whose profession was being neglected by every segment of society should not be overlooked—and let it be remembered that the generals who engineered the first radio controlled Tank Brigade experiment in 1931 did so in the shadow of a pay cut and an International Disarmament Conference.

The armoured experiments of 1927–28 had been registered by the publication in 1929 of an official booklet written by Brigadier Charles Broad entitled *Mechanised and Armoured Formations*. Between its purple covers (conferring on it the nickname the 'Purple Primer') there were dourly printed a comprehensive description of mechanised forces, their capabilities and limitations, the organisations that it was envisaged they might adopt, and a forecast of the way they should be employed in war. The

'Purple Primer' was a look into the future because, although it assumed the continued use of horsed cavalry, it left the reader in no doubt that mobile, mechanised formations incorporating tanks, artillery and infantry, working in co-operation, would be the decisive element in fighting formations of the future. It assumed that control would be exercised over the radio in a year of an official trial which rashly reported that it was impossible to use radio between moving vehicles.

Gradualness had now become enshrined in delay and not until 1931 was another armoured force gathered together. But, unlike the 1927 organisation, it matched within itself only fully tracked elements (that is tanks, since no other fully tracked vehicles were yet available), and these were being equipped with a new crystal-controlled radio set that permitted a higher quality of speech between tank commanders than had ever been achieved before. In fact, the main aim of the 1931 Experiment, in which 2nd, 3rd and 5th R.T.C. came together as 1st Brigade, Royal Tank Corps, under the command of Broad, was to demonstrate the feasibility of manœuvring a mass of vehicles controlled by the brain and voice of one man. Tactics and the evolution of a balanced organisation could only follow after this principle had been established, but because tanks alone were employed, fresh fuel was added to the furnaces burning within those who feared a take-over bid by the Tank Corps. The All Tank Idea stalked Salisbury Plain to the terror of the reactionaries who overlooked the insistence of the 'Purple Primer' on all arms co-operation.

Major Eric Dorman Smith, who at that time was brigade major to Brigadier A. P. Wavell, the commander of the 6th Infantry Brigade, watched a demonstration by the tanks from the 2nd R.T.C. against light anti-tank guns in a dug-in infantry position at Aldershot, and imagined how complete would be the destruction of unsupported tanks when thrust headlong against anti-tank guns. He considered it unrealistic in that the unsupported tanks ought to have been decimated by the anti-tank guns and, in the friendly discussion that followed, detected what he felt was resentment on Hobo's part that the infantry anti-tank gun might be a threat to the tank as the arrow had been to armoured knights. Unfortunately it would appear that the claims of the contending factions were never submitted to a scientifically controlled test. So the assumptions for all the subsequent trials were unchecked and based on guess-work, thereby permitting an unbridled argument to develop which, in the end, could only be settled by a close study of the real thing in actual warfare. But Dorman Smith shrewdly understood that he was in the presence of a tank enthusiast (as he himself was an anti-tank-gun enthusiast) and that his master, Wavell, appreciated enthusiasm from any quarter.

What might not have been apparent to Dorman Smith was the revolution taking place in the 2nd Battalion, Royal Tank Corps. On taking over, Hobo set himself to turning a battalion which was already in good shape into an élite. Like any other British Army unit, life was governed by a gentle peacetime routine—surprises were rare and so their new C.O. struck them like a bomb. The 1931 Experiment was due to start but a few weeks after his arrival: the 2nd had to be trained impeccably before then. Any activity detracting from this aim came suddenly to a halt—even the cricket fixture list collapsed before his zeal and the milage run by tanks on training, that had averaged three hundred miles a year before he came, climbed steeply to an annual average of over a thousand. To his own satisfaction he demonstrated that even the temperamental medium and light tanks could cover great distances without breaking down, provided their crews indulged in the most meticulous routine inspection and repair at every opportunity under the eye of officers, who were expected to know more than their N.C.O.s and not be frightened of getting dirty.

The 2nd vibrated to the scouring by their new C.O. of every corner of the barracks. It was borne upon the officers that they were at the beck and call of a man whose philosophy stemmed from Sparta. Every activity was made to reflect a fierce sense of militant urgency; everything had to be speeded up to coincide with 'tank time'. Young officers were encouraged to ride motorcycles and not horses; their lives had to be dedicated to acquiring a faultless knowledge of their task, and if this induced long hours of work, causing them to forswear the company of the ladies (and other entertainments), it all fitted in with the Spartan theme. Not everyone could stand this pace and there were those who openly resented it; but for the hardy and the quick-witted it was a richly rewarding inoculation against the ravages of war that were soon to engulf them. The secret of survival was knowledge of facts gathered by hard work, and then their use with gallant frankness in the teeth of the C.O.'s scepticism.

Hobo overflowed with ideas which lapped unceasingly across the main stream of his policy. Every officer had to be an expert map-reader—not just of the easy-to-read one-inch Ordnance Map, but of the difficult quarter-inch one, and anyone found carrying a one-inch map hidden under the quarter-inch was made to dismount and walk home. Every officer had to be able to speak concisely over the radio—commonplace now, but in those days quite revolutionary and written off by the majority of soldiers as impossible. But Hobo simply said, 'If you really believe in wireless it will work.' And it did—although sometimes extra instruction had to be applied during those hours of the day when it was customary to play tennis.

Methods such as these enabled the 2nd Battalion to perform feats that at first appeared outlandish. Once the whole battalion was made to move on its tracks from Farnborough to Lulworth in one day—against the advice of the experts. There were no major breakdowns: nevertheless an emphatic order came from above saying that the return journey must take two days—an order received by Hobo in the nature of a challenge and outwardly obeyed by the device of driving from Lulworth to Hartford Bridge Flats (a few miles from Farnborough) in one day and harbouring for the night there, before driving into Farnborough to complete the trip into barracks early the next morning. This presumably was his interpretation of advice, given a year or so later in the course of a reprimand to Lieutenant Mike Carver, 'The secret of success in the Army is to be sufficiently insubordinate, and the key word is sufficiently.'

Drawing deeply upon his own experience, and deep understanding of what others thought, the new C.O. set out to brace his men's minds against the terrors of war. Nigel Duncan, who was in the 2nd at this time, remembers:

The way he painted for you the actual picture of what war was like; what you in a tank would face and have to do when somebody loosed off at you. It is difficult to recall the Army's state of mind in 1931 when Hobo was almost alone in preaching of war, telling you that you must prepare yourself and your men for the eventuality.

The men found the new regime almost as hard as did the officers, but for them there were rewards of another sort. For a start, he had an innate and invaluable ability to speak to them lucidly and make himself abundantly clear: a strict disciplinarian, his justice was not of the oppressive kind, and he freely took the advice of his adjutant, Bill Yeo, who sometimes had the impression that his commander might be more at home administering the law to Indian rather than British soldiers. There was no attempt at ingratiation, but his efforts to improve the men's comfort were far above normal, and vividly interpreted in striking improvements to accommodation, the construction of a highly modern cookhouse in which the men sat at tables for four instead of the old-fashioned rows, and withall a sharp rise in the standard of catering that began to make the home of the 2nd something of a show-piece.

Because he thrust his nose into every activity and levelled uninhibited criticism at all who faltered, he could not fail, even if by 'fear', to revolutionise. Soldiers love their officers to be 'characters' and this Hobo grew to be. They felt he was hard—very hard on the officers—but they could follow the direction in which he was leading them and began to learn, after he had talked to them and explained his ideas, that what he was trying to create was something new, exciting and at variance with accepted practice. To recognise and enjoy innovation is to acquire high morale: to consolidate it by success is to breathe life into a soldier's existence.

In the sports arena there were few battalions in the British Army to equal the all-round achievements of the 2nd at that time. In the boxing ring, on the soccer field, in the swimming pool, round the athletics track, on the pistol range or across the motor-cycle track there would be, as a matter of course, individuals or teams in the 2nd colours who were winners or runners-up. Hobo fostered those sports that seemed to him to develop individual character. The lone man running long distance was to him the epitome of endurance; although not good at ball games himself, he suffered them provided they were played at speed. He thought cricket on the same plane as golf, slow and lacking any element of danger, and once wrote in a report, 'This officer plays cricket. Need I say more!'

*   *   *   *   *

In one way it was unfortunate that Hobart's first year in command coincided with the Tank Brigade Exercise and clashed with his own priorities. The exercises were welcome enough but would have been doubly so if he had had time to shape the battalion exactly to his desire. As it was, he often had to struggle when the priority of one jostled the other making it difficult to put Broad's demands for the brigade above his own programme in the battalion. Both Broad and his brigade major, Ralph Cooney, remember some lively tussles to persuade Hobo to bend in their direction, and the need to get their way by demonstrating that a radio trial, for instance, would benefit 2nd Battalion R.T.C. as much as 1st Brigade R.T.C. Nevertheless Cooney considered Hobo as co-operative as any of the other commanding officers. Yet it was in his dealings with the unconverted that Hobart increasingly raised resentment, for he sought conformation in a singularly uncompromising manner. Those who followed him willingly found the ride enervating and entirely rewarding: those who dragged their feet or refused to be persuaded were met by an unseemly devastation. Hobo, with his enthusiasm balked, sometimes became quite unreasonable, and Bill Yeo recalls bracing himself more than once to remonstrate at indiscretions saying, 'You have made an enemy there,' as some outraged reactionary departed, and then being surprised to see Hobo blush, abashed at his impulsiveness. Unfortunately the men he upset were sometimes those who later might have become valuable allies. One was a senior artillery officer, Robert Gordon-Finlayson, who could not visualise shell-fire being projected from a moving tank. But the tide within

Hobart ran strong and the call of the task deafened him to politics and influence.

The 1st Brigade, Royal Tank Corps, only worked as an entity for a fortnight in 1931 on Salisbury Plain. A progressive series of exercises, all written to practise the essential elements of control (to which the evolution of tactical doctrine took second place) with each company and battalion systematically being put through its paces so that, in the end, Charles Broad had no further need to give orders by any means other than wireless. Eventually it became possible for the whole brigade of one hundred and eighty tanks to be manœuvred at once in response to the demands of one brain, and on the day that could be done the Army Council came to witness it.

But on the great morning there was a thick fog lying between the demonstration arena and the tank park at Tilshead. Completely confident, Broad had refused to allow orders to be written or for the demonstration to be rehearsed: now the fog was to be ignored, and it was left to Ralph Cooney to lead the tanks through the fog across the featureless Plain to the arena whence Broad would take over on the air. From this calculated risk came so awe inspiring a spectacle that there were many present who expressed frank disbelief that what they saw was not a well-arranged trick, for as the fog lifted and the sun came out, the phalanx of tanks rolled into sight and at Broad's orders paraded and wheeled non-stop with an almost inhuman precision. It was breathtaking in its apparent simplicity, unforgettable as a spectacle; a preview of the future charged with an inescapable impact.

Broad's example was infectious. Proof positive of the new-found power of wireless, making it a weapon in its own right because it increased the power of the commander to weld all his elements into one homogeneous implement, redoubled the claim of the Tank Corps that a tank brigade possessed an inherent battle-winning capability. From this day those who resisted the Armoured Idea began to falter, and those who stood to lose most by opposing mechanisation had to choose between continued resistance or capitulation prior to acquiring the new fashion. And although the next edition of the 'Purple Primer', with its revised title of 'Modern Formations', incorporated the organisation and roles of horsed cavalry, informed participants in the argument realised that the time for compromise was past. The part of the horse in war was, mercifully, ending.

Not that the next two years epitomised a great revolution. The Ten Year Rule was abolished in 1932 but not until 1934 did a brigade of tanks reassemble on Salisbury Plain and if by then the tank men had refined their techniques, there existed little to encourage the hope that the rest of the Army was following their lead. The artillery had yet to decide on the vehicle to carry their guns into battle, although they already had one machine, the Birch gun, that could keep up with tanks: two regiments of cavalry had made the first change of mount, and climbed aboard armoured cars: the infantry inclined to hope that the anti-tank gun would subjugate the tank and leave them untouched. Corporate action by all the elements of the Army seems to have been pushed aside by sectional interests. It was generally agreed that tanks needed protection from enemy artillery and anti-tank-gun fire; that the tanks would normally come into action with infantry and artillery to break the enemy front, after which the tanks might drive deeply into the enemy rear. But the need for protection could never be absent and it could be given by light armoured vehicles whose main armament was a machine gun, the mirror of Ludendorff's 'Infantryman with a machine gun' and the essence of one of the trials carried out in 1932 and 1933 by Wavell's 6th Brigade.

Here was a choice acceptable to all. The Tank Corps had its own light tanks charged with the tasks of protection and reconnaissance. The mechanised infantry battalion could now be given something similar to a light tank and take over this work from the tank battalions, at the same time acquiring their own armoured machine-gun carriers to enable them to join in the armoured battle. In other words, the infantry could have armour but would need to adjust their speeds to keep up with tanks on the one hand yet stay with their marching colleagues on the other.

For two years the infantry experimented with the light-machine-gun carrier until there came the day when a demonstration at the Machine Gun School powerfully argued the strength of the claims by its sponsors. Then it was that, in the presence of the C.I.G.S., the pundits rose up to rain blows upon the idea largely on the grounds that it introduced a rate of operation that transgressed the customary speed of infantry action. Eric Dorman Smith, who, as brigade major of the 6th Experimental Brigade and an expert machine-gunner himself, was deeply involved in the trial, has written that this was the most disappointing conference he had ever attended. That silent officer Wavell, nominally responsible for the experiment, never said a word in defence of the carriers and so the idea went temporarily into cold storage. It was one thing for Wavell to claim, in writing, *after* the conference, 'I remained quite clear on the value of my proposals, even if they were unorthodox', it was apparently something else to say it in public with senior officers present with the risk of censure that that might incur—particularly after one of the pundits had already called him 'an unsound iconoclast'.

But to the Tank Corps the effect of Wavell's acquiescence was critical since, if for a few more years the infantry were to remain barely mobile, quite incapable of accompanying tanks and yet wholly reliant upon the tanks to protect them in battle, the tank force would have to look to itself for its own protection by using its light tanks primarily in that role in lieu of infantry. No less important was the whisper of early claims by the cavalry to step where the infantry feared to tread, and to take over the light tanks and with it the protection role.

This extraordinary state of affairs in which the Army allowed its vital basic elements, the mobile and the foot arms, to bargain their future structure against the role they might carry out, was the background to Hobart's entry into the forefront of the struggle. In the spring of 1933 he relinquished command of the 2nd to become Inspector of the Royal Tank Corps. Leaving a battalion he knew to be the mirror of his own conception of an armoured élite, he rode forth to spread his teaching over a wider field—a field covered by the traps and snares of vested interests fighting for their lives.

His future policy is plain in a paper written for the C.I.G.S.'s

Research Committee in April 1934. Outlining demands by the infantry for a light tank in large numbers to carry their machine guns, mortars and anti-tank guns into action, *or* for a slow heavily armoured tank to accompany them across country, he wrote:

No existing vehicle exactly fulfils the demands of either school. Special experiments will be required in either case.

The proposals therefore are:

(a) To design a pilot model of the most suitable type:
   (i) A heavy close co-operation tank carrying a cannon.
   (ii) A cheap, simple, small and inconspicuous light close co-operation tank carrying either machine guns or .5 inch.

(b) To experiment on the best feasible modification to existing Medium Mark II tanks and Light Tanks Mark I to IV, to enable them to carry out the role under consideration.

(c) To equip the 4th Battalion RTC entirely with one of the above types.

(d) To try out the other type simultaneously would require another Tank Battalion.

A letter in explanation clarified his proposals:

1. The preservation of the Tank Brigade and all it stands for, and avoidance of having it misused or split up.

2. Completion of 6th Battalion to full size, as a nucleus of a 2nd Tank Brigade in Egypt.

3. Expansion of the RTC.

The paper and the letter contain the background to Hobart's work and the development of British armour up to the outbreak of war. They lay down the lines upon which British practice in war was to evolve, because from them stem the fundamental designs of the armoured vehicle with which war was fought; they go further by laying the foundations of armoured warfare as designed by the British and copied by the Germans to the ultimate confusion of every conventional European army; finally they set the stage for the struggle for supremacy within the British Army between tank, horse and footmen, because Hobart, abandoning the backward arms in disgust at their slowness, set out to create at least one forward-looking organisation which could partly take care of itself and eventually lead the rest of the Army across the armoured threshold. The first act in the drama played to a full house in the Summer of 1934 (the year which marked the official birth of the new German Armoured Force) when Hobart led a tank brigade across Salisbury Plain for the first time since Broad had led one in 1931. The fact that his dual appointment as Inspector of the Tank Corps as well as commander of its first brigade was the result of the current financial freeze detracted not in the least from the impact.

Broad's foundling was now a lusty youth entering upon its primary education. True its vehicles were the same medium and light tanks, curbed by unreliability and restricting the speed at which the formation could move; but they in no way curtailed Hobart's intention to extend his operations well beyond the necessarily limited manœuvres that had been executed by Broad. Each succeeding exercise demonstrated the variety of ways in which the force could move seventy miles on the first day or one hundred and fifty miles in three days, along selected routes from one position to another making use of every vestige of natural cover and the welcome cloak of darkness. These exercises were projected outside the tactical battle into the realms of strategy, their designer embroidering an outline pattern on the tapestry of future war.

Enthusiasm within the brigade was all-consuming, for many of those taking part had been brought to believe that their radi-calism was like a crusade. Expanding the system he had in-herited when he took over the 2nd Battalion, whereby the com-mander explained each exercise beforehand and drew forth the lessons learnt to the troops, Hobo held the most elaborate and exhaustive briefings, something of an ordeal for those taking part since at any moment might come a brisk command to explain the reasons for a particular decision, action, or message to the whole assembly. As often as not the sharp request arose out of some tactical sin, the lesson from which Hobo intended to rub in to the bone. He was quite unsparing in praise and blame, the former probably gruff and cut short—its meaning savoured and never forgotten; the latter taking a vituperative form, often reinforced

THE FIRST TANK BRIGADE

by the imposition of some penalty designed to inflict physical
discomfort on the culprit. There was, for instance, a particularly
well-cratered zone on the Plain through which it was most in-
advisable to drive one of the badly sprung light tanks; but
through this stretch of corrugated country more than one unfortunate crew was sent knowing full well that the loss of a track
in addition to a hideous ride were inevitable. As with schoolboys,
the punishments were designed to fit the crime.

Nevertheless under the impulse of Hobart's hard driving there
was bred a unique comradeship and pride in self-recognition
of the hazards with which their commander beset them. At night
the men could be heard discussing tactics with a most unusual
fervour and in the officers mess 'shop' was talked unendingly,
egged on by judiciously selected, provocative statements by
Hobo. The pressure he exerted was unending—the man seemed
inexhaustible and his staff, led by Captain John Crocker, lived on
the verge of crisis. The 'yes' man was unwelcome, but contradiction had to be accurate if disaster were to be avoided.

He had his own way of showing approval, as Horace Birks
found when he decided, after a few months as Hobo's staff
officer in the War Office, that he had not made the grade.

I went in and saw Hobo one morning and said I was sorry and
would he save my face and get me a simpler job? He looked at me
with the most extraordinary expression, took his glasses off, shuf-
fled his papers and said, 'Well you've worked for me for three
months now and I didn't realise you were a bloody fool. I'm going
off for nearly three weeks skiing and I would certainly not have
gone there if you had been useless—now get out!'

The results fully justified the means. By the end of August a
pitch of training had been reached that transcended anything
ever seen before: of greater importance was the appearance,
in startling simplicity, of the undeniable feasibility of the armoured idea in the dominant role on the battlefield. Hand-in-
glove went the making and breaking of reputations—Hobart's
made as a great organiser, trainer and a visionary; Crocker's as
a superb, unruffled staff officer under the most harrowing cir-

A.C.—I

cumstances, having his feet firmly planted on the rungs to success by Hobart; Birk's dashing backwards and forwards between
his desk in the War Office and Hobo's tank on the Plain, bridging
the gap between officialdom and action, and remembering once,
travelling in his car at eighty miles per hour, trying in vain to
catch the flow of Hobo's conversation, but at last having to complain, 'I am sorry, sir, I can't hear a word you are saying because
we are going too fast.'

'So we are—Robinson, slow down to sixty—ah, that's better
—now we can talk.'

The soldiers closest to him became for ever his devotees.
Lance Corporal Carmen was given an inscribed silver cigarette
case by Hobart when he left after driving him for two years
and recalls:

Most of the miles we travelled together were done around eighty
m.p.h. Once in our early association I had just got on to the open
road and doing sixty and he said, 'You're not in a built up area, you
know! !', so after that it was just as fast as the car would go—and
the only reprimand I ever had, if you could call it that, I negotiated
a tight squeeze at high speed—and he said 'You're chancing your
arm a bit aren't you! !'.

He had great patience, and if for instance, on occasion we had
some mechanical trouble with the car, he would sit on the fence and
ask me how long it would be, and off he would go for a walk.

It seemed that he was indefatigable and very rarely did he go to
sleep in the car, even after an exercise when I could hardly keep my
eyes on the road, he would be analysing some point with the B.M. or
whoever was with him.

Most of those early disciples who worked with Hobo that
summer he guided upwards thereafter, because he was constant
once he came to trust a man: the problem lay in winning that
trust in the first place.

Hobart's directive to the Tank Brigade in 1934 was highly
ambitious, calling, amongst many things, for resolution of all
aspects of control, supply, repair and recovery, co-operation with
the R.A.F. and with other arms. He visualised the brigade being:

employed on a strategic or semi-independent mission against some important objective in the enemy rear . . . to create uncertainty and doubt : to induce the enemy to deploy in one direction and then to attack in another . . . to avoid strength and attack weakness. . . . In addition [the directive said] it must be capable of more intimate co-operation with other arms where the situation demands such action.

Taken in isolation, the 1934 exercises were merely a delayed extension, one stage higher, of the company and battalion exercises in 1931 and 1932 and it is quite apparent from the Training Instruction that Hobart saw them in this light, particularly when he saw fit to include in the objective 'To make a start in practising co-operation with other mobile forces'. Just as Broad tentatively exercised as a brigade after intense company and battalion trials, so Hobart tentatively linked the Tank Brigade with other brigades as part of an embryo division.

On its own the Tank Brigade did all that Hobart said could be done, but co-operation with other arms led into deep waters, even when the other arm happened to be the 7th Experimental Infantry Brigade commanded by his fellow armoured enthusiast, Lindsay. A combined exercise in September fell under the control of the G.O.C.-in-C. of Southern Command, General Sir John Burnett-Stuart, a forward-looking soldier but one endowed with a destructive sense of humour ('anything for a laugh,' was Hobart's comment), and the chief umpire was Major-General A. P. Wavell.

For the first time mechanised artillery, a mechanised infantry brigade, an armoured car regiment and a tank brigade were brought together, forming the earliest recognisable shape of an armoured division of the future—all under the command of Lindsay. But the exercise devised by Burnett-Stuart paid scant heed to the future: instead it concentrated on hampering the Tank Brigade as a fillip to the morale of the infantry—the very opposite of the spur in which they were of need. The embryo armoured division was launched on a raid along a circumscribed route towards a limited objective, tied to a schedule that gave insufficient time for the approach to be made at night. Furthermore, Lindsay was told he was not to incur heavy losses during the raid in order that the force might be preserved for use in another more important task later on. In consequence the enemy had only to block one route and the surprise inherent in the mobility of the force was sheered off.

Lindsay tried to solve an almost insuperable conundrum by expedients, not one of which satisfied Hobart or himself. Both were loath to split up the armour, both convinced that speed was essential and that, if possible, the direction of their thrust should be disguised. The sheer speed of their first plan, in which, as it happens, a battalion of tanks was grouped with the infantry, achieved complete success, by taking the 'enemy' and, above all, the umpires, by surprise, catching everybody unprepared and forcing the exercise controllers to adopt bogus measures (by means of an enforced halt for the tanks to allow the enemy in-fantry to get in position) to restore the situation.

From that moment the umpires under Wavell lost sight of reason in their effort to hamper the mobile force with measures outstripping subterfuge, and as the farce dragged on Hobart got angrier and refused to take part in what appeared to him to be a charade. The knowledge that officers' wives had been employed to guide the 'enemy' into position and that infantry had been told to lie in the road to prevent his tanks passing drove him to fury. This, to him, was a vital experiment upon which the future of armour depended—to make a mockery of it was a senseless waste of time and opportunity.

The last phase of the exercise, watched by an influential body of spectators, became channelled into a withdrawal by the frus-trated mechanised troops, suggesting to the less-perceptive on-lookers that the experiment in long-range penetration had failed as it would invariably fail. They overlooked the fact that, once again, an unmatched force, which had never co-operated before, had accomplished much.

It had certainly not failed. In adversity Hobart rose to supreme heights, skilfully filtering the whole of the Tank Brigade through a defensive barrier which had been strung across the country in his rear, and then rallying again ready for battle. Nigel Duncan marvelled at him that night, for his cheerfulness, resource and inspiration beyond words, as he led them out of the trap in the face of acute disappointment, and recalls seeing him in the early morning sitting on top of his tank and refusing to listen to despatch riders' reports till they had been given a tot of rum.

Back in the War Office ideas floated up. Eric Dorman Smith, by now a staff officer in SD2 in the War Office, drawing forth a paper which had been written by Lindsay and in which lay the genesis of the Mobile Division, saw this as the right time in which to launch it while the lessons of the exercise were fresh. Delays there were to be, but progress was continuous tortuously slow. In the autumn of 1934 a tentative agreement that the old Cavalry Division should be replaced by a Mobile Division marked two important innovations, firstly that the cavalry were to be mechanised and secondly that the sort of organisation described in Hobart's 1926 paper was to be utilised. There was to be a Reconnaissance, a Fighting and a Support Group with the cavalry given the role Hobart had considered belonged to mechanised infantry. Thus the cavalry took a step into the future while the infantry elected to remain in the past. The significance of the group organisation is Lindsay's acceptance of Hobart's ideas and the indication of the latter's influence in persuading the War Office of the validity of his radical 1926 views.

The exercises held on Salisbury Plain in 1935 frustrated Hobart's desire to practise long-range penetration, since the C.I.G.S. had insisted that it was to study action when close to the main battle line. Nevertheless this was the year in which he led the brigade into night actions (mounting searchlights on tanks) as well as a host of original manœuvres which in the next war were to be everyday routine. Sometimes his tank tactics grew from the ambushes he had laid in Waziristan—always they were fluid and fast-moving, ahead of the thinking speed of his contemporaries in every department.

And in 1936 the work went ahead against every handicap, lack of machines and men since a whole battalion had been shipped to Egypt to meet the threat of Italian aggression in the Western Desert, shortage of wireless sets and spares, and crews who were

universally new to the work. By improvisation and a double in-
jection of enthusiasm, Hobart somehow continued to get value
from next to nothing, drawing forth a shout of approval from
the Chief Instructor of the R.T.C. Schools, Colonel Justice
Tilly:

Hobo put up a first class show with the Bde this year with no
tanks, only lorries, and no wireless . . . he can train a *show* from
zero—where it was this year, all the personnel being new.

*   *   *   *   *

For Hobart 1934, when the Tank Brigade achieved permanent status under his command, had been all-consuming. He
had seen his directive tried out sufficiently to carry the Armoured
Idea forward by a great leap, and although his efforts to involve
the Royal Air Force had met with a cool reception, enough had
been demonstrated to indicate the influence air power was to
have on the next battlefield. Penned behind the wall of independ-
ence constructed in the twenties by the Air Staff, under the
forceful influence of Air Marshal Trenchard, the R.A.F. could
hardly be warm, since Trenchard had envisaged the resolution
of national policy by bomber air power in much the same way as
Hobart foresaw the resolution of campaign strategy by the use of
armoured forces. The similarity of the problems facing both
men—the need to persuade, educate and convert the uninitiated
—are at once apparent along with their single-minded determination to have their own way. However, Trenchard could stake his
claims higher as befitted a superior appointment, but whereas
the Army based its concepts on a series of actual limited armoured successes in the First World War, the Air Force rested its
case for the effectiveness of the bomber on a totally untested
theory, finding whatever credence it could from a few months'
pin-prick bombing of West German cities, when seven thous-
and bombs caused a mere fifty deaths.
    The strain, even for Hobart, must have been crushing. At the
height of the training season he confessed to Dorrie:

I have not been a big enough man to carry through the burdens of these three years and able at the same time to keep hold of all my interests and social side. I have narrowed and hardened. I have had to get like that to carry on my job.

And I resent becoming dull in the home and a bore to my old friends. The resentment is really at the bottom of my occasional outbursts and my demands to see more of my old friends—who, very naturally do not want to be bothered by anyone who has become a bore.

And it must be uninspiring for you to live with a man 9/10ths of whose thought and energy is given to RTC.

I used to maintain that a soldier had no business to marry. If he wanted to be a good soldier he must inevitably be a bad husband.

It looks as if I were proving this.

Self-denigration such as this was only half-serious. The driving force within him could barely be assuaged by a confession, yet there stands revealed a frank introspection, an awareness of his faults and a half-hearted unwillingness to curb them, linked to the birth of a positive effort on his part to strive harder to give more and take less from the fabric of his home life. Yet, contrarily, he was in need of a source from which he could replenish the copious energy expended during the intense working week: home was the well from which this refreshment was drawn and so efforts to impart an increased share of time to it became subconscious aids to the ultimate military aim. More than ever he endeavoured to segregate his family interests from those of the Army, throwing himself wholeheartedly into the life of Dorrie and Grizell whenever he could be with them, rarely discussing the subjects that dominated his work, and never allowing even the most harrowing events to spill across their happiness. Yet here, in his home, although he was all important as elsewhere, he was not dominant; Dorrie was given the whole of their income to use as she thought best without interference by Patrick, and he was content to give up all his old, most expensive sports, such as riding and hunting (keeping fit with daily runs) and be given just enough pocket money to meet his daily needs. It was true that he could be over-demanding on the lives of all who surrounded him, but in his home he relaxed most and here the selfish aspect became almost entirely submerged by his adulation of family life and his tender kindness to wife and child.

Conversation and argument absorbed his off-duty hours, although occasionally he visited the theatre and remained an admirer but not a worker in the garden. His eyes cast about in search of beauty and gloried in aesthetic delights, and he could enthuse others with what he loved best.

Yet the soft subtleties of music evaded him. Not that he was completely tone deaf or had no wish to partake in the most direct of all the arts, but perhaps because he could find no logical, intellectual pattern in music which suited his own analytical mind. He liked the sound of brass bands because it stirred him, just as he found the movement of ballet gripping, and the bawdy atmosphere of the music hall satisfying to the coarse facet of his character, but further than that he could not go. There is only one recorded instance of Hobo singing, once when Alan Herbert persuaded him to perform at home with Dr. Malcolm Sargent as accompanist on the piano. The singer's rendering of a conventional drawing-room song lacked the remotest association with pitch and tone, but was sufficient to excuse him, when asked on subsequent occasions to perform, to claim he only did so with Sargent as accompanist!

Personal ambition spurred him—there can be no doubt of that—it is an attribute of greatness that it should have been so, but the primary cause of his pursuit of power went far beyond personal aggrandizement. Two years later, when the battle for the existence of the Tank Brigade in the shape that he believed right was raging, he wrote to Liddell Hart, with whom he had developed a strong friendship as well as profitable collaboration:

But what I am afraid of is the spoiling of this wonderful instrument of war. Do you remember Oliver Cromwell's early letter to Hampden: 'I have a lovely Company. If you could see it you would love it too.' It was that Company that was the model and kernel of the New Model.

I suppose that the elder generation are still amateur soldiers at heart. Still unconsciously look on soldiering as a part-time occupation for a land-owning gentleman. . . .

Cromwell said : 'I must have men who make some conscience of their work.'

I'm rather ashamed of grouching. But the Tank Brigade is very near my heart . . . I cannot look with cynical detachment on the prospect of it being broken or spoilt through carelessness—or ignorance.

Notice his reversion, oft repeated, to the Cromwellian analogy at a time when Puritan zeal was at a premium, when the Tank Brigade ran close to a New Model. Written in 1936, when nobody could afford to look complacently at the state of the Armed Services (although there were plenty who did), men such as Hobart and Liddell Hart, who foresaw and cared, recognised the need to educate every section of opinion, official and private, to the paramount need for modernisation of the Armed Forces. Their ideas introduced to the military environment the product of a regular exchange and refinement of views adjusted to a worsening situation. As often as not the opinions of one are to be found in the written works of the other and vice versa.

An exchange of letters in late 1942 does as much as anything to express this relationship.

30 November 1942 Hobart to Liddell Hart
Originality . . . rare in conjunction with power—and opportunity—of expressing it and exposing it to fellow men. In conjunction with opportunity for executive action—rarer still.

7 December 1942 Liddell Hart to Hobart
No thought is completely original—a spark from one mind sets light to an idea which is incipient in another man's mind, and he in turn sets light to others.

Hobart drew deeply upon Liddell Hart, while without doubt appreciating that many of his more unconventional conclusions stood a better chance of seeing the light of day if projected through the mind and pen of the Military Correspondent of *The Times*. Liddell Hart has stated that Hobart was not one to give away the innermost councils of the War Office, but there undoubtedly took place a free exchange of ideas to help combat a deadly threat, and from Hobart, Liddell Hart received a considerable amount of the up-to-date information so essential to a military correspondent. Intuitively Hobart was acquiring a method that, with the passage of time, was to be his main tool in the role of a kind of *éminence grise* behind the seat of military thought.

In the same role he arranged what must be considered a clandestine meeting with Mr. Winston Churchill, as the latter endured his spell in the political wilderness. During a lengthy discussion Hobart put the facts of the deteriorating balance of tank power before Churchill, but it seems with only partial effect, for of the German breach of the Allied front in 1940, Churchill later wrote:

I had seen a good deal of this sort of thing in the previous war, and the idea of the line being broken, even on a broad front, did not convey to my mind the appalling consequences that now flowed from it . . . I did not comprehend the violence of the revolution effected . . . I knew about it but it had not altered my inward convictions as it should have done.

Nevertheless, a contact was renewed which had first been made at an R.T.C. Dinner in 1935, and the fire of Churchill's criticism of Britain's unpreparedness fed by rich, volatile fuel.

Yet it was the re-emergence of Hitler's Germany in 1933 as a threatening military power that elevated the debate on tanks from the threshold of experiment to the level of precipitate development. The restrictions imposed by the Versailles Treaty had effectively muffled but not obliterated German investigations into mechanisation. Within the framework of an army only a hundred thousand strong and forbidden to have its own tank or air arm, mock-up machines were used to simulate the various elements that they thought should compose the new mobile arm. The actual development of tanks took place by clandestine methods, often outside Germany, mostly in Russia. From secrecy to a brash, overt display was a short step in parallel with

Hitler's assumption of power and the formation of the first German tank battalion in 1934. The philosophy guiding the evolution of the German tank forces was essentially similar to that which was uppermost in the minds of Broad, Lindsay and Hobart. As Guderian, the greatest German exponent of armour, wrote of 1931:

We were quite convinced that the future development of our armoured troops must be directed at making them into an operationally decisive weapon.

Nevertheless the German tank enthusiasts encountered the same sort of opposition from their 'old guard' as did their British counterparts, and for roughly the same reasons. But they possessed a decisive advantage, culled from the conviction that it had been the tank that had brought about their defeat in 1918. Moreover they had no need to consider the cost of scrapping obsolescent equipment to make room for machines and, above all, Hitler as Chancellor, with overwhelming financial control, was thoroughly convinced of the decisive power of tanks.

Looking around for examples upon which to hang the assumptions for their theories and early experiments, the German pioneers were attracted to Britain as if by a magnet. The Americans had scrapped their tank troops after the war, the Russians were secretive, and the French had not carried out a serious study of the use of tanks beyond the point reached in 1918. The reactionary military in France, feeling deceptively safe in the comforting shelter of victory in 1918, believed that tanks were still only an important adjunct to infantry fighting *en masse* in straight lines, so when the French cavalry started to experiment with an independent tank division in 1933, it was on the lines of horsed cavalry in the reconnaissance and screening role and not as an element of decision in its own right.

Thus the Germans could only learn from the British and it becomes permissible to ask, therefore, what rate of advance in technique would have been made by the Germans from 1933 if there had been no progressive and vociferous British school, and what effect this would have had on the outcome of political events? The question is perhaps academic, for there is no doubt that the Germans were already thinking along independent lines, but undoubtedly knowledge of the British experience reinforced the arguments of the German enthusiasts against their more conservative colleagues and speeded up the whole process.

Of those days it was reported that, after a successful exercise, Guderian had brushed aside the opinions of an anti-tank expert saying, 'That is the old school and already old history. I put my faith in Hobart, the new man', and in champagne giving a toast —'To Hobart'. Guderian does not confirm the incident—but it is at least symbolic.

From then the speed of progress was cumulative as each advance in technique pushed the thoughts of the strategists and planners another stage ahead of current practice. Towards the end of 1935 three Panzer divisions were formed. The tanks themselves were lightly armed and thinly armoured; but the composition of these all-arms formations, predominantly strong in tanks, reflected the organisation of the British 'Mobile Force' and in no way copied the French cavalry concept.

By adopting this method, the Germans simplified the work of their tank designers since they were not burdened at first by consideration of the construction of a slow heavy infantry-accompanying tank; they could concentrate their limited resources on the kind of vehicles that were closest to Hobart's imagination—light machines for scouting and protection and a medium one with an all-round combat ability and a wide radius of action. The initiative was rapidly passing to the Germans, for as yet the danger of German ambitions were not fully understood in Britain, the financial purse strings remained drawn and nothing was being done on a noticeable scale to manufacture new equipment.

In Britain in 1935 the heated discussions revolving round who should crew the tanks—the Tank Corps or the Cavalry—took an equal priority with reflections that the existing machines were worn out and irreplaceable in the necessary quantity or quality for at least another four years.

In his dual role as Inspector in the War Office and commander in the field, Hobart struggled with undiminished energy to hammer home the truth of his convictions, the perils of the weakening condition of the British tank force and, above all, the need for the War Office to acquire a realistic policy. There was no agreed plan for the British Army to intervene on the Continent in the event of war, as it had done in 1914, and so an exposition of the future of the mobile armoured army was weakened since it was not related to a defined task.

In February 1936, just one month before Germany remilitarised the Rhineland, Hobart debated Liddell Hart's propositions concerning the balance of British forces. In *The Times* the latter had discussed the merits of using the Army to police overseas territories, suggesting that the offensive on the Continent might be carried out by the Royal Air Force, subject to an investigation that might disclose 'the prospects of reviving the power of the offensive on land'.

In a letter that reflected a mass of his own personal experience in Mesopotamia, India and on Salisbury Plain, Hobart reiterated the gist of a paper he had written the year before for the Director of Military Training.

What is called 'Internal Security' in India is really police work, which could actually be much better performed by people especially trained for the purpose, yet we keep 26 battalions of British infantry tied up for this job, mostly in places where they cannot be sufficiently trained for modern war. . . .

. . .To put it in a nutshell, I believe that we require two categories of troops :—

(a) Mobile divisions.

(b) Combat troops, i.e. those who follow up and hold areas, bases etc.

From the latter, efficient garrisons abroad for naval and air bases can be found in peace and war. The former, of course, are the offensive Armies. I believe that by insisting on India :

(a) Doing her own policing,

(b) Using Indian troops only in the covering force, we could maintain at least one British mobile division in India, another in Egypt and two or more at home which would give the necessary reliefs.

Here again is a fuller development of all foreshadowed in his 1926 papers.

*   *   *   *   *

In his long paper to the Director of Military Training (D.M.T.). Hobart had summarised the tasks that tanks would have to undertake as :

(a) Action by a Mixed Tank Brigade, the essence of which is that tanks can get themselves through S.A. fire but do not attempt directly to clear a way for unarmoured troops.

(b) Action by Infantry Tanks whose object is directly to assist an infantry advance through hostile S.A. fire and probably also through wire.

If no open flanks are available it may well be necessary to use the latter type of attack to enable the Armoured Brigade to break through to more vulnerable areas.

There in about eighty words is a definition of the Armoured tactics of the British Army during six years' war and the foundation of tank design policy for the next decade.

Although not a trained mechanical engineer, Hobart never failed to impress engineers by his rapid, intuitive understanding of the kernel of an engineering problem. He could see through technical matters with extraordinary perception and interpret the language of technology with fluent ease.

An example of this rapport is quoted by General Sir John Evetts who, after the Second World War, took Hobo round the firm of Rotol to show him developments in the intricacies of controllable-pitch aircraft propellers. At first the designers and engineers treated their visitor with the nicely calculated patronisation reserved by experts for the amateur, but, as the tour progressed, Evetts noticed with amusement that the experts were not only losing their scepticism, but were becoming engrossed by a man who displayed an unusual awareness of their problems. The climax of the visit came after an explanation of a particularly complex piece of machinery had been greeted by one or two searching questions, followed by a simple comment, proving not only had Hobo fully grasped all they had said, but that his mind had raced ahead to the very core of the difficulties they had been experiencing for months with this propeller. There is always a need for an understanding between the meticulous, painstaking and necessarily slow assessment of research workers and engineers on the one side of industry and the urge for speed to exploit time, capital and opportunity on the other. Gifted staff officers with technical leanings give yeast to the dough of the engineers, the former not always aware that the analytical world of the technician could be offended by brash intrusion; the latter equally blind to the essential demands of haste.

For these reasons a close understanding between Hobart and Colonel G. le Q. Martel, that ingenious engineer who, in 1936, was moved to the War Office as Assistant Director of Mechanisation, became essential. Hobart once wrote: 'I had a great quack with G. le Q. Martel—which is a thing I always enjoy. He is one of the *most* intelligent people in the Army. And a man'; and probably overlooked Martel's resentment of a man who appeared to him as a novice in the engineering as well as the tank world. For Martel was not the sort to forget that he had been with tanks in 1917, six years before Hobart, and expressed it by forbidding Hobart to deal direct with R.T.C. officers in his, Martel's, department.

The task awaiting Martel was Herculean. Apart from a series of unbattleworthy light five-ton tanks armed only with machine guns designed primarily to execute the policy of imperial policing at least possible expense, and secondarily the protection role in continental war, only experimental tanks had been built since the last of the Vickers medium tanks came off the production line in the mid-twenties. Projects there had been in plenty, but the overriding demands of financial retrenchment, and a public opinion that abhorred the arms traffic and stifled new ideas, had restricted the scope of engineering development to what was virtually a monopoly shared between Vickers and Woolwich Arsenal, and scrapped each new vehicle before production could be started. Building tanks was, most certainly, an extremely expensive pastime because these heavy and rugged machines were

unique; in those days there was no significant civil demand for
the sort of engineering or components which they required and,
therefore, the development of a new tank more often than not
called for protracted and costly original research and development. Moreover, as weight and complexity increased in response
to the demands of Hobart and the tacticians, so did the costs of
the end product mount and make Martel's argument with the
Treasury all the more difficult.

There was complete understanding between Hobart and
Martel on the need to compromise between tactical necessity,
cost and engineering feasibility. Simultaneously they felt that
tank manufacture should be undertaken by a wider range of
firms to raise productivity and instil a measure of competition.
In 1934 the design of a new medium tank known as A9 had
been started by Vickers, but, as Martel discovered, its suspension
was quite inadequate and another eighteen months were needed
for redesign. The discovery did nothing to endear the designers
and manufacturers to Hobart—and he said so! Coming along
were two Infantry Tanks—neither of them satisfactory—since
A10, a derivation from A9, was not thickly enough armoured
and A11 was a comical little vehicle with very thick armour, an
engine that could barely push it along at 8 m.p.h., only one
machine gun and just two men to crew it. But in the summer
of 1936 Martel visited Russia with a mission headed by Wavell
and saw a mass of tanks carried on a new type of suspension
originally designed by an American—Mr. Christie. The involved
(and at times clandestine) negotiations which followed culminated in a contract whereby Lord Nuffield (who had collaborated
with Martel in the construction of a 'private venture' tank in the
twenties) bought the Christie patent rights and set up a tank
factory. Here was the competition and increased capacity sought
by Hobart and Martel : here too was the strain from which all
subsequent generations of British cruiser tanks was bred.

Neither Hobart nor Martel bothered at this stage to press
for vehicles they knew to be beyond the capability of industry
to manufacture—and in this desire to accommodate their sights
may well have been set too low. They wanted a machine as
stated in Hobart's 1935 paper to D.M.T., with all over armour,

all round traverse of weapons, that could fire on the move, had wireless control and speed across country.

In a specification drawn up by Martel, with Hobart's concurrence, in February 1937, these characteristics were converted into a close compromise between the requirements of mobility and armour, but proposals for armament sowed the seeds of subsequent mischief.

(a) one high velocity gun, say 2 pounder . . . Bigger projectile not required; it means fewer rounds to carry.

(b) one high-angle smoke projectile mortar.

A key figure in the deliberations to procure new weapons was the Master General of Ordnance (M.G.O.) whose departments actually arranged, amongst other things, for the production of armoured vehicles. At this time the M.G.O. was General Hugh Elles, a fine, handsome figure, the man who had commanded the Tank Corps with such distinction in the First World War and who only as recently as 1935 had been appointed a Colonel Commandant of the Royal Tank Corps. Elles had been a brother officer of Hobart in India and since the war had followed a successful conventional career leading to his appointment to the Army Council as M.G.O. Without doubt, the Royal Tank Corps hoped for sympathy and help from this prominent man and it might be expected that he would be in the lead to espouse the cause of armour. Yet, by 1935, Elles had arrived at a totally opposite view, having reached the orthodox conclusion that 'tanks were useless owing to anti-tank guns, rifles and mines'. In mind he was wedded to the tactics of Cambrai and quite unreceptive of Hobart's concept of tank versus tank combat and deep penetration.

In October 1936 he 'again changed his mind', because he thought that a heavily armoured tank working closely with infantry might survive. The motives behind Elles' changes of mind are not clear. At best he must be considered confused and unreliable, but that was of no help to Martel or Hobart or to the consolidation of a progressive armoured policy. Knowing the way Elles thought and anxious to get tanks of some sort, even if of

A.C.—K

the wrong type, they wrote accommodating specifications. In so doing they conceived a stunted, ill-bred vehicle—one that could not later be satisfactorily adapted to carry a more powerful weapon than the two-pounder gun.

Unfortunately, not only armour defeating ability was sacrificed, since the rejection of a larger gun made it impossible to equip the next generation of tanks with a gun capable of firing a satisfactory high explosive shell. Tragically this to Hobart in 1935 was acceptable for, as he wrote to D.M.T.:

When the task of the tanks, however, is to assist unarmoured troops they must move more slowly and seek out and silence the chief enemy of the unarmoured troops, i.e. hostile machine guns. In this process they will inevitably expose themselves to anti-tank devices, e.g. anti-tank guns, minefields etc. It is then that the close co-operation of artillery and particularly of infantry is helpful.

Obviously, Hobart envisaged artillery as the proper agent to dispense high explosive—emphatically he was convinced of the need for all arms co-operation. Here the misconception of his obsession with the 'all-tank' concept, to the exclusion of the traditional arms, is nailed at the expense of his perception in not foreseeing the day when their inability to fire high explosive against anti-tank guns sentenced many tanks to destruction. Even as early as 1940, in the first tank battle between British and Germans at Arras, the inability of the infantry tanks to engage enemy guns with high explosive when the artillery were unable to keep up with the pace of the battle, was decisive.

Martel's position in these arrangements was interesting and throws his understanding with Hobart into sharp relief, for, as a member of Elles' Staff at H.Q. of the old Tank Corps in 1917 and 1918, Martel had a deep regard for his old chief who was, in any case as M.G.O., the man to whom he owed direct allegiance. And Martel, while accepting the concept of independent, armoured operations, believed also in the need for heavy infantry tanks. His was a carefully thought out position, balancing an assessment of operational requirements and personal survival with an astute understanding of the workings of the political, doctrinal and financial factors. It is clear that Hobart understood the need for careful compromise and manœuvre too—however abhorrent; it is also to be noted that nowhere can any written criticism of Elles be found in his documents—a sign that, in his efforts to achieve his aim, he was utterly determined to contain himself. To know that a Colonel Commandant of his own corps was not convinced of its *raison d'être* must have been galling and when in a later day the abolition of the Royal Tank Corps was mooted, it can have been no conciliation to Hobart to consider that Elles, as a Member of the Army Council, might do nothing to sway the final decision in favour of the Tank Corps.

Towards the end of 1936 his period in office as Inspector drew to a close bringing with it words of approval from those in power. From General Burnett-Stuart:

My dear Hobo,
    I appreciated your nice letter—and hate to think that an association for the furtherance of the interests of the Tank Brigade is over. I don't think anyone could have carried it along thro years of depression and disappointment as you have done, and brought it through cheerful and tempered in the fires of adversity—I give you more than full marks.
    I don't expect to meet you in a bowler hat all the same, but still in the garb of power. Anyhow I shall always enjoy seeing you and being argued with. . . .
                                        Good luck,
                                          Yours ever
                                          J. Burnett-Stuart

and his notes on a confidential report initiated by Major-General Arthur MacNamara, the Director of Military Training, and seconded by Field Marshal Sir Archibald Montgomery-Massingberd, the C.I.G.S., mark the approbation in which he was held at the highest level.

                                        The War Office,
                                          London S.W.1.
An officer of definite personality untiring drive and energy and an infinite capacity for work. He is exceedingly able with a good, orig-

inal and quick brain, capable of bold conceptions which are basically sound if perhaps apt to be overstated. He is highly proficient in his profession and is full of keenness with special reference to the R.T.C. whose interests he has very much at heart. With strong and definite views, and by nature impetuous and impatient of delays, and full of enthusiasm for the efficiency and progress of the R.T.C. he faces up to the difficulties of peace time conditions in the best spirit, and has been always loyal and helpful in giving effect to decisions which have been made.

In his somewhat difficult role of I.R.T.C. while comdg. the Tank Bde, he has carried out his duties as Inspector with characteristic zeal and energy. An enthusiast, alive, physically fit, active with great powers of endurance. As I.R.T.C. he has done much towards the progress of the R.T.C.

A.E.M.

I agree with all Gen MacNamara's remarks.

Brig Hobart by his enthusiasm and drive has done much to bring the Tank Bde. to a high standard. A real enthusiast and with great knowledge on Tank matters he has the interests of the Corps very much at heart. I have found that he accepts decisions most loyally even though he may not entirely agree with them, and this has made his assistance and advice of the very greatest value to me during somewhat difficult times, when the interests of the Tank Corps must be weighed against those of other arms and a sound balance maintained between the interests and claims of all arms.

A.A.M.M

In recommending Hobart for command of a mobile division (still not formed) or an ordinary division, both reporting officers cleared the way for advancement to the pinnacles of power, and it will be noticed that neither one of these officers resented Hobart's forceful methods, and indeed acclaimed his loyalty in the face of adversity. Their judgements at this time bear comparison with those of their successors three years later. Moreover, these were the generals who were pilloried by their successors for lack of appreciation of the need to modernise the Army; General Ironside on becoming C.I.G.S. in 1939 while making no criticism of his immediate predecessors, said of Montgomery-

Massingberd (and also of Milne): 'Those are the two men who ought to be shot.'

*   *   *   *   *

In March 1937 Hobart was nominated to fill a new post at the War Office to take care of the interests of the expanding armoured arm and called the Deputy Director of Staff Duties (Armoured Fighting Vehicles) (D.D.S.D.(A.F.V.) for short). He re-entered the War Office hating the place, yet thoroughly versed in the by-ways of the dull corridors where an ability to walk the shortest distances from one desk of power to another was as decisive as the short cuts his mind took in solving every problem.

The appointment attracted widespread press attention: typical of the comment was that in the *Evening Standard* on 24th March.

His chief characteristics are abounding energy, an unusual fertility of mind (almost to the point of unorthodoxy), complete fearlessness, both physical and mental, and an outspokenness which has not always worked to his personal advantage in the service.

As a battalion and brigade commander he knew everything that went on under him, and looked personally into everything.

'The eye of the master maketh the horse fat' is one of his favourite sayings. It is due to him that our Tank Brigade, despite its out-of-date machines and shortage of equipment, is to-day the most lively and flexible fighting organisation in Europe.

Comment such as this had political undertones. Inevitably it brought him into the public limelight for the first time as a symbol of policy, representing a half-suggestion that the British Army was about to take tanks more seriously.

He must have been well aware of the conflicting influences affecting decisions at the top and known that, without a declared role in Europe, the Army was bottom of the rearmament league. Yet nothing in his notebooks or letters indicates his resentment of this, or an appreciation of his own significance, for he appears absorbed in the work, satisfied only that the chance

to further the armoured idea in his own way was now his. Inevitably he stood as a beacon for those who espoused the cause
of armour and a target for those who distrusted the concept—
and neither side were likely to find him in a mood to compromise
when the tide seemed to be running in his favour.

Those associated with him knew a hard master; those against
whom he was to pit his wits and strength were soon to learn to
fear his knowledge, dislike his 'difficult' ways and, eventually,
from their fear was to grow its natural offspring—hatred.

Horace Birks, speaking of the attitude of many officers in the
War Office at that time, thinks :

They approved the War Office hours which were ten till five. They
dressed nicely, they walked quietly, they had a horror of anything
approaching a row and anything in the nature of 'go-getting' was
viewed with abhorrence. Direct contact with suppliers and inventors
was viewed with distinct disfavour. There was, however, a small minority who were determined to achieve something—of which Hobo
was a leader—but it was extremely unpopular and unfashionable.

But in one place, in the Tank Brigade, there was a corner of
affection that nothing could eliminate, as Hobo discovered himself when he went to visit the brigade in camp in 1937 to present
his boxing trophy. At the end of the evening's sport, as he climbed into the ring, the men began to cheer him uncontrollably
and it went on for over five minutes unchecked, officers and men
standing together in a display of emotion such as they could not
explain. And he stood there, stooping forward slightly, as he
now did, and they saw that this man was one with them, looking
at them through a blur of tears trickling down his cheeks.

Against the background of Germany's blatant reoccupation of
the Rhineland in March 1936, and the rapid growth of her
armed forces, Hobart became imbued by a rabid sense of urgency.
No sooner in his new chair than he pressed the new C.I.G.S.,
General Sir Cyril Deverell, to summon a Research Committee to
consider the specification for the new medium tank. But a month
later, in April, when the Committee met and Elles showed them
the wooden mock-up of the new vehicle, the temporising tone

of this meeting graphically foretold the future. For although there was agreement on the specifications of the model, Elles poured cold water on its prospects by saying, 'It would be two or three years before we go to production on it'; that he was prepared to accept it as 'a long shot'; that it was 'putting too many eggs in one expensive basket', and thereby he exposed his preference for the 'I' tank and his desire to give it priority in production.

The importance of the meeting lies in the priority given to the 'I' tank, spiralling into an over-production of these machines in the early days of the war to the detriment of 'cruisers'. Unavoidably, from 1943 onwards, it was American production of Sherman tanks which chiefly filled the 'cruiser' gap. Above all, this meeting marked the beginning of hostile disenchantment between Hobart and the Army Council because from now on he was in open conflict with Elles.

As the war clouds gathered and the German armoured division multiplied, trained, practised in action in Spain, and acquired a confidence based on success, Hobart found himself more and more alone in the War Office stubbornly defending principles he was convinced were right. The Army as a whole leaned on the theory that the forces to combat the new German Army should be similar to those of 1918 with the assistance of as many modern aids as could be assembled. The 'aids', tanks, mechanical cross-country vehicles and aircraft were not, it was thought, likely to prove decisive elements in the struggle.

The official view in October 1937 was summarised by the Director of Staff Duties, General Squires, Hobart's immediate superior, as

1. The Mobile Division (excluding the Tank Brigade) has the task of protecting the Main Field Force when on the move and medium reconnaissance at all times. It would thus find itself between the Main Force and the Enemy until the battle front was formed at which moment it would be withdrawn.

This represented the old role of horsed cavalry transposed to the Cavalry who were now being given light tanks. It was the same as that being adopted by the French, leading to the impotence and destruction of their tank forces in 1940.

2. The Tank Brigade (kept separate from the Mobile Division) would have the task of striking a heavy blow at an opportune moment, exploiting success or carrying out deep raids, but because the increased power of anti-tank weapons was all the time whittling away the power of tank formations, the chances of the Tank Brigade prosecuting its role successfully are getting more remote with the passage of time.

The contrary view was Hobart's: its vindication was to be Guderian's triumph.

7

PROPHET IN HIS OWN COUNTRY

On the 10th May 1940 Germany launched an offensive against France and the Low Countries. Awaiting her onslaught behind fixed frontier defences stood the fully alerted French and British armies and the semi-mobilised armies of Belgium and Holland. To all intents and purposes the invasion came as no surprise except in timing and direction for, although the governments of the Low Countries had clung to neutrality in the hope that they might be spared involvement in the war that had broken out in September 1939, they were fully aware that a German offensive against France was almost sure to follow precedent and engulf them as well. In any case, France and Britain planned to move into Belgium when this happened.

So, even when the Germans moved at an unexpected moment, the prospects of Allied survival, in theory, should have been better than in 1914 when the invasion had come quickly after the declaration of war and caught them less well prepared. Indeed, in May 1940 there was virtual equality in numbers on either side, both in men, guns and tanks. In the air, it was true, the Germans had superiority in numbers and quality, but in tanks, the other key weapon, there was little to choose overall between the machines of Germany, and France and Britain.

Yet within ten days the Germans had forced capitulation on

Holland; Belgium was on the brink of surrender; German troops had reached the Channel coast by cutting a swathe through northern France from the Ardennes to Abbeville; the French armies lay in ruins on all sides; and the British Army was struggling back to Dunkirk in the hope that it might reach this last exit from Europe before the German tanks in their rear got there ahead of them. Not only had the German Army entered France through the least well defended part of her frontier, the Ardennes, but invariably whenever French tanks met German tanks they were defeated, leaving nothing to oppose the German panzer divisions once they had cut through the lines held by the relatively immobile French infantry formations.

At Gembloux in the first three days of the invasion the concentrated German tank formations virtually eliminated French tank divisions (called D.L.M.s), that fought strung out in emulation of the cavalry vedettes of old. Only once after that was a French tank formation to make any sort of impression on the Germans, but General de Gaulle's inexperienced tank division was powerless in the rout going on around; and only once was a British tank formation to shake the Germans when seventy of their lightly armed, slow and heavily protected 'I' tanks (mostly Elles' comical A11s) struck at the German flank at Arras on 21st May. There the British attack under Generals Franklyn and Martel broke down not only because it lacked sound preparation and numbers, but also because the marching infantry and wheeled artillery were unable to keep up with the tracked tanks. Here, tanks that were not armed with a gun that would fire high explosive were stopped by opposition that could best be destroyed by shell-fire and found that their own artillery had fallen behind out of support because they lacked the mobility to keep up: here infantry on their feet could only mop up after the tanks had passed through the German anti-tank-gun screen, but a few infantry mounted on carriers and on motor cycles did invaluable work in the van of the battle with the tanks: here it was confirmed that unarmoured infantry unaccompanied by tanks were easy prey to massed tank formations and that anti-tank guns usually only exercised a temporary restraint.

The débâcle of the Allies had been engineered almost entirely by methods that had been foreseen by those in Britain who understood the potential of the German tank formations in relation to the weakness of the other European armies. Hobart was not entirely alone in fighting to prevent the coming catastrophe but only a handful shared his views to the full, and of these none were permitted to play a part in the lead: Broad had been sent to India, after serving in an administrative post, Lindsay too had gone to India, and Pile had commanded infantry before being diverted to command an anti-aircraft formation. In the War Office from 1933 until 1938, helped by Martel between 1936 and 1938, Hobart fought for the Armoured Idea and for the formation of mobile divisions in a shape that seemed to him battleworthy. Because he believed fervently in what he was doing and fought hard for his principles, he became a lonely figure.

*   *   *   *   *

In 1932 the Ten Year Rule had been abandoned by Ramsay MacDonald's Government—a significant decision by a man of pacifistic persuasions involved at that moment in intense negotiations on disarmament—but vital in the interests of survival as the spirit of Locarno started to dip in decline. Yet, the only visible threats to British interests arose on the periphery of the Empire, whence the ill-equipped Army sent its main strength. Consideration and preparation for general war on the Continent attracted only passing attention and what little exploration there was grew only discursive since the nature of the enemy remained undefined. Without knowing that the advent of Hitler presaged a serious threat to peace, Hobart wrote the scenario in 1933 of the shape of war to come, projecting his vision through the eyes of a nation possessing an armoured striking force similar to that which was to be developed by the Germans by 1940. At the outbreak of war he thought:

Caution will be rampant by reason of the fear of modern arms of which there is not much experience amongst General Staffs, e.g. air, gas, armoured fighting vehicles. No chance of elaborate march tables, with every road filled with long columns. Will concentrations at bases even be possible? Dock areas?

We should play on his [the enemy's] fears. Both by air and mobile land force. Threats (or rumours even) of an armoured force in his rear, near mobilisation centres at different places : probably little material damage (lorries here and there, detachments of troops etc) will be necessary or advisable. We must avoid losing tanks.

When we have played on his nerves sufficiently, and when the preparations for our main strategic stroke are ready, then we strike in combination with all our forces. Tank thrust in this case will be at a vital point, and pushed really home, i.e. we must accept our losses.

But here, as at all times, tanks' true role is to ATTACK WEAKNESS. Use the Line of Least Resistance : Speed; Surprise.

Exact timing of this depends on many factors. The great cavalry exponents of mobility i.e. cavalry in the past did not send their mobile masses ahead to indulge in a cavalry battle of mutual extermination, but kept them in hand to use at the crisis with decisive effect to finish the battle. Certainly they 'covered' their main forces with clouds of light skirmishers, and this is essential. But . . . they were a screen, and a means of protection by giving information of attack.

He went on to argue the case for similar protection for the Tank Brigade and for a mobile base for operations protected by infantry skirmishers, anti-tank and anti-aircraft guns, and for means (implying infantry) to collect prisoners, hold defiles and vital points and to secure town or other centres.

This conception of the shape of war to come coincided with discussions with Liddell Hart in which the latter suggested, as a result of his own observation, that a tank thrust might be directed through the Ardennes, at that time considered by the General Staff as impassable to tanks : from it came the Charter in 1934 for the 1st Tank Brigade, described in the previous chapter. But by June 1936, after the new C.I.G.S., Field-Marshal Sir Cyril Deverell, had been in Montgomery-Massingberd's chair for two months, Hobart's uneasiness was transmitted in writing to Liddell Hart :

Generally speaking I feel that there is no refusal to consider novelties and that there is a diminution of certain prejudices in some ways. On the other hand I feel great weight is still given to factors which would disappear if boldly handled, such as social factors, the Shibboleth of Tradition and so on. Moreover the tendency to suspend all action until further consideration, while it would have been admirable six to eight years ago, is to my mind now impossible. The economic pressures on dictatorships will not wait for us. 'They cry Time, Time, and there shall be no time given unto them.'

The general lines of policy which have been beaten out during the last three years . . . should at least be adhered to . . . but if we altogether stop the machinery . . . now it will take some time to gather momentum again and we will be caught with our trousers down. . . .

By January 1937 these views had hardened to the suggestion of desperation. Again to Liddell Hart:

I can never get anyone to paint any sort of definite picture of what the battle-area might look like (in their opinion) in the next war. Nothing but cloudy generalities . . . but all agree in condemning my practice. (I wrote out one in some detail and presented it to DSD who was so shaken that he tore it up and forbade me to use it in any TEWT.)

And then the mention of a threat by Deverell to abolish the Royal Tank Corps: '. . . a return to the old anarchy, divergence and faction', an idea that lay dormant until later that year, but whose existence was symptomatic of the state of flux in Army thought at that time.

Deverell was a man whose mind lay open to suggestions—admirable qualities providing each suggestion was correctly weighed in coming to a solution and that, in 1937, a time of peril, they arrived at a permanent decision in quick time. The very open-mindedness of Deverell seems to have encouraged those around him to press a variety of personal convictions when the new War Minister, Hore-Belisha, was looking even further afield for yet more advice because he was sceptical of that given by Deverell and other members of the Army Council.

At this critical moment when the scope of Britain's participation on the Continent in conjunction with her own defence had to be defined in order to build a viable force by 1940, the seeds of decision fell broadcast. Government policy still did not envisage the despatch of an Expeditionary Force, although the General Staff had prepared plans to send four conventional infantry divisions and a mobile division of undefined composition. This was a unilateral proposal since the main element of British intervention fell upon the bombers of the Royal Air Force, on the fancied assumption that long range penetration by aerial bombardment would be decisive at least cost. When the Prime Minister, Mr. Baldwin, had said in 1932 that the bomber would always get through, he may well have had it in mind that Britain's defence depended as much on attack as defence and permitted priority being given to bomber production ahead of fighters. Only on the eve of war did the Government reverse its thoughts, give priority to fighters and decide on intervention at the side of France in Europe. But in 1937 the official defence of Britain depended on establishing bomber bases as close as possible to Germany while keeping German airfields as far as possible from Britain. The composition of the Expeditionary Force and the structure of the Army depended on the resolution of this problem.

Hence the protracted discussions revolving round the composition of the first British Mobile Division (just after Germany formed three of her own) were particularly vulnerable to wild fluctuations. Common to all was the loosening of the Treasury purse strings in permitting rearmament. Divergent were the traditionalists planning with Deverell to build a larger army on conventional lines, against Hore-Belisha, advised by Liddell Hart, searching for something new—the unconventional, armoured idea.

In the midst, Hobart, trying to persuade his masters through official channels to accept the unconventional, became identified indirectly with Hore-Belisha in connection with Liddell Hart. If, later, Liddell Hart discovered, to his dismay, that his association with Hore-Belisha was restrictive, the product of Hobart's collaboration with Liddell Hart was even more damaging since it smacked of intrigue and undermined the trust of his colleagues in the War Office.

Just as he was about to become D.D.S.D.(A.F.V.) Hobart wrote in February 1937:

I am convinced that the faster a Formation moves the smaller it must be. The striking part of a modern mobile force must be its Tank Brigades . . . I would therefore add to the Tank Brigade only

(a) minimum of holding troops necessary for its protection at rest, for temporarily holding an enemy's attention and forming a pivot of manœuvre and for holding an obstacle for a short time. Carried in tracked machine gun carriers.

(b) In addition the other essential is reconnaissance . . . for this the RAF is required. Also a reconnaissance formation consisting of both Armoured Cars and Light Tanks.

Becoming more specific in September 1937, after the annual training season, he wrote a twenty-six-page paper for D.S.D. and the Director of Military Training (D.M.T.), 'to tender my advice on the subject of the organisation of Armoured Fighting Vehicles'. The subject of mechanisation could no longer be discussed in isolation, and had to encompass the full range of army organisation but this did not permit Hobart to blink the deplorable realities of current equipment in the Army, for he had refrained from considering the ideal, and had confined himself strictly to the best employment of units already existing or improvised. His suggestions, therefore, involve no increase, no major reorganisations and no new expense. They were 'merely a reshuffle of the cards we hold to enable them to be played with maximum effect'.

He had written his paper with the object of surveying the armoured forces proposed for the Regular Field Force, and to consider whether present proposals for provision and grouping were economical and efficient.

The main recommendations were:

(a) To provide more economically for the more intimate scouting and protection requirements of the main columns by the provision of mounted riflemen in each Infantry Brigade.

(b) To provide for the co-ordination and control of Army Tank Battalions.

(c) To provide more economically and efficiently for the needs of the Field Force as regards strategic reconnaissance and protection by grouping Cavalry Tank Regiments into formations for the purpose.

(d) To exploit the great offensive power of the Tank Brigade to its maximum by including it in a formation especially designed for the purpose. In outline the formations recommended were:

(a) *An Army Reconnaissance Formation*

Two Cavalry Brigades each of three cavalry tank regiments.

(b) *A Tank Division of*

(i) *A Tank brigade*

(ii) *A Cavalry Brigade* of one or two cavalry tank regiments

(iii) *A Holding Group*, of mounted rifles, A.A. & A.T. medium, and artillery and R.E.

Thus the number of tank units (other than army tank battalions) then being planned for the field force (i.e. eight Cavalry Tank Regiments and the Tank Brigade) were to be regrouped to provide two types of formation, with no additional provision.

If later it became possible to form a second tank division, Hobart argued, manœuvre would become far more effective when more than one formation was available. The possibilities of deception and surprise would be more than doubled: attack from more than one direction became possible, the use of geographical features facilitated, and many strategical possibilities opened up. The proposals made in his paper provided for the better grouping of tank units, but the question still arose of whether there were not too high a proportion of reconnaissance units. There were eight cavalry tank regiments, plus the light battalion of the Tank Brigade, making nine reconnaissance units as compared with only three striking units in the Tank Brigade. But the inclusion of a second tank brigade in the field force would go far towards correcting this proportion. And so, he thought, a reduction in the number of tank battalions allotted as army tank battalions would give the nucleus of a second tank brigade and further mechanisation of cavalry, or a reduction in the requirements for strategic grouping create a second tank division. But this ran contrary to the policy of the Army Council in their desire for each infantry division to be supported by tanks. Yet all his proposals, and more, were to come to pass in due course as the inexorable pressures of the deteriorating political and military situations squeezed forth decisions during the next three years. However, the presentation of the paper to the C.I.G.S., with unwelcoming comments by two General Staff directors, came at a bad moment in the affairs of the War Office hierarchy.

To begin with, they had already committed themselves to re-building the new Army on the lines of an infantry and artillery mass, capable of being expanded in war to over fifty divisions. The rapid loss of sympathy between the C.I.G.S. and the War Minister was being converted into an atmosphere of suspense and vacillation of which an example was the instruction that officers connected with tanks were not to discuss plans with Hore-Belisha if they met him. By October 1937 Hore-Belisha was closely engaged in seeking ways to effect the removal of his C.I.G.S.—an exercise known subsequently in the War Office as 'The Feast of the Passover'.

As part and parcel of Hore-Belisha's campaign to reform the Army and change the members of the Army Council, the selec-tion of senior officers to fresh posts became an absorbing pastime upon which much else had to wait. The new Mobile Division was to have been formed on 1st October, but by then still had no commander because of disagreement on who was the right man for the job. On the assumption that the main striking power of this division was to be a tank brigade, it was logical, as Liddell Hart suggested to Hore-Belisha, that its command should go to a tank expert, and so the names of Broad, Pile and Hobart automatically came to the top of the list of contenders. But if the Mobile Division was only to be the heir and successor of the old Cavalry Division, carrying out reconnaissance and screen-ing, but not the 'striking' role embodied in the function of the Tank Brigade (and therefore to the exclusion of a tank brigade) then the command could go to a cavalryman.

At this point it may well have been that personal prejudice entered into the deliberations. Liddell Hart knew that the idea of turning over the Mobile Division to the cavalry role with a cavalry commander stemmed from the Director of Military Operations and Intelligence, Major-General Robert Haining, the Director of Military Training, Major-General Alan Brooke

A.C.—L

and Hobart's chief, the Director of Staff Duties, Major-General Squires, who had already consigned Hobart's T.E.W.T. to the waste-paper basket. All three, being committed to the policy of a conventional army, were certain to oppose Hobart's unconventional solution and thereby seek to prevent him commanding the Mobile Division by excluding the Tank Brigade from it— a sentiment sharpened by fear and dislike of Hobart's close association with Liddell Hart.

From this confrontation there derived an impression by Hobart that Alan Brooke (a future C.I.G.S.) was against armour, although one suspects that Alan Brooke's reticence was caused not so much by dogma as by lack of experience since he had yet to command armoured vehicles. Moreover it should not be forgotten that these men were by way of being in competition with each other for key appointments in a future overshadowed by the imminence of a change of C.I.G.S. And casting his shadow over all, as a sort of interlocutor, the Military Secretary, Lieutenant-General Lord Gort (responsible to the C.I.G.S. for officers' appointments) watched and guarded his own position. Thus a triumvirate who were at the Staff College in 1919, Brooke, Hobart and Gort, became intermingled in the struggle for power.

To Gort, acutely conscious of the social prejudices at work, the circumstances of Hobart's marriage was a factor in the selection process. Since the days at the Staff College he had kept in touch and had frequently dined with the Hobarts on friendly terms. He had himself suffered the tribulations of the divorce courts, as the innocent party, thus he was more aware than many of the stigma involved, and he it was who suggested to Hore-Belisha that he was 'rather anxious about Hobart's old divorce case', conveying that 'the cavalry would object'—which Liddell Hart doubted. So Gort proposed Brooke, an artillerist, to command the first Mobile Division, a neat compromise between the claims of the Cavalry and Tank Corps, qualifying it with the suggestion that 'while Hobart was the best leader for war, Brooke would be a good man to think out the problem of training'— an illogical argument which merely crystallised the views of a segment of the General Staff, who chose to forget Hobart's unchallenged supremacy as a trainer while conforming to the view that he was a 'monomaniac' about the Tank Corps.

In the midst of these negotiations, Hobart's paper on A.F.V. Organisation found its way to the C.I.G.S., and thence, in due course, Hobart himself went, to quote Liddell Hart:

... 'on the mat' in front of Deverell and admonished ... Deverell had told him that his paper was contrary to the views of the directors, and 'that if he could not reconcile his conscience with their views, he had an alternative—to resign'. Deverell had 'ended on a note of appeal, that the Army must stand together and "show a united front to the politicians" '. Deverell had also said that it 'didn't matter' if a gunner or infantryman commanded the Mobile Division for the time being, and that Tank Corps officers 'might get their chance in two or three years time'.

Time for Deverell still moved gradually—or so he thought.

Ossa piled on Pelion that grim October month. On 19th October Hobart's sister Betty, Bernard Montgomery's wife, died after a heart-rending fight for life against the poison from an insect bite in the leg that continued unchecked despite amputation of the affected limb. His letter to Liddell Hart two days later barely reflects the profound misery he suffered, but carries a strong belligerence at a critical moment in armoured affairs.

Dear Basil—The paper I wrote (of which I showed you an early draft) on the immediate reorganisation of A.F.V. units, was put forward to CIGS with some very tendentious comments by the GS Directors.

They suggested that I was completely obsessed by Tanks, and had quite lost sight of the FF in general and the nature of the operations in which it might be engaged.

This to me! who have been imploring them for years to define the nature of those operations so that we can organise and train for an understood purpose.

So I felt constrained to produce the attached. And thought you might be interested. So send you a copy.

I am rather battered at the moment. I have just lost my sister, a very close and intimate friend, in circumstances very painful and depressing.

'Fight on, my men' said old Sir Andrew
'I am wounded, but I am not slayne.
I will lie down and rest awhile
And then I'll rise and fight agayne.'

And well I know you are fighting. All I can say to hearten you is that you've got the whole thinking younger part of the Army behind you: and they realise anxiously that if this fight is not won and drastic steps quickly taken, there is little hope for the Army—or the nation.

Good Luck!
Hobo

Undoubtedly he drew unnecessary fire upon himself by reason of his utterances, for in debate he did not take the same care as in his papers and the loose use of the word 'tank' led (as it does to this day) to many misunderstandings. There is little doubt that Hobart thought overall of armoured fighting vehicles but did not always speak so precisely when arguing his point face to face.

The paper to which the letter refers was yet another attempt to analyse the peril in which Britain and her forces stood. A few quotations taken at random are enough to illustrate the breadth of his vision.

. . . The lack of an authoritative definition of the character of the operations in which we may be engaged is the cause of much dis-agreement as to organisations and tactics. It is also the root of wide-spread misgivings in the Army, and in the public mind with regard to the Army. . . .

(a) For us, defeat by Germany would be decisive. Setbacks else-where might cause severe embarrassment, but with Germany elimin-ated, other things could be restored subsequently.

(b) We cannot achieve complete security everywhere and must concentrate on what is decisive. As far as the Army is concerned, it is the Western theatre that is important. The Mediterranean position depends on naval and air action. Elsewhere in the world, similarly, naval and air operations are the governing factor, and the Army's part is largely Imperial policing. Moreover the ultimate fate of the outlying areas must depend in the end upon the decision in the West.

(c) For us, the prime concern is to keep German air bases at a distance, and then, if we are to bring the war to an end, to advance our own air bases to decisive ranges.

Our ability to put forces on to the Continent is severely curtailed. In the early phases, at any rate, the forces which we send can only be small. Such forces must therefore be of the maximum value in relation to their size, and in relation to the forces of our Allies, and the character of the operations.

(d) Our Allies already dispose of such a number of defensive formations, reinforced by fortifications, that a contribution by us of further, and relatively few, defensive formations is of comparatively little value. On the other hand, a contribution of armoured (i.e. offensive) formations, able to delay by mobile counter attack, would be of high value relatively.

It will be realised from the above that I hold that such forces as we send at the outset should mainly consist of armoured formations.

Moreover, such formations should be offensive, for mobile counter attack and counter offensive. Unarmoured formations, I (and many others) believe to be seldom capable of profitable attack under modern conditions, though Infantry, of course, will always be required for holding and occupying.

In the intervals between defended strategic centres, there will still be scope for mobile operations, aimed at disrupting the enemy's control and maintenance organisations. Such mobile operations could, however, only be successfully effected by air formations and by armoured formations.

War cannot be won by defence. The serious effect on our civil population of long-drawn out operations, of another slaughter like Passchendaele or even of a real stalemate might be serious. There is no hope therefore in relying purely on defensive power.

With these considerations in mind, I wrote the paper on A.F.V. organisations for the Field Force. In writing that paper I purposely confined myself to a consideration of the requirements of the Field Force composed according to present plans of 4 Infantry Divisions, and certain mobile troops grouped at present into a Mobile Division.

Another, and critical aspect of the circumstances in which our troops may be engaged seems to have received little consideration.

The German Army has three very large Armoured Divisions and these are further organised into a higher formation, viz. an Armoured Corps.

The Tank formation in each Division disposes of some 700[1] tanks. The exact proportions of mediums to lights is not yet known and, in fact, probably still depends on the type of medium adopted.

But in any case the Division is much more powerful than our proposed Mobile Division.

If, as may be supposed, the Germans make a drive to secure air bases from which air attacks of greater intensity can be launched, their Armoured Formations leading can only be countered by either static, and previously organised, anti-tank defence, of where static defence is not ready, by powerful offensive Armoured Formations superior either in numbers of offensive vehicles or superior in quality, gunnery and handling.

In reply to criticisms that his September paper had not considered the field force, nor the nature of the operations in which it was likely to be engaged, he went on to point out that:

the danger of the power inherent in the German Armoured Divisions and their ability to seize offensive air bases close to Britain, before our slower Infantry Divisions could be brought into action, was such that the Mobile Division with its Tank Brigade might be the only British element that could come into action in time.

And underlined:

the 'opportunist' nature of armoured mobile operations and pointed to the lessons of his experience that formations of this nature had to be homogeneous in composition and could not be an heterogeneous collection of all arms flung together under commander and staff without specialist knowledge.

He saw:

no purpose for a force mounted in light vehicles that could not stand up to the massed strength of the German tanks,

and he was

adamant of the need for infantry to be capable of their own reconnaissance in order to develop their offensive power to the full, but pointed out that his proposal would cause very little change to the Organisation already in use by a General Rifle Battalion.

1. In fact it turned out to be only four hundred.

But his masters were no longer prepared to listen. They wanted to leave the Tank Brigade out of the Mobile Division, linking their decision with a renewed proposal (ascribed to Alan Brooke) to abolish the Royal Tank Corps.

In October 1937 everything most dear to Hobart was under attack; indirect shots were being fired at his marriage, for he was aware that it was weighed in the scales against his next appointment and promotion; indirect, too, was the blow at himself, through the attempt to eliminate his beloved Tank Corps. A more direct assault was the rejection of all he stood for in relation to armoured divisions. Finally, and striking to the core of his feelings as a patriot, the threat, from neglect, to the security of his country by undervaluing the German armoured divisions building up in the east. Better than most he foresaw how invincible such a force would be if pitted against the other European armies in their present state. In desperation he turned to fight harder, but often with less finesse—sure he was right and his masters wrong.

*   *   *   *   *

As the struggle for succession in the War Office moved towards its culmination, the appointment of a commander to the Mobile Division became the key to the battle of wits. Hore-Belisha at all times seems to have refrained from proposing any one contender for the Mobile Division by name, but insisted that whoever got the job must be experienced in training armoured troops. Deverell could not be persuaded to name anyone in this category, and was unwisely supported by General Elles, for the latter had forgotten (what Hore-Belisha already knew) that he had recently given it as his opinion that Hobart was the only man capable of doing the job. Gort continued to seek a compromise and actually told Hore-Belisha that Deverell had been arguing that, because of Hobart's marriage, the cavalry officers' wives would not call if he were appointed. Looking for a new way out, Gort proposed that Hobart might replace Brooke as D.M.T. if the latter took the Mobile Division.

On the 3rd November 1937 a decision was nearly reached during discussion between Hore-Belisha, Deverell and Gort at which it was agreed that Brooke should go to the Mobile Division. Thereupon, to quote Liddell Hart's report of his conversation with him that day, Hore-Belisha had told Deverell

. . . that he would only accept Brooke for the Mobile Division if a Tank Corps man was appointed DMT in his place. . . . Deverell had seemed to admit the force of the argument [were it not done this way there would be nobody experienced in mechanisation in an influential post of the Army when mechanisation was in full swing] whereupon Hore-Belisha had asked him who he considered the best of the Tank Corps men, Deverell had said 'Hobart', although complaining that he was difficult, whereupon Hore-Belisha had said definitely that Hobart was to be DMT.

Liddell Hart adds that the Selection Board had intended to send Hobart to India (the backwater reserved for all 'difficult' progressives at that time, it seems). Now that Hore-Belisha had received the name of a Tank Corps general, graded 'suitable' by the C.I.G.S., he had a keener purchase in the argument— and needed it.

On the 5th November Hore-Belisha started the day by deciding to dismiss a member of the Army Council—General Elles— and appears not to have relished the task. Later the C.I.G.S. told Hore-Belisha that Hobart was doubtful of his ability to undertake D.M.T. This was a fatal error, made in absence of the knowledge that Gort had already told Hobart what was in train, and had also told Hore-Belisha that Hobart was willing to take the job. Only later was Hore-Belisha to hear that, in fact, Deverell had not told Hobart of the revised scope of the job and that, in any case, Hobart prudently had asked only for twenty-four hours to consider his decision.

Fully prepared, Hore-Belisha took the breath out of the C.I.G.S., saying: 'In that case Hobart goes to the Mobile Division and Brooke stays as D.M.T.' There the matter dropped, leaving Hobart as D.M.T. and part cause of the downfall of a C.I.G.S., for as the War Minister told Liddell Hart, 'he had never known such obstruction' and 'he was getting very tired of it'—an ominous exasperation, for this was not the only example the War Minister had experienced of the C.I.G.S.'s stubbornness and trickery. Since he meant to have his way in reform, the C.I.G.S. would have to go. A month later, on the 2nd December, the blow fell with ruthless suddenness, and Gort found himself nominated as Deverell's replacement.

Gort's new Army Council, said to contain in its three new members men receptive of new ideas and possessed of a very thorough military knowledge (one, the substitute for M.G.O., called Director General of Munitions Production, was an engineer vice-admiral) did not have time on its side. Even if they actually envisaged war as only two years off they could not, with the best will in the world, catch up all the time lost in the years gone before.

Nothing was more important to Hobart's success as D.M.T. than the goodwill and co-operation of his fellow directors on the General Staff, yet it was already likely that both those in office, the Director of Staff Duties, Major-General Squires, and the Director of Military Operations, Major-General Haining, were opposed to him before his appointment. The overselling of Hobart to Hore-Belisha and the manœuvring to secure the appointment of Brooke to the Mobile Division had placed Hobart in an invidious position. If he acquiesced to the stated policy of his colleagues his integrity as well as his convictions would be forfeit. It was unlikely that he would persuade them to change their views: therefore he could choose between passively standing by and watching much go wrong, or fighting his colleagues in an effort to achieve as much reform as he could.

In electing to pursue his own convictions Hobart was as one with Hore-Belisha driving eagerly ahead with a multitude of new ideas, but from Gort through Major-General Adam, the new Deputy Chief of the Imperial General Staff, had to come the passwords to unlock the doors that had held back progress and disarmed the Army throughout nearly twenty years. It was then up to the three directors to interpret this freedom in a practical and energetic manner by injecting a new, revitalising spirit. But by now the senior army officers, for the most part, no longer trusted Hore-Belisha, not only because he appeared to be going too fast but because his methods of acquiring information roused their suspicions and offended their sense of propriety. In his anxiety to uncover the untainted ideas of progressive officers, Hore-Belisha sometimes short-circuited the formal and accepted channels of communication and came up hard against the barrier that most besets those who enthusiastically assail entrenched, administrative machines in their desire for speed by impelling vested interests to close ranks, instinctively, in self-protection.

The new D.M.T. tore into his new work with customary vigour, producing the same reaction as that thwarting Hore-Belisha. Taking over from Brooke created the need to overcome the prejudice of those on his staff who had been devoted to his predecessor. Their widely different methods jarred: nevertheless changes came to be made. Writing to Liddell Hart on the 31st May 1938 after six months in office:

Not very easy to sit down and applaud what has been accomplished. One is so acutely aware of how much has been hung up and how much remains to be done. Training has to wait upon
(a) organisation
(b) provision of equipment.

The letter then ranged across the whole field of training, from the methods of turning horsemen into tank crews; the expansion of the Royal Artillery, beyond conventional support in the field, to include searchlights, anti-aircraft and anti-tank guns, and research; through an insistence on every man being instructed in anti-gas precautions, to the education of the officer into the needs of a mechanical army. He hammered away at the sin of waste, pointing impatiently at the practice of using men in the training depots on administrative duties instead of making them get on with learning their craft as soldiers; on the need for an infantry grouping system to improve flexibility in posting men to where they were most needed and thereby make the fullest use of every resource (measures which had not been fully implemented twenty years later). He turned to the desirability of cutting formal drill, reducing ceremonial and producing a field or battle drill—ideas that were in train when he took post, the inventions of many minds that had been waiting for a chance to give air to their creative ability. Hobo it was who breathed invigorating winds through his part of the War Office and rustled the leaves of

improvisation. Undoubtedly he tried to do too much and could
have acquired more goodwill if he had adjusted his priorities to
exclude some of the more contentious proposals. That all was not
well comes in the warning note:

The attitude of those in authority—well, one point is that so
long as you continue to provide the Cavalry officer with 2 free charg-
ers, although his unit is equipped with tanks, so long, psychologically, will he be wedded to the horse and indifferent or adverse from
'getting down to' the machine.

The new régime was bound to take a little time to find its
feet before it could drive full speed ahead, yet even before it had
an opportunity to do this, Liddell Hart, in conversation with
Gort on the 21st January 1938, discovered a trend that betokened
the reverse of urgency, the latter remarking, 'We mustn't upset
the people in the clubs by going too fast—we must give them
time to get over the shock of the Army Council changes.' This
was, in a way, right and proper, for it might have been dangerous to shake confidence in the lower levels of the Army by a
heedless display of rash immoderation at the top; but it was not
the remark of 'the gangster' whom Hore-Belisha had intended
to fill the post of C.I.G.S. Nor did it bode well for a man of
Hobart's inclination who wished to push ahead at all costs.

In a talk with Hore-Belisha a day or so after his conversation
with Gort, Liddell Hart referred to the need in reforming bodies
of '. . . the right combination—combining men of drive, men of
balance, men of originality, and men of comprehensive outlook',
and reckoned Hore-Belisha's Army Council contained men with
all these virtues less those in whom drive and orginality predominated. It followed that pressure from below from one as
dynamic as Hobart was bound to be resented, Liddell Hart noting: 'I should not be surprised to see Hobart moved out of the
War Office on some convenient excuse', a premonition confirmed by Hore-Belisha saying he had come to realise that Gort
was 'the most reactionary' of the new team and that he could already feel in the atmosphere that Hobart was not really looked
on with favour by the new lot. He added that the case was a
parallel with the Prime Minister's, Neville Chamberlain's, atti-

tude to Winston Churchill who admitted that if Churchill, with his abler brain, were in the Cabinet '. . . he will dominate it—won't give others a chance of talking'. The analogy reminds one of Chamberlain's criticism of Hore-Belisha, saying in effect that his impatience and eagerness, making him careless of other people's feelings, were the defects that came from his principal qualities of courage, imagination and drive. We may doubt if a combination of powers to force the rate of progress with patient persuasion can ever be found in one man. History refutes the suggestion that they can, and from Socrates to Churchill tells a tale of self-destruction.

Hobart's misfortune, in parallel with Churchill's, was an inability to relate burning enthusiasm and brilliance with a rapid rate of progress in peacetime that was acceptable to public opinion. But whereas Churchill possessed a marked talent for gentle persuasion in debate when he chose, Hobart lacked the soft touch in public. What always had been the weakest part of Hobart's armoury now made very little difference to the outcome because the scales were being tipped against him by men whose natural reaction to 'go-getters' and those who 'rocked the boat', was one of mistrust and ultimate fear. It was his crowning virtue that, knowing these things, he persisted in his policy regardless of personal advantage.

Meantime affairs in Europe were being raised to fever pitch. Spain seethed with civil war, Abyssinia had fallen to Italy, Austria had been absorbed by Germany and now the heat grew in the Sudetenland as Germany bore down upon Czechoslovakia. The German Army that four years ago had been an embryo was now strong, healthy and more than half-grown. The teething troubles of mechanisation were being overcome by biting on the hard food of small wars.

And in May the C.I.G.S. asked the War Minister to allow him to remove the most senior and experienced expert in mechanisation from the War Office and give him command of an Anti-Aircraft Division because Hobart was '. . . no use—want to get him out'. It would have been easy for Hore-Belisha to reject the request, but in the long run this would have achieved the reverse of good, for the simple reason that the Army Council were no longer prepared to make full use of their Director of Military Training. Hobart was being cut off from the main stream in a way that prevented him from making his rightful contribution, but as Hore-Belisha told Liddell Hart, Hobart was not alone in this:

. . . they evaded carrying out his [Hore-Belisha's] wishes or came back again with fresh objections.

Towards the end of June, Hore-Belisha partly gave way, agreeing to permit Hobart's removal from D.M.T. on condition that he was appointed commander of the Mobile Division that, under the clamour of events, was to be formed in Egypt. A sad little note to Dorrie announced the impending change:

30th June 1938
My beloved woman,
    I have just had a letter from the M.S. offering me command of 'the Mobile Divn to be formed in Egypt' not earlier than Oct.
    It seems to be a very half-baked affair.
    I have asked to see M.S. tomorrow and shall have to alter my programme to enable me to do this. An awful rush.
    Keep this to yourself, of course: but consider.
    I feel that I shall have to accept: but may get situation clarified in my talk with M.S. tomorrow.

Much love   P.

The stresses and strains of bargaining had thrown Hobart into the chair of the D.M.T. as a sop to the prejudice of one side in the power tug o' war. The post might have been well suited to his talents had those with whom he had to work been attuned to the dire necessity for speed. As it was, they found the new D.M.T. moving too fast on a divergent course and, in self defence, concentrated more on controlling than using him, probably from fear of being dominated themselves. In a sense he had failed, but not in a way in which he had need to be ashamed, nor was it a hard-luck story to have fought for a belief that was to be proved right.

    Could a compromise have been reached between the positive progression of Hobart and the negative conservatism of the Army Council? It is hard to visualise one, for it seems the evolution of the British Army of the 1930s followed separate paths, characteristic of the revolution through which it was passing. Up one road went the more conservative members who sincerely believed that a fast-moving modernisation would do more harm than good because it would overwhelm the mystique of confidence based on traditional discipline and morale: with genuine concern they rallied to protect a well tried system which, to them, appeared to be in danger of instant demolition by radical hot heads with unethical contacts with civilian critics. Along another road marched those who feared the oncoming collision with a highly mechanised foe and fretted at the frustrations that inhibited their warnings and attempts at counter-action: it was to be their misfortune to be proved right by events at a time when the opportunity for compromise had passed. But in late 1938, those who held to tradition were in power and those who outwardly disagreed were not: there could be no meeting point between them.

Those with forward tendencies who withheld from controversy did so because they wished not to risk their careers by appearing to join the radicals: prudently they acquiesced in public to the will of those in power, happily provoking, in private, those who might instigate progress while they waited to reap the benefit themselves, in the hope that by then it would not be too late. As Wavell wrote of his relationship with the Members of the Army Council and some of the army commanders, 'We prepared for war as well as we could.'

A fourth element, the complacent ones who could or would not grasp the magnitude of the perils undermining all they lived for, provided a mute unthinking chorus in tune with the political appeasement of the day. Of them Hobo wrote:

> You think these plotted? Those designed
> The War with deadly craft? and some
> Made money out of Kingdom Come
> On purpose?—Nothing of the kind.
> God! how much better such hell's
> Cunning than that crass ineptitude
> Which, like a slattern bringing food,
> Just slipped, and let the whole world crash.

8

THE JOURNEY TO EGYPT

When the uneasy summer of 1938 culminated in a political débâcle at Munich leading to the sacrifice of Czechoslovakian sovereignty to German intransigence, the Government and the Armed Services found themselves propelled into a series of half-measured repairs to patch the gaping holes in the defences of the British Empire. More exposed than it had ever been during the First World War, that jugular vein of the Empire, the Suez Canal, lay betwixt the newly expanded Italian possessions in East Africa, their restless colonial armies in Cyrenaica and the sleek, outward efficiency of the Italian Mediterranean Fleet. Through Palestine the festering sores of an intractable dispute between Jews and Arabs pinned a large British garrison to internal defence, while in the Western Desert a scratch force of mobile units was assembled around Matruh to guard the Egyptian frontier against the threat of an Italian invasion from Cyrenaica.

In Cairo Lieutenant-General Sir Robert ('Copper') Gordon-Finlayson, the G.O.C.-in-C. of British Troops in Egypt, did what he thought best with fragmentary resources to provide against the threat with shadow forces supported by next to no Base Organisation. Those closest to the C.-in C. are unanimous in their praise of his upright nature and his thoroughly Christian outlook and behaviour. He was an orthodox soldier, on the verge of nomination as next Adjutant General, second to Gort as a Member of the Army Council, but not even his friends or personal staff credited him with a quick or comprehensive mental capability, and one is actually on record as saying after the conference following an exercise:

It was very dull having to sit there listening so long to dear old 'Copper's' rusty brain slowly creaking round.

Beyond doubt he was not convinced of the revolution inherent in mechanisation and appears not to have grasped the philosophy of High Mobility—or sympathy for Hobart and the petrol engine. At a luncheon, when Egyptians were present, and the news had first come in June that Hobart was to form a Mobile Force in Egypt, he was heard to remark, 'I am fed up with Hobo and his petrol engines.' But that was in June and the September crisis was not in sight.

At about 3 p.m. on the 25th September 1938 Lord Gort came into Hobart's room at the War Office and told him that war was very probable, an attack on Egypt to be expected, and that he considered Hobart must go there at once to form an Armoured Division to oppose the Italians. It was confirmation of Gort's conviction that Hobart was the leader for war, an urgent assignment, made more imperative because it created the new division several weeks earlier than originally intended. At first there would have to be improvisation, but a full staff, commanders and supporting services were promised and Gort said they would be sent as soon as possible. The day before, General Ironside, without warning, had been sent in equal haste to become C.-in-C. designate of an, as yet, non-existent Middle East Command—an appointment foreshadowing the one taken up by General Wavell in 1939. Gort's exhortation to Ironside, 'We shall expect you to win the war for us out there,' in all its ironic perception indicates the importance to which he assigned Hobart's dispatch next day, for Gort rated Italy the greatest threat to Britain while France took care of Germany.

In company with the British Ambassador to Egypt, Ironside and several other senior officers, Hobart took off in the flying boat *Centaurus*, arriving at Alexandria on the 27th September —two days before Mr. Chamberlain flew to Munich to talk with Hitler and Mussolini. The events of 1914 were being repeated, officers being sent from their desks at the War Office to become field commanders on the eve of war at the expense of continuity.

To Gordon-Finlayson, who happened to be meeting Ironside, the arrival of Hobart in the same flying boat came as a complete surprise, and so his welcome, 'I don't know what you've come here for, and I don't want you anyway', was that of a man off balance. Coming on the heels of a friend's warning that Gordon-Finlayson could be 'dangerous to him', the greeting was not calculated to set Hobart's mind at rest, but the task set by Gort overrode all personal prejudice. On the brink of war time was not to be wasted on recrimination.

Waiting in the desert were the Founding Desert Rats, consisting of a Mechanised Cavalry Brigade with the 7th Hussars mounted in light tanks, the 8th Hussars in Ford trucks (that were later to be replaced by light tanks) and the 11th Hussars in World War I Rolls-Royce armoured cars; its Tank Group with 1st and 6th Battalions R.T.C. in light tanks and unbattleworthy Vickers medium tanks; and the Pivot Group, which at that time comprised only the 3rd Regiment Royal Horse Artillery equipped with 3.7 in. howitzers, and the 60th Rifles (its second infantry battalion did not arrive until April 1939). The headquarters, communications and administrative services had to be dredged out of the base garrisons—although Hobart's additional responsibility for Abbassia Garrison proved more help than hindrance, since amongst the windfalls from its branches came two Grade 2 and two Grade 3 staff officers.

Right from the start Hobart found himself at odds with the general lack of urgency permeating Gordon-Finlayson's headquarters and a staff which, at the height of a national emergency, did not work much in the afternoons. Possibly the tempo merely extended Burnett-Stuart's policy from the days when he had greeted the arbitrary 10 per cent cut in army pay by the

A.C.—M

reprisal, 'All right, we'll not work on Wednesdays!' but it was out of place in September 1938. Writing to Dorrie on 13th November:

HQ BTE seems so complacent and apathetic. I am trying to go slow and not rush them, I have kept it fairly in mind chafing inside myself because I wasn't doing more, but even so I seem to have aroused resentment. It seems to me that instead of wanting to get things right, to try and profit by the awful disclosures of this last emergency, they resent being told what went wrong, or any suggestions for improvements. I don't say that is due to Copper himself, but he seems curiously in the hands of his staff and they influence his reactions.

There were those who thought it unlikely that Hobart and Gordon-Finlayson could ever have seen eye-to-eye because they were not the types who would, but the relationship galloped to destruction from mutual resentment as Hobart's superior mental agility capered across Gordon-Finlayson's slowly acquired beliefs; each disagreement pushed them further apart while staff officers, instead of repairing the rift, seemed sometimes to have gleefully widened it themselves: eventually contact was maintained by Hobart applying for a weekly interview with the C.-in-C. Nevertheless, Gordon-Finlayson visited two exercises run by Hobart's division and afterwards, in March 1939, expressed his satisfaction with what he had seen.

Indeed, by then a miracle had been wrought. The amorphous collection of units was beginning painfully to acquire a recognisable shape, hanging its operational efficiency on a shoe-string. With an incomplete staff, Hobart had to train a brand new type of division from scratch, convert several of its units to new establishments with unfamiliar equipment, and devise an entirely original system of supply for totally mechanised forces working in the undeveloped desert wastes.

For the cavalry conversion came hardest of all. The 11th Hussars had been mechanised for ten years, but the 7th and 8th had said farewell to their horses but a year before and had yet to acquire the philosophy and knowledge essential to their new role: and, unfortunately, there was not time to break them in gently.

Moreover there were those amongst the more senior cavalry officers who made no secret of their abhorrence of radical change,
although fortunately many of the younger ones adopted a far
more open-minded attitude to mechanisation and some were
openly enthusiastic. Not least of the latter was the brigade
major of the Cavalry Brigade, but then Charles Keightley had
only recently spent a period in Germany living with one of the
new Panzer divisions to see and understand for himself the
power and meaning of fast moving armoured formations. To
the cavalry die-hards these were sad days symbolised by the decision to group them with the Tank Corps in a Royal Armoured
Corps, but on the 31st October 1938 they were left in no doubt
that the time for mourning was past. Shortly before setting out to
join her husband in Egypt, Dorrie had a letter which touched
on this problem:

. . . I had the Cavalry CO's in and laid my cards on the table. They
are such nice chaps, socially. That's what makes it so difficult. But
they're so conservative of their spurs and swords and regimental
tradition etc., and so certain that the good old Umpteenth will be
all right on the night, so easily satisfied with an excuse if things
aren't right, so prone to blame the machine or machinery.

And unless one upsets all their polo etc.—for which they have
paid heavily—it's so hard to get anything more into them or any
more work out of them. 3 days a week they come in 6 miles to Gezirah
Club for polo. At 5 pm it's getting dark: they are sweaty and tired.
Not fit for much and most of them full up of socials in Cairo. Take
their clothes and change at Club. Don't return to Abbassia till 2 am
or 3 am. Non-polo days it's tennis or something.

Well, well. But I am trying not to be impatient and to lead gradually, not drive. The result is I get depressed by how little is happen-
ing: and impatient with myself.

In a report after nearly a year of experiment and training,
Hobart outlined his aim and how far he had travelled to achieve
it.

I decided to concentrate on dispersion, flexibility and mobility this
season: to try and get the Division and formations well extended,
really handy, and under quick control. To units unused to the speed

and wide frontages made possible by mechanisation these matters present considerable difficulties.

There is the isolation due to the wide intervals necessary in the desert, involving the necessity of being able to keep direction, to navigate a unit, to keep a dead reckoning, to learn to watch for small indications and to use one's eyes in spite of mirage, etc.

Maintenance in newly mechanised units is not, of course, of a high standard, but great interest is being taken and as knowledge increases the standard of inspection, which is the secret of good maintenance, will improve.

It must be a matter of course for all officers not only to wear overalls but also to take part in the maintenance work on their vehicles.

It has not yet become instinctive for crews and commanders to get down at every halt and look round their vehicles at once. If this were the case many oil leaks, loose bolts etc., would be seen and remedied and many subsequent demands on fitters avoided.

I am certain that we have to encourage in all crews the sense of ownership which makes it a point of honour that they should be able to keep their vehicles running without assistance from outside; even if we have to do it at first at the cost of some damage by unskilled enthusiasts.

Once again he laid stress on the vital need for other arms to assist the Tank Group in its task. The Light Cavalry Brigade provided reconnaissance and protection of the sort he had once envisaged infantry carriers carrying out, the Pivot Group with its infantry battalion and artillery were invaluable for holding areas vital for manœuvre against which enemy forces might be drawn, and for the protection of key administrative points. The field, anti-tank and anti-aircraft artillery, he wrote, would maintain the traditional role of the Royal Horse Artillery in support of mobile troops. There was plenty for everyone to do, no redundancy envisaged, but a redeployment of skills inescapable. Above all, this was a team of all arms working in close co-operation.

There was too much for the divisional commander to do, and he knew it. Appreciating that it would be his task to fight the division as a whole, Hobart sought decentralisation by creating a Tank Brigade headquarters free to fight the tank battle at close quarters while he ranged across the whole battlefield. But at first this could only be created by another improvisation using officers, men and equipment borrowed from regiments already hard pressed by their primary functions. Thus one sort of short-age bred another, but may also have strengthened the concern of those who fretted against the 'All Tank' misconception and be-lieved the divisional commander centralised too much control in himself.

By concentrating before all else on teaching the division how to live and find its way in the desert and by building up a sound administrative organisation at the same time, Hobart applied the lessons he had learnt in Mesopotamia, passing on his own fund of knowledge and experience from which all desert fighters would draw one day. The majority of men disliked the desert and preferred to avoid living in it. Throughout that winter, when the nights grew chilly, Hobart cast back over twenty years to when he had been a staff officer on the Tigris, the old desert habits carrying him on personal reconnaissances more than one hundred miles deep into the void, away from the sea, to sample the conditions for wheeled and tracked vehicles for himself, far away on the desert flank. Inevitably geography determined tactics by dictating that the only open flank was deep inland from the coast: the soldier who could go furthest away from the sea with confidence, would have most room in which to manoeuvre and increased opportunities of striking a surprise blow out of the wastes: essentially the confidence to do so had to be based on desert-craft and a comprehensive knowledge of every possible square mile of sand. The quest for both, which had gone on sporadically for years before, became an integral part of routine training and, as the distances travelled increased, the shortcomings of the vehicles became more apparent and the load on the repair facilities of the base workshops unbearable.

Here was grit for further friction with H.Q., B.T.E. New trucks had arrived but there was no way of knowing if they were desert worthy without putting them to an arduous test. From the treatment given at Hobart's direction, certain defects appeared, as was to be expected in untried equipment, but it was not a bit to the liking of B.T.E. who regarded the trial as 'a gross misuse of War Department transport'. The trucks were abruptly withdrawn for use in the base and the battle between commanders extended to their staffs. Major C. Smith, who as D.A.A. and Q.M.G. of the division, worked closest with Hobo, as his chief administrator, recalls two senior staff officers at B.T.E. who did not

. . . hesitate to make disparaging remarks about Hobo to me and as one of his chief staff officers I naturally resented them—and probably said so.

That such a state of affairs should exist between headquarters is more than reprehensible—it should not have been tolerated. The solution lay squarely with Gordon-Finlayson—to report there and then that he was unwilling to have Hobart as a division-al commander. But this, amongst other things, he shunned, and staff officers who disliked Hobart's 'disloyalty' (a term which could be stretched to mean attempts to acquire increased resources for the division) could hardly complain that the fighting arms were being trained contrary to their commander's ideas, since no training instruction was ever issued. Thus, without official guid-ance except of a negative kind, Hobart had either to disobey orders or do next to nothing at all at a time of national emerg-ency.

The normal rules of the Services require that a commander shall write a confidential report on each of his commanders. Before returning to England to become Adjutant General, Gordon-Finlayson used this document to appease his pent-up frustration with Hobart without offending his own conscience. Unhappily, in its very first sentence incomprehension was regis-tered, and what followed is at one moment apt and the next con-tradictory, indicating unhappy confusion in the mind of the writer. Hobart's notes of the report read:

Difficult to serve with or understand. Active in body and mind. Very hard worker. Brain quick and full of ideas. Considerable drive. Impetuous in judgements which are not as consistent and confi-dence-bearing as a Commander's should be. Manner and tempera-ment not usually sympathetic. Personality average. Interested in wel-fare and carries out well his administrative responsibilities.

Wide technical knowledge Royal Armoured Corps. Unduly optimistic about its capacities. Marked reluctance to listen to others' opinions and is too impatient with staff officers too jealous with regard for his own formation. Gives impression not placing much value on other arms : has caused misgivings and shaken his position as a Commander, result is he does not get the willing best from his subordinates and has not welded them into a happy and contented body.

General Hobart's methods of managing officers and men do not give the best results. I cannot regard him as a suitable commander in the field nor for promotion. Credit due for much hard peacetime work here both to the Mobile Division and Administrative Area.

Better scope for undoubted energy, peculiar temperament and particular abilities in such spheres as that of Technical Adviser AFV or in administrative capacity on staff. Not likely to qualify for the highest command and appointments.

A report such as this was utterly damning, as it was meant to be, the more so since its arrival in the War Office would coincide with that of its writer, who, in due course, could draw it from the records in his official capacity. It has more than passing interest because not only did it halt Hobart's career, it set the pattern for every subsequent attack on his character, and because of this it must be treated as of great importance when studying the remainder of his progress, particularly the last paragraph with its grim, yet paradoxically happy prophecy. The criticisms require more detailed consideration to evaluate the differences in outlook that separated Hobart from Gordon-Finlayson or, for that matter, any other officer of the latter's temperament.

Hobart was certainly difficult to understand, not least because his range of knowledge and ability covered such an enormous span, and undoubtedly his explosive grasp of problems and short cuts to their solution could be unnerving to slower intellects. But the charge that his manner led to uncertainty amongst his officers and men is not substantiated by those who served closest with him (the minority who could not stand his pace were in any case as often as not of insufficient calibre), and it could be demonstrated that many who had worked most successfully under him were already on their way to the highest places in the Army, indicating that his influence on them was the complete reverse of destructive. It is strange that in one sentence there is censure on the grounds of lack of sympathy and in another praise for his welfare work. But then, contradiction is the essence of this report.

To say that his personality was average was quaint and diametrically opposed to the good qualities extolled in the report. The old charge of lacking appreciation of other arms was to be expected, even though it held less water than ever in view of the fact that the only 'other arms' he had had in the division during his time under Gordon-Finlayson had been a regiment of artillery and one infantry battalion. However, since Gordon-Finlayson had never visited the division in person to meet the officers and men, it must be assumed that he drew many of his conclusions concerning confidence from what others told him, and so one asks where loyalty began and ended in Gordon-Finlayson's mind?

It was neither likely nor indeed necessary that Gordon-Finlayson should justify the contents of his report and in answer to Hobart's request that he might do so, replied:

Needless to say, I do not agree with some of what you have said, and the War Office can judge. But whatever I have reported and whatever you think, I am sure you will agree with me that loyalty to the Service forbids that there should appear to others any marked opposition between us, either professionally or socially. Indeed, on my side the latter has never existed at all, it was news to me that you thought it had.

Which may well have been quite true; nevertheless it was a fact that there had been very little social contact between the Gordon-Finlaysons and the Hobarts and it had been made abundantly plain to Mrs. Hobart, after she arrived, that she could not be received in Egyptian (Mohammedan) court circles since she was a divorcee. If Gordon-Finlayson had grounds for serious complaint and felt as strongly as he suggested, Hobart should have been removed before the handover. In so doing the measure of Gordon-Finlayson's sincerity would have been authenticated, and his successor saved embarrassment.

* * * * *

On 1st April 1939 the mechanised cavalry and the R.T.C. became married, taking the name 'Royal Armoured Corps' and thereby signalising the fusion of the old and new mobile arms in one task, manning a common type of equipment. The work of welding them together was unusual and, as Hobart realised, delicate: for help he yearned for encouragement from above, for it was he, the divisional commander, who had to merge cavalry to tanks. From Gordon-Finlayson's successor he hoped for a change of heart and at the outset found it as the new C.-in-C., Lieutenant-General Henry Maitland Wilson, a fellow student at the Staff College twenty years before, wasted no time in coming out to the desert to see for himself, spending three days with the men and machines and looking at the country. Of that visit Wilson wrote in his book:

During July I visited Mersa Matruh and carried out a reconnaissance of the desert to the south of it, being conducted by Hobart, who commanded 7th Armoured Division. . . . At Mersa Matruh the escarpment stood back in a circle with three miles as its longest radius, the harbour and town being covered by an inner ridge some 100 feet high. . . .

The main responsibility for defence fell on the armoured division allotted the role of playing for time pending the arrival of reinforcements. . . . In the country south of Matruh the escarpments are duplicated with a flat desert plain about three miles wide between them, the surfaces varied considerably between good, sound, hard going, stone slabs and sand hummocks, the last two slowing down at times the rate of movement of A.F.V.s and M.T. to as low as five miles per hour.

A force with thorough knowledge of such conditions possessed a great advantage over an adversary which was new to the country. We spent two days travelling over the country to the south, enabling one to get acquainted with desert conditions including navigation and location finding. One was at once struck with the fascination of those open spaces, devoid of outstanding landmarks, the only features being low, flat-topped ridges with striking similarity so that every small object such as a cairn of stones or an empty tar barrel assumes great importance.

Wilson contemplated the condition of 7th Armoured Division's equipment with horror:

> It was at that time very short of mobilisation equipment, especially as regards tanks and M.T. Each armoured brigade consisted of only two regiments, the Cavalry Regiments being equipped with light and the Tank Corps regiments with medium tanks. The latter gave me a shock at my first inspection seeing the same medium tanks which one had seen performing at the Aldershot Tattoo for many years and whose armour was questionably proof against A.T. small arms.

but inadvertently shows ignorance of the tanks when he referred to their armament:

> Their one advantage was the six-pounder gun which if modernised would have proved far more effective than the two-pounder which had just been introduced.

The gun then in service was, in fact, a three-pounder and not in the least suitable for upgrading to six-pounder.

At a rate of four a month new medium tanks were beginning to arrive in Egypt, welcomed by Wilson as 'a ray of hope for improvement in the armour of the medium tank units'. Wilson's understanding of tanks and tank warfare is of interest. Obviously he had grasped the relationship of gun-power to armoured protection, the essential elements in the tank versus tank engagement, and clearly he understood the part that mobility would play and the manner in which this depended on the defence of a fixed base: here Hobart's influence can be detected. That he had swallowed whole the misconception of the All Tank Idea without understanding the more subtle merits of All Armour can be seen when he writes:

> One had to check a pernicious doctrine which had grown up in recent years, aided by certain civilian writers, that tank units were capable of winning an action without the assistance of the other arms.

Already the anti-tank gun had appeared in the order of battle of armies as a counter to the tank; in consequence without incurring the risk of heavy casualties in tanks which, with our limited resources we could ill afford, these A/T guns required to be neutralised by artillery. Also, during operations situations would frequently occur where the presence of infantry with tanks would be invaluable. These principles were borne out in the subsequent fighting. The chief agents in debunking these and many other fallacies of our pre-war pundits were the Germans.

Although he wrote with the full benefit of hind-sight he fails to describe the pattern of desert fighting as it took place from 1940 to 1943: nor does he seem to have understood the relative state of the armies in 1939, the way the Germans employed armour, or the course of events in France in 1940. Indeed Wilson cannot claim much credit as an exponent of mobile war: throughout Wavell's highly successful mobile operations in late 1940 he was merely kept informed by Wavell of the project under consideration and the orders being passed to O'Connor for execution: and later, shortly after being sent to Greece, the static organisation Wilson had set up to defend Cyrenaica was swept away by Rommel in his first fast moving desert campaign. The importance of Wilson's comments lie not so much in their propagation of the All Tank legend (linked with a side blow at Hobart's association with Liddell Hart) but in their demonstration of his continued mis-reading, even after the greatest armoured war in history, of the vital significance and application of mobility.

At the end of July Wilson attended the final phase of a week long exercise held by Hobart for his commanders, and at the end made a speech praising the exercise and endorsing its teaching. There was no vestige of criticism. A few days later, on 2nd August, the Hobarts returned to England on leave, no shadow lying across their departure, happy in the belief that a sound personal understanding had been established with the new G.O.C.-in-C.—as it probably had. On the same day General Sir Archibald Wavell arrived in Cairo to become Commander-in-Chief, Middle East, responsible for co-ordinating British war plans in the Near and Middle East and North Africa, France, Turkey, and possibly Greece and Rumania.

A month before the declaration of war, Wavell took post at the centre of a vast strategic complex: his task to plan for any eventuality that could arise at any moment on a multiplicity of fronts ranging from Malta, the Balkans, the Cyrenaican frontier, or at several points in East Africa, his resources pathetically meagre when matched to the task. Since he never had the use of a personal aeroplane in which to fly to the extremities of his Command, his opportunities to view even the most important fronts were limited. Rightly he decentralised wherever he could, so perhaps it was for this reason that he left the Cyrenaican front to Wilson and even by November had still not visited there or seen his only Armoured Division. Yet it is strange that this man who believed so keenly in seeing for himself did not hasten even by road to look at the front closest to Cairo, where early contact with the enemy was first to be expected.

The signature of the Russo-German non-aggression pact on 23rd August, followed by the proclamation of formal guarantees by the British Government to Poland, restarted the alarm bells of war. An immediate recall brought the Hobarts post-haste to Egypt, he to rejoin his division at Mersa Matruh. War came, Poland fell, the German armoured divisions making short work of their outdated adversaries, and then the blaze died down to the guttering flicker of phoney war. The lessons of the armoured holocaust and the way it had overcome Poland could be ignored from a distance and had to be slurred over because public knowledge of its true import could have led, to say the least, to a disastrous decline in morale. Poland, in any case, had no Maginot Line behind which to shelter and so the base fallibility of this sort of modernised fortification had yet to be demonstrated: until it had been, the old theories remained intact. Therefore, although the overwhelming power of massed tanks had been exposed to view, the fatal meaning of its real threat to Western European security became hidden in a cloud of propaganda, and, since Italy elected to remain neutral for the moment, the opportunity to try out Hobart's ideas in the desert was not immediately forthcoming.

Gradually the tension in Egypt relaxed to the point at which Wilson could safely withdraw the Armoured Division to the base to re-fit, but before doing so he decided to hold a large signal exercise in the desert to test its state of training. The arrangements were as unusual as the operations the exercise was meant to simulate. It would have been customary for Wilson to discuss his aim and scheme with Hobart and invite the latter to submit an appreciation and plan. By so doing the manner in which Hobart intended to overcome the problems set by Wilson would have been disclosed and a sense of collaboration created. But no such arrangement was made and so Hobart, interpreting the spirit of the exercise as a test of his division, tackled each new situation as it arose in a thoroughly realistic manner, leaving the exercise controllers (who by inference became the enemy) in the dark as to his hour by hour intentions. To complicate matters the fog of exercise war became thicker as the result of a total breakdown in communications between the division and the controllers. As Wilson's staff should have known, Hobart directed operations in a unique way from a small, mobile Advanced H.Q., keeping touch with his Rear H.Q. by radio. But, for security reasons, the keys to all codes had to be left at Rear H.Q. and therefore the coded messages sent direct to Advanced H.Q. by Wilson's H.Q. could not be broken. Thereupon Wilson set out to make personal contact with Hobart in the desert, an adventure doomed to failure from the start because, according to Major Smith, at Rear H.Q.:

His ADC did not seem to want to understand the instructions given him regarding map references and compass bearings which were essential to enable him to guide his General to General Hobart.

Indeed an offer by Hobart to provide a guide was declined.

After many frustrating hours coursing about the desert, when the angry Wilson found and lost a series of signal terminals scattered about, the two met at last, but by then the mood went beyond the simple re-establishment of communications.

We have noticed Hobart's habit of hammering out the lessons of his own exercises in public and his ruthless criticism of all and sundry regardless of rank and seniority. Perhaps it came as no surprise to him that General Wilson now proceeded to level at him the same sort of vituperation in front of the officers and soldiers of his own division at Matruh after the Signal Exercise. Yet within the division there was disquiet at this exhibition. They thought they had performed rather well. To be told the reverse in forceful terms by the G.O.C.-in-C. was disconcerting and could have been damaging. To Dorrie on the 27th October Hobart wrote:

We had a conference on our exercise to-day. C-in-C found a lot of faults: almost all small matters of detail (or stupidity on the part of individuals) but it was the querulous tone he adopted that was so curious. It seemed that he was bent on finding something wrong. A good many of the points were incorrect, but he hadn't even troubled to ask me beforehand.

I know this sounds like 'the inefficient officer excusing himself by saying his superior is prejudiced'. But I have looked carefully at all the points and gone into them with my staff—and cannot feel that they were justified. They were the sort of thing I'd have asked one of my Brigadiers about quietly: unimportant details that had gone wrong through personal error. But were magnified by C-in-C to appear as enormities.

Well, Well.

Much love, P.

That same day he signed a simple but reasoned letter addressed to H.Q. B.T.E., answering Wilson's criticisms point by point. But it really did not matter—and one suspects Hobart surmised that it did not.

On the 12th November he was called to Cairo and later that day received a copy of a letter from General Wilson which read:

Headquarters
British Troops in Egypt
Cairo.
10th November, 1939.

To: General Sir Archibald Wavell,
K.C.B., C.M.G., D.S.O.

I regret to report that I have no confidence in the ability of Major-

General P. C. S. Hobart, C.B., D.S.O., O.B.E., M.C., to Command the Armoured Division to my satisfaction.

Though an excellent trainer of an A.F.V. Formation as regards technical detail and the work of small units and at the same time possessing a first rate knowledge of all problems connected with the organisation, armament and maintenance of tank formations, he shows many defects in the handling of his Command.

His tactical ideas are based on the invincibility and invulnerability of the tank to the exclusion of the employment of other arms in correct proportion.

These ideas combined with the excessive centralisation of his Command under his own hands are in my opinion unsound and are already beginning to reflect themselves in the training of units.

Being self-opinionated and lacking in stability I do not consider that Major-General Hobart can be relied on to discard his own ideas and carry out instructions from his superiors in a spirit of loyalty and co-operation—His personality does not make for harmonious working with those with whom he comes in contact and though commendably keen on his own formation, he shows little consideration for the feelings and wishes of others.

I request therefore that a new Commander be appointed to the Armoured Division and that Major-General Hobart be given an appointment where his methods of organisation and his intimate knowledge of Tank Armament etc may be given full scope.

H. M. Wilson
Lieutenant-General,
General Officer Commanding-in-Chief,
The British Troops in Egypt

The pattern will be recognised, for Wilson's letter repeats much of what had already been written by Gordon-Finlayson—in places it is almost a replica—and the reason became quite evident on the 14th, when Hobart had a personal interview with Wavell. There is only one account of this meeting and it is Hobart's, but since it was described by him in his plea to the King for reinstatement, we may assume that it is close to the truth, since General Wavell would have a full opportunity to comment.

At my interview with General Wavell, he stated that he agreed with General Wilson, and ordered me to hand over my Division and proceed home forthwith. I asked General Wavell to give me some instance of failure, or at least specific facts in substantiation of the charges made. He said he was unable to do so. He told me however that General Gordon-Finlayson had not only spoken to him about me at home, but had shown him a copy of the adverse confidential report, which he had written on me.

Now, King's Regulations stated in those days:

A confidential report will be furnished annually to the Under Secretary of State, The War Office, on every officer. It will be strictly confidential as between the officers reporting and the officers reported on.

Therefore, if what Hobart says is true, a clear charge of impropriety could be laid at General Gordon-Finlayson's door, and neither General Wavell nor General Wilson come out of the transaction with credit. Wavell may well have come to Egypt with the premeditated intention of sacking Hobart, and Wilson, who appeared not displeased with Hobart's formation shortly before Wavell's arrival, swung the other way within two months of Wavell's arrival. In fairness to Wavell, it seems he had no intention of removing Hobart entirely from military employment. In his letter to the War Office he wrote:

I hope, however, that it will be found possible to use General Hobart's great knowledge and experience of Armoured Fighting Vehicles in some capacity.

He was saying, in essence, 'this man should serve on—but not under General Wilson or myself'—and that they were right to get rid of Hobart if they could not agree with him cannot be denied. Sufficient justification for their act is less easy to find and Wavell could never be persuaded to give it. It is difficult to understand how a man commanding what was predominantly a tank formation could do other than base his tactical ideas primarily on the tank: or how somebody who sticks sincerely to ideas of long standing can be 'unstable'. The refutation of the accu-

Hobo, by Eric Kennington

Above: Second Lieutenant Hobart in 1907 (second from
left in the front row)
Below: Lieutenant Hobart in 1914 (extreme left in rear row)

Top: Rolls-Royce armoured cars
Centre: After the crash—British and Indian troops examine the wreckage
Bottom: After the rescue—Hobart (fourth from the right) confers with his late captor. Tennant is third from right

Top: Vickers Medium Tank Mk I—the work horse of the
armoured experiments. Weight 12 tons
Bottom: Birch gun—the 'tank' the artillery did not want

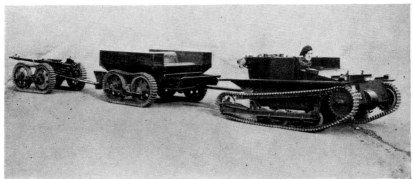

Top: The Vickers Light Tank Mk I—a cheap fighting vehicle of five tons weight
Bottom: Carden Loyd Carrier Mk VI with trailers
mounting 20 mm. anti-tank gun and crew—its pace too fast for infantry thought

Above: The 1st Tank Brigade on Salisbury Plain
Below: Hobo in the turret of the 16-ton Vickers Medium Tank
directs operations on the Plain

Top: A 9 Cruiser: 12 tons of compromise
Bottom: A 10—the project for an Infantry Tank which produced another, heavier cruiser of 14 tons

Top: Elles's comical Infantry Tank Mk I—the thick-skinned, slow A 11
Bottom: Christie Cruiser at speed—the sire of the Nuffield cruisers

Assessing 11th Armoured Division in 1941—Churchill with Hobo

General Montgomery escorted by Brigadier Duncan (*left*),
with Hobo and Lieutenant-Colonel Jolly in rear. Taken shortly
before D-Day

Above: Valentine Duplex Drive. Good enough for training but rejected by Hobo
Below: Sherman Duplex Drive—spearhead of the invasion

Top: Scorpion Flail on Valentine—only a training device
Bottom: Crab Flail on Sherman—a most efficient mine destroyer and combat fighting vehicle

Top: A.V.R.E.—a central feature of the assault team—shown here after dropping its S.B.G. bridge
Bottom: A.V.R.E. with Bobbin—a rushed project to satisfy a special need

Above: Churchill Crocodile—most spectacular of the Funnies
Below: The moment of truth—Hobo inspecting 1st Lothian and
Border Horse

Above: D-Day. Specialised armour on the British sector
Below: Walcheren—where specialised armour dominated

A special cargo crosses the Rhine in a Buffalo. Hobo is accompanied
by Churchill, Alan Brooke, Montgomery and Dempsey

sation that training and 'feelings' were suffering came later from his officers and men in another salutary way.

Both Lieutenant-Colonel 'Strafer' Gott and Horace Birks, who had just arrived to take over from Gott as G.S.O. 1, were astonished at the news brought by Hobart after the interview with Wavell, but Birks was even more astounded at the supine manner in which his general accepted it.

I was aghast and asked Hobo where his reply was, but he said he didn't propose to fight the matter: it was the personal opinion of the C-in-C, and that he was finished in any case and the only sensible thing was to go home.

This reaction, remarkably similar to that adopted by Wavell himself when Churchill sacked him in 1941, far from suited Birks who thereupon spent a long exhausting night walking up and down with Hobo in the desert persuading him to put in a letter of protest and not look on the disaster as 'the Will of God'.

Nothing of this sort could be of avail, as Hobart knew. Since he could not stay, the best course was to go with dignity. In the event he went in triumph, for as his car drove the mile and a half from his H.Q. to the airstrip it was to find the route lined by the men of his division, gunners, rifle, cavalry and tankmen, all cheering their general in a spontaneous and unforgettable farewell. They none of them knew why he was going—simply that he was and they must pour out to see him off with a demonstration of outright confidence and affection. To the General and his wife came a flood of letters from the C.O.s of all the units expressing their shock and dismay at his departure, and from Major-General Richard O'Connor, commanding the 8th Infantry Division at Matruh, who had found co-operation with Hobart easy and with whom had worked in close accord, a sorrowful letter saying of the Mobile Division: 'It is the best trained division I have ever seen.'

The following June came the first unmistakable justification when, from the beginning of operations against the Italians, the 7th Armoured Division, using Hobart's methods from the desert

A.C.—N

flank for the first time in earnest, dominated the numerically superior enemy who clung to the coast: and just under a year later the crowning mercy—total victory by 7th Armoured Division at Beda Fomm after O'Connor's triumph in the desert. At that supreme moment one of those he had trained sent him a signal reading: 'Recent success mainly due your previous training and organisation', and reflecting the opinion of Major Smith, when writing his tribute in the history of 7th Armoured Division, *The Desert Rats*, by Major-General G. L. Verney:

> The Divisional Staff may well have felt discouraged. But one great asset they had, a Divisional Commander of great initiative, drive and leadership who was prepared to make bricks without straw . . . his spirit was to remain with them after he had gone and many were the times when he was quoted—' "Hobo" always used to say . . .'

'He made bricks without straw'—indeed there was his great strength and, perhaps, a hidden weakness. Could it have been that, under the test of war, he might have overrated his own ability to succeed? Never once had he failed to achieve his aim, by hook or by crook, and produced astonishing results with meagre resources. Against the Italians it worked: against Rommel, as he tentatively advanced in April 1941, the outcome could have been more in doubt in the uproar of one great improviser meeting another—yet the blows to the fortunes of a British Army handled in a semi-mobile manner by Wavell from the static H.Q. (set up by Wilson shortly before he went to Greece) can hardly have been harder than they became in the event.

Let it just be said that, when the bitterness had faded in the distance of time, and the tempo of war was scorching every waking moment of his life, Hobart's only lasting regret was the lost opportunity to cross swords with Rommel. It would have been a fascinating encounter and who can say how many months of desert warfare might have been saved if Rommel had been defeated on his first appearance? For Rommel enjoyed his first success largely by luck and not least at the invitation of bungling by the generals opposed to him.

Part 3

PRODUCTION

*The invention all admired, and each
how he to be the inventor missed, so easy
it seemed once found, which yet
unfound most would have thought
Impossible.*

Milton in 'Paradise Lost'

9

WHEN THE THUMBS ARE TURNED DOWN

An unpleasant voyage back to England in a crowded troopship as part of a slow-moving convoy threatened by the hazards of mine and torpedo; a pre-Christmas arrival in a home country groping amongst the frustrations of food rationing and the black-out—these were the parting gifts of the Army in Egypt to the Hobarts. His reception by the War Office was surreptitiously cool, as a letter from a friend in the Military Secretary's Department on 14th December foretold:

I have been trying for over a week to find out some news for you, but everyone treats my requests with a certain amount of suspicion. All my usual channels are quite mute.

Step by step the climax approached. On the 15th December came a letter informing Hobart that he would remain on full pay pending a decision as to future employment. With the post on 7th January 1940 came a notification that, in accordance with regulations, if no suitable opportunity had occurred of making use of his services by 9th March he would be retired (three months then having elapsed since he officially relinquished command of the Armoured Division). On the 9th February, at his own request, he had an interview with the C.I.G.S., General Sir Edmund Ironside, and came away in a happier frame of mind, having been told that he would be employed in command again and that it was only the stagnant state of the war and the consequent lack of vacancies that had held up his reappointment. Ironside's final words, to the effect that there was no cause for anxiety and that an administrative post would be found to tide him over, while comforting, were hedged by a request that they should not be repeated outside.

Then, less than three weeks later, there came another letter saying that, as no further employment could be found, 'you will be placed on retired pay . . . with effect from 9th March 1940'. There is no reason to suppose that Ironside ever fully appreciated the hollowness of his promise, although as president of the Appointments Board which decided major-generals' appointments he cannot have been unaware of the situation; but the C.I.G.S. could not necessarily be expected to follow up individual cases under the conditions of war. Equally, there is no vestige of proof that anybody deliberately omitted to find Hobart employment in sufficient time to stave off his enforced retirement, although General Gordon-Finlayson's position as Adjutant General and a member of the Appointments Board may not have been without significance. That Britain's leading tank expert came to be placed on the retired list at the outbreak of a war that was to be dominated by tanks is merely, at best, a reflection on the shortcomings of a myopic bureaucracy.

Bereft of the only employment he knows in time of war, what can a dynamic soldier do to absorb his energy and assuage the bitter insinuation that personal honour has been sullied? Some small portion of his efforts must, of course, be dedicated to looking for a home and to the reorganisation of an everyday life subject to reduced financial resources. As a half-measure, while the search for a suitable house went on, the Hobarts took up residence in the charming little Gloucestershire village of Chipping Campden. From here, stage by stage, were directed the attempts to restore his fortunes, submitting an appeal to the King, pleading that the decision in Egypt should be set aside, permitting a return to the Active List. Matters such as these never move at a great pace, but when the details have to be referred to Egypt for comment by the C.-in-C. in time of war, speed is impossible and delay its handmaiden. A wearisome round of notes, cables, enquiries and then more delays faded meaninglessly into the blurred background until suddenly everything was illuminated by the crimson flash of war on England's doorstep.

The abortive naval and aerial warfare which overshadowed the disastrous land campaign in Norway in April 1940 at first gave vent only to an instinctive uneasiness in the minds of the public. But then disquiet, fanned by the newspapers, was transmitted in ripples of annoyance, billowing into waves of oratory breaking across the floor of the House of Commons to sweep Neville Chamberlain out and Winston Churchill into office as the new Prime Minister.

And as that great man came to power the roar of German tanks could be heard rumbling into Belgium, through the Ardennes, following the bombers deep into the northern plains of France. As Hobart had foreseen in detail, aeroplanes and armour began to paralyse a whole nation by a stroke to the heart. But while Churchill sprang to lead his country in defiance of the danger, one of his most devoted admirers, Hobart, had perforce to take his place in the ranks—and in the ranks of the newly formed Local Defence Volunteers at that—as one of the guardians of Chipping Campden.

Promotion came rapidly. Within a few days he wore the stripe of lance corporal as under his leadership the defence of Chipping Campden grew to fanatical importance. Nigel Duncan, who happened to be living in the village at the time, coming home occasionally from his job in the War Office, used to enjoy his walk from the station to the hotel in the cool and peace of the evening until, invariably, he would be halted by a peremptory command from a Volunteer, demanding his identity. As time wore on the persistence of the sentries became such that it was well-nigh impossible to convince them that he had any right in Chipping Campden at all. This was a strong-point organised with ruthless efficiency—a living example of the manner in which the lance corporal's enthusiasm could seize the loyalty and co-operation of all kinds of his countrymen.

This release from boredom was heaven sent. If the Regular Army would not make full use of his talents, the budding Home Guard certainly could. Within a few weeks he was asked if he would act as Deputy Area Organiser of the L.D.V. South Midland Area, with its H.Q. in Oxford. He gratefully accepted: Chipping Campden was altogether too small to absorb his talents. Once again the floodgates holding back his torrential energy opened wide, and again his letters to his 'beloved woman' are the best guide to his activities. Throughout that torrid summer he lived off and on in Hertford College, Oxford, relishing the lush isolation of the academic scene, dinner with the Warden at high table, the successive moves to ante-rooms for port and coffee and smoking, the dignity of it all, the absence of a wireless set from any common room to preserve the donnish life undisturbed—'until the bombs arrive'. From here he motored miles in any car, with whatever rationed petrol he could procure, to urge on the ill-equipped barely trained L.D.V.s, and persuaded an author, John Brophy, to become his staff captain—an appointment eventually leading to the production of the first handbook for the L.D.V.

Simultaneously he engaged in protracted negotiations to arrange the lease of a house in Deddington, and larded a letter to Dorrie with details of a new recipe—of an unusual kind from a tankman-turned-tank-hunter.

> *Cocktails:* each bottle
> either $\frac{1}{2}$ petrol
> $\frac{1}{2}$ tar
> or else
> $\frac{1}{2}$ petrol
> $\frac{1}{4}$ paraffin
> $\frac{1}{4}$ tar

depends on quality of tar. Best to make one up of each and try. Ignition: easiest way is to keep a rag (not too small: about $\frac{1}{2}$ duster is right) tied round bottle.

When time comes man uncorks bottle, soaks rag, unscrews cork, knots soaked rag round neck of bottle and lights it with an ordinary match and throws at once.

His whole conduct took on a strange mixture of cynicism and idealism: one moment he was writing with tongue firmly embedded in cheek, the next enthusing those who might enhance the value of the L.D.V. as a whole, but always tireless and direct as ever in endeavours to clear the approved channels when they became clogged. On the 17th July he wrote:

I am trying to get in touch with the NUR and other Railwaymen's unions: but am being ridden off, politely but obviously, by the management. They seem frightened of them. The GWR idea of getting men to join the LDV seems limited to sending them messages for the managers down the official channel. It hasn't worked. Perhaps the men are suspicious of the management: perhaps they don't read them: perhaps they are merely fed-up with everlasting appeals. Anyway the result so far is not wonderful. I can't help feeling that if one could get at the Trade Union leaders it would have much more effect.

The letter sheds a most interesting sidelight on Hobart's political inclinations, for as a radical he was moving away from the traditional army officer's commitment to Tory sentiments to seek other agents who might shake the Government out of its apathy. At the heart of discontent, of course, clung a soured view of a system which had cast him out and a desire for reform, root and branch, above all, at the War Office.

In those days there is no doubt that his mind followed four tracks. One pursued concern for the welfare of his family (leasing a house and pondering the need to send Grizell to safety in America—a course rejected by the 10-year-old with characteristic Hobart pugnacity); another the proud duty of serving his country at her most perilous hour; a third, wider road, carried a despairing wish to see the Army restored to esteem in the nation's opinion; the fourth, narrower avenue, constricted by anger, intruded on all the other tracks—an insistence on the imperative need to wipe out the slur on his honour. Yet his associates at this time received no indication of his worry and depression: they guessed his torment but never heard a grouch or complaint. Nor was he to be heard in public castigating those of whom he could justifiably round and say, 'I told you so', as the German Panzer army ground Western Europe under its tracks.

Gradually all four tracks began to converge under the guidance of war. In no other way could it have been done, for normally when the thumbs are turned down on an army officer he can hardly ever expect a reprieve.

However, once the issues had become fairly stated, once France had fallen in June and Britain stood on her own, the British strategy could revert to its traditional defensive, offensive nature. Within the defended perimeter of the British Isles the incentive to hold on did not obliterate the search for means to strike back. First priority went to the Royal Air Force since it was already engaged in the skies above its own airfields: in a lower priority came the rebuilding of conventional army formations into much the same shape as they had been in France.

The tank lesson from France was fresh in soldiers' minds and bandied freely in the press. It was apprehended that the best antidote to the tank was the tank itself, but since only a handful of machines had not been lost in France and the factories were still not producing a sufficient flow of new ones, the demands of the British Army were unlikely to be satisfied for many months to come. Moreover the tanks that were coming off the factory floors would be obsolete once the Germans, seeking an overwhelming technical advantage, up-gunned and up-armoured theirs. Nevertheless, because anything was better than nothing in the summer of 1940, production of existing designs had to be stepped up regardless of quality and the distant future.

Neither the organisation nor the tank manufacturing capacity of Britain were equal to the task that circumstances forced upon them. Just a month before the outbreak of war a Ministry of Supply had been formed charged with the task of providing the Armed Services with equipment, absorbing amongst other departments, that of the M.G.O., although the Navy and the Royal Air Force managed to stay out.

Thus, to the lasting discomfort of the Royal Armoured Corps, the entire staff of the Director of Mechanisation assigned to the design and procurement of vehicles in the M.G.O.'s Department, was lost from the War Office to the Ministry of Supply. At a stroke the War Office lost what few experts it possessed to another Ministry, depriving it of an educated opinion on the affairs of mechanisation: from then until the Army General Staff could re-create its own tank department, its views became subordinate to those of the Ministry of Supply, making it go cap-in-hand to ask for what could be given instead of what it wanted.

The new and extremely complex organisation, exposed to the demands of a vast expansion, had simultaneously to grapple with a search for the best way to practise its charter. And in 1940, a year later, the Ministry of Supply was still finding its feet while under ever increasing pressure to provide boundless quantities of equipment. In theory the creation of this Ministry to centralise procurement may have been praiseworthy; in timing its arrival, to say the least, was unfortunate: in application an extra level of decision was introduced into the procurement of weapons which, inevitably, multiplied the opportunities for misunderstanding and delay. The outcome was all but disastrous to tank production.

Yet even when at last the tanks reached the troops there was still no guarantee that they would be used in the most effective way. Mostly the men in command at the top were those who had failed to understand the nature of modern tank warfare in 1939, and the lessons of one disaster could hardly be thoroughly digested in a few months. In any case it was almost a case of the blind leading the blind because owing to the retrenchment of the previous decade, there was a shortage of tank experts, both in factory and field, capable of interpreting and disseminating their art to the untrained masses in the ways of armoured warfare on the grand scale.

*   *   *   *   *

In August work had been offered to Hobart in connection with tank production at the Ministry of Supply. A Tank Board had been formed—a purely political creation—charged with the co-ordination of new ideas with industrial capacity and matching them to the insistent demands of the fighting troops: because it had responsibility but hardly any power, it could do little more than exchange views and suggest ideas and, partially, as a result, no significant progress was made in 1940 in the way of research and development into the next generation of tanks. Indeed, research and development was practically halted as a deliberate act of policy to enable everything to be concentrated on production.

Hobart was not keen to get involved in this field as a member of the Ministry of Supply because, as he wrote, 'I can't see that there's room for anyone but Pope in that line, and I don't want to jockey him.' Major General Vyvyan Pope, late of the R.T.R., was then head of the Armoured Fighting Vehicles Directorate in the War Office, responsible amongst other things for stating and co-ordinating the design of future tanks. Hobart, by nature, would have tended to adopt a War Office attitude instead of that required by a representative of the Ministry of Supply, and might have complicated affairs through not being fully aware of current production problems.

That summer it was decided to raise five new armoured divisions in addition to the three already in existence, but an expansion such as this could only be effective over a long period of time and only then if carefully geared to the availability of men, machines and training facilities. And the latter were almost as critically short in supply as the others since land across which tanks could drive and shoot was equally vital for agricultural purposes to help meet the country's need for food in the face of the tightening German naval blockade.

Once satisfied that the Battle of Britain had been won and measures for immediate defence well started, the Prime Minister addressed himself to the tank game, looking far into the future for ways and means to attack. His interest may have been sharpened by an article from Liddell Hart in the *Sunday Pictorial* of 11th August 1940 (circulated to key people in July), although three days before that Justice Tilly, one of Hobart's C.O.s from the Tank Brigade, had written to Hobart saying: '. . . I am certain you are going to get a command in the near future. I can't say much on paper but "our Winston" knows all about it and I think quite a lot will happen before long.' Liddell Hart's article, entitled 'We Have Wasted Brains', drew attention to the tank generals who no longer commanded tanks, mentioning Martel, Lindsay, Pile, Fuller and Hobart. At that time Pile, as head of Anti-Aircraft Command, and in the thick of the opening rounds of the Battle of Britain, found himself brought into

close touch with the Prime Minister and he recalls how concerned both Winston Churchill and Lord Beaverbrook were
over the tank situation and how, at the end of September, the
former was looking for somebody to put in overall charge of
tanks. Pile writes:

> I told him we had a superb trainer of tanks in Hobart but he had
> just been sacked. He asked me to get him to come and see him.
> I saw Hobart, but he was very difficult; said he could do nothing
> unless he was first reinstated and said that his honour had been un-
> satisfied. I took him to the bar of the Ritz and at last persuaded him
> to accept Churchill's offer.

From the moment the Prime Minister's interest became known
Hobart returned to the lead in tank affairs, formulating a policy
designed to give economic employment to the men and machines
which soon were to be ready for use. It seems to have made no
difference that he was still only a Home Guard officer. Early in
October he was circulating proposals for an Armoured Army
and receiving comments in turn from Pile, Crocker and Tilly,
and later from Pope. The aim was the creation of a doctrine
'that is aggressive': the essentials to be an adequate air force
co-operating with 'Wholly Armoured Battle Formations, un-
hampered by unarmoured formations and not tied to or clogged
by Infantry formations'. Backing this great force of twenty divisions with ten thousand tanks was envisaged a huge training programme run by a General Officer-in-Command Armoured Army
who 'must have the full support of the Army Council to carry out
his task and be himself a member of the Army Council'. Responsible to the new commander would be one General Staff for
armoured forces, another for design and production. The paper
went on to outline the need for the Air Force to train with the
Armoured Army, for types of tanks with specifications very similar to those which eventually began to appear three years later,
for the need to develop supply by air and for ancillary troops,
such as mobile anti-aircraft formations, motorised artillery and
infantry, engineers and, in addition, parachutists—all as part of
an Armoured Army (not a tank one) separate from the rest of
the Army.

Armed with these ideas and a mass of figures, Hobart met Churchill at Chequers on the 13th October, and records sitting next to his charming hostess Mrs. Churchill, and after lunch being conducted by Mr. Churchill on an inspection of some bomb craters made a week previously within three hundred yards of the house.

On the way back I talked to Randolph and we stopped at a pram to see his infant who looked to me absurdly like Winston. When we reached the house Winston said 'Come into the Library, General, I want you to tell me about Tanks'. Only Attlee accompanied us. I remember feeling myself to be unwisely foolhardy when I put our initial need at ten armoured divisions, but all Winston said was 'How many Tanks?' and when I said ten thousand, nodded his head.

After half an hour or so he looked at the time and said he must hurry off as he was already very late for his daily rest, but told me he wanted to talk to me again at tea time and meanwhile to go into details with Attlee. I had about two hours with Attlee, and then some more, including some personal facts,[1] with Winston.

There followed one of Mr. Churchill's most eulogistic minutes to the C.I.G.S., Sir John Dill (who had taken over from Ironside at about the same time as Gordon-Finlayson had given up as Adjutant General):

Prime Minister to C.I.G.S.   19.x.40.

I was very pleased last week when you told me you proposed to give an armoured division to Major-General Hobart. I think very highly of this officer, and I am not at all impressed by the prejudices against him in certain quarters. Such prejudices attach frequently to persons of strong personality and original view. In this case General Hobart's original views have been only too tragically borne out. The neglect by the General Staff even to devise proper patterns of tanks before the war has robbed us of all the fruits of this invention. These fruits have been reaped by the enemy, with terrible consequences. We should therefore remember that this was an officer who had the root of the matter in him, and also vision.

In my minute last week to you I said I hoped you would propose

1. At this point he unburdened himself of his grievances, for Pile says Churchill told him Hobart had only asked to be reinstated in Egypt to restore his honour.

to me the appointment that day, i.e., Tuesday, but at the latest this week. Will you very kindly make sure that the appointment is made at the earliest moment.

Since making this minute I have carefully read your note to me and the summary of the case for and against General Hobart. We are now at war, fighting for our lives, and we cannot afford to confine Army appointments to persons who have excited no hostile comment in their career. The catalogue of General Hobart's qualities and defects might almost exactly have been attributed to most of the great commanders of British history. Marlborough was very much the conventional soldier, carrying with him the goodwill of the Service. Cromwell, Wolfe, Clive, Gordon, and in a different sphere Lawrence, all had very close resemblance to the characteristics set down as defects. They had other qualities as well, and so I am led to believe has General Hobart. This is a time to try men of force and vision and not to be exclusively confined to those who are judged thoroughly safe by conventional standards.

I hope therefore you will not recoil from your proposal to me of a week ago, for I think your instinct in this matter was sound and true.

This minute is of multiple importance, for it shows the Prime Minister's fascination for Hobart, seeing in him a kindred spirit, and reflects his distaste of the attitude of those in the War Office who had still not woken to the magnitude of the revolution that had taken place: but it also reports Dill's fear of the difficult character who seemed about to be re-introduced into the army hierarchy, bringing in his portfolio a vast take-over bid.

A week later came a telephone call to Hobart for an interview with the C.I.G.S., greeted by a priceless moment of farce as Hobart insisted on being told if he was to appear dressed as a civilian, a major-general or a lance corporal in the Home Guard: a problem beyond Dill's knowledge of protocol to answer, although in the end the dress of major-general was decided upon. Dill offered Hobart the command of one of the new armoured divisions, but said that he would rather he took on the new job —envisaged in the earlier paper—Commander of Armoured Forces.

But the proposal fell far short of the powers the paper deemed necessary for the fulfilment of its aim, and thrust into broad relief the confused state of official thought in its attempts to graft an Armoured Army on to the old infantry one. The paper on an Armoured Army had already been shown to the G.O.C.-in-C., Home Forces, General Alan Brooke, who appears to have agreed with Dill in a wish to water-down the most revolutionary aspects of the proposal. The reaction is not surprising, but, inevitably, it pointed to Brooke as a formidable adversary to the Armoured Idea. In essence, Dill saw a Commander, Royal Armoured Corps, raising and training a sort of private tank army separately from the rest of the Army with which it was to fight. It was the All Tank Idea gone mad, the more so since the C.R.A.C. was specifically excluded from control of design and procurement of new machines and not given a post in the War Office from whence the major direction of the war and rearmament came. Instead, the C.R.A.C. was to be permitted to make suggestions and placed under two chiefs—the C.I.G.S. (Dill) and the G.O.C.-in-C Home Forces, Brooke, who would train the actual formations for war. Emphatically, there was to be no seat on the Army Council.

In Hobart's opinion the offer was 'merely a prop to a rotten organisation—destined to failure—and when this became apparent I should, of course, be a convenient scapegoat'. Power had to go with responsibility: therefore a seat on the Army Council was essential, and from this would spring the post of C.-in-C., something the Army Council could never accept. In any case, as he told Dill, he did not want to return to the War Office, he would be very pleased to take an armoured division, but first wanted action taken on his appeal to the King; noting that Dill appeared genuinely disturbed no proper reply had ever been received to it. For the moment there was an impasse.

It is speculative if Hobart genuinely believed in the viability of the demand for an Armoured Army with its commander an Army Councillor. Little faith can be adduced from his notes or recorded comments: why then did he propose, even in the circumfusion of a desperate wartime situation when the British traditionally put their wrongs to right, what virtually amounted to the upturn of the long established structure of the Army? Was he being blindly unrealistic or, perhaps, quirkishly humorous in prodding the Army's leaders with an ideal of the sort which was embarrassing yet so near to an acceptable solution that it could not be rejected out of hand? Or had he decided, as had Fuller after the First World War, that 'if you don't stake your claims high, no one will listen to you'? The truth, arrived at partly by reasoning and partly by instinct, probably drew inspiration from these reasons and others unfathomable in so complex a character—but urged on most of all by a desire to do something positive in the face of disaster—right or wrong— bearing in mind that the Prime Minister was backing him.

Perhaps it is worthy of notice that the Germans, faced themselves with disaster after Stalingrad, appointed their greatest tank expert, Guderian, Inspector General of Armoured Forces with a charter remarkably similar to Hobart's ideal of 1940. The subsequent revival of German armoured formations linked to prodigious strides in production can hardly be dismissed as trivial.

On the 4th November came another interview with the Prime Minister, shortly before a Cabinet meeting, 'back to fire, glowering at me: very disappointed that I had refused employment'. But Hobart stood his ground, and reiterated his insistence upon action in response to the appeal to the King. In appearance it was deadlock; in effect the Prime Minister had won his point in the only way possible, by asking as they parted, 'Will you leave it to me?' and by writing two days later:

Private   10 Downing Street,
                                                         Whitehall.
                                                    November 6, 1940.
Dear General Hobart,
    The matter is one for you to settle, and personally I could not attempt to sway your decision. I should have thought however that in times like these the Command of an Armoured Division about to be formed gave high opportunities for useful service.
    Pray let the CIGS know what you are doing as other arrangements must be made.
                                    Yours etc.
                                        Winston S. Churchill.

    In appealing to patriotism and to Hobart's devotion to tanks,

A.C.—O

Churchill revealed unerring insight into the leading impulses motivating a most diverse personality. The response was instantaneous, made, in fact, before the letter arrived. 'I felt I could not refuse a direct request from Mr. Churchill', he wrote to Dill.

More letters passed.

8th November 40.   Leadenporch House,
                                                    Deddington,
                                                    Oxon.

Dear Prime Minister,

Thank you very much for your letter of 6th, which has just reached me.

I greatly appreciate that you should have found time to see me and to write.

I am most anxious to be of any service I can to the country—or to you. I will undertake the work you mention or any other to which I am appointed.

I will do my best.

I realise that I must be re-employed now as a retired officer. Please do not think that I am attempting to make any conditions when I say that I would like my Appeal to the King still to go forward, as I conceive it to be the only means of removing the slur which, I feel, rests on my honour and reputation as a soldier. But, if you consider such action to be in the public interest in these times, I will withdraw my Appeal.

I am informing the CIGS.

                          Yours sincerely,

                                              P. C. S. Hobart

In explanation of his insistence that the appeal should go forward, Hobart had written to Dill on the 4th November:

. . . I felt that the unmerited disgrace inflicted on me could only be removed by restoring me to my old place on the Army List: and that no measure less than this could be expected to give the necessary confidence to those called on to serve under me.

Eventually the appeal went forward, only to be rejected, and ensuring that Hobart's name could appear only amongst the list of retired officers—a position offering small hope of further advancement, while in no way reducing his effectiveness.

On the 19th November, at yet another meeting between Dill

and Hobart, it was formally proposed the latter should become Commander of the R.A.C., responsible for the individual training of officers and other ranks, but not of units and formations. Dill said the appointment was urgent, a new division for Hobart to command would take time to form and, anyway, an armoured division commander should be a good bit younger than fifty-five: Hobart replied that he wanted time to consult Pope and one or two others to find out what the job entailed. He was given forty-eight hours to do so and on the 21st November submitted a paper which virtually tallied with the one he had discussed, unofficially, with Pile and the others and to which Dill and Brooke had taken exception. He re-emphasised:

1. Essential—Army Council status to get an Armoured Army ready for 1942. He, himself, was willing to serve *under* this Commander in any capacity *providing* he had power.
   2. (a) A Training Commander with a small H.Q. *not* in the War Office.
   (b) Two Major Generals in the War Office for General Staff and Adjutant General, and for Equipment.
   3. Close co-operation with the Royal Air Force.
   4. Pick of personnel (quality, not quantity).
   5. First Priority on equipment production.
   6. Grouping of Training Establishments.
   7. Recalling of a number of RTR officers and NCOs from overseas to train new units and formations.

In his opinion only Charles Broad or Tim Pile could do the top job 'and the War Office hate both of them'. He added, in a letter to Liddell Hart:

. . . I said they might find themselves forced to put the Armoured Corps under the Air Ministry instead of the War Office: the former did, at any rate, understand machines and mobility.

That must have gone down well! The rest of the story is best told from Hobart's own handwritten notes made at the time.

Sat, 23/11/40 Lunched at Chequers. Had 30 or 40 mins with Churchill afterwards. He said Dill and shown him my letter (of 21st). Discussed general question of Armoured Formations. I explained necessity for a Head for AFV and how essential it was for him to be on Army Council level if the thing was to be done in the time. Mentioned a few difficulties. He asked who could do it. I said Charles and Tim were the only 2 with the 'necessary' qualifications. Before he went off to bed he said, 'You will hear officially of your appointment soon.' 29/11/40 Interviewed Dill at W.O. (re my note to him on AFV Reorgn of 21/11/40). He pressed me to take on the Training job. Said he could not agree to a member of Army Council for RAC only. I merely maintained my position and said that I had no confidence in being able to do the job without that backing and would prefer to go back to his original offer of an Armoured Division. He said it was awkward as they had already selected another man, but it might be changed perhaps. Anyway there'd be another Armoured Division available in Jan for certain. He said, of course, Armoured Divisional Commanders should really be younger. I agreed. (Alan Brooke went into CIGS as I came out. Auchinleck came in before me.)

29/11/40 After reaching home I was rung up by Dill personally. He said he had consulted Brooke and would be prepared to appoint Martel as a Lt-Gen to command RAC .Would I accept the job under him? I said I was convinced he must be on Army Council level and any other arrangement would only be a waste of time. Dill asked whether I would not change my mind. I said no.

Martel had returned from France via Dunkirk having to his credit one major tank action fought close to Arras. To some his handling of the battle had looked like a mismanaged shambles, although the British 'I' tanks had performed well against the triumphant Germans. But in a deteriorating situation wherein the state of affairs was constantly blanketed by the fog of war, Martel could not justifiably be held wholly responsible for the errors committed, and it was not until the war was over that it became known just how successful the British tank action had been. On his own assessment not a good commander in the field, Martel was more at home as an engineer, and in the environment of the War Office, perfectly in tune with the system, malleable to its pressures, and managing to make limited progress without ruffling too many feathers or becoming labelled 'difficult', as had so many of the other tank addicts (the band of crusaders as he calls them in his book *An Outspoken Soldier*).

From the beginning, the task of creating an Armoured Army was hampered by his lack of power and confused by the dual responsibilities to Dill and Brooke. As Martel wrote:

This was obviously a delicate position for a commander and I asked if I might have a charter. The reply was that the War Office had tried to prepare one but it had proved to be so difficult that they asked me to do without one. I did so, but I am not sure if it was very wise. There was every opportunity for friction in this dual post, but fortunately no major conflict arose.

From the day the post of C.R.A.C. was created, Hobart's fears were being realised, for even if the War Office could not devise a charter, it was at least adamant that no one arm of the service should be permitted to predominate. In Martel a willing co-operator had been selected, one who, unhappily, appears to have taken a complacent view of the future, in a manner bound to bring him to cross purposes with Hobart. Forgetting that in the affairs of man the authority of the individual has almost invariably been decisive Martel wrote after the war:

I do not think that it would have mattered very much who had been chosen for this Command as long as it had been one of our band of crusaders. I think that the result would have been much the same whoever had been selected. Having studied these matters for many years I was able to settle on the organisation that we required in a comparatively short time and establish a technique for armoured warfare which had the full support of all the formation commanders. Neither the organisation nor the technique can have been very far astray for they remained practically unaltered throughout the War and led us to our final victories.

This inflexible position was neither sound nor true in the act. It does not even benefit from hindsight, although many of the ideas were more those of the band of crusaders than himself— and the organisation of training had been outlined by Hobart and Pope before Martel was consulted. The technique of armoured warfare never ceased to evolve as the war progressed, as experience ripened into new practice and quantities of the new and much more powerful equipment that Martel had envisaged, appeared. Along with tanks that could carry bigger guns pro-

tected by thicker armour, there had to come changes in the composition of armoured formations so that they could work as
closer-knit, All Arms teams in the battle against the rising power
of better anti-tank guns in campaigns taking place in a wide
variety of terrain from the Western Desert and the steppes of
Russia, to the closer farmland of Western Europe.

The current organisation of the Armoured Division had
grown top-heavy in tanks as the three balanced groups evolved
by Hobart and integrated so successfully under his hand in 7th
Armoured Division became mis-shapen under the hammer of
battle. At first the Cavalry Group was supposed to act as the
reconnaissance and protective element to the Tank Group revolving around the Pivot Group; but since autumn 1940 the
light tanks of the Cavalry Group had been replaced by the same
kind of tank as those in the Tank Group (a change brought
about by the failure of light tanks when used as maids of all
work in the absence of sufficient battle tanks in France). Leaving
the Pivot Group much as it was, reconnaissance now fell only
to a single armoured car regiment, and protection to the two
motorised infantry battalions belonging to the Pivot Group.
Whereas Hobart's concept of an armoured formation was in the
proportion of three parts reconnaissance to three parts strike,
three parts protection and three parts pivot, this new formation,
the design of which owed nothing to him, was six parts strike,
one part reconnaissance, two parts protection with a pivot lacking infantry. Indeed the word 'pivot' was dropped and replaced
by 'support'. This came nearer to the All Tank Idea than ever.
It was for a reversion to Hobart's original concept, modified to
suit new equipments, that he called as he took up his new command, something Martel would not countenance because there
had been too much changing about already. Thus at the outset,
as Martel drew on the mantle of command, he was to find himself in conflict with the man who had designed his command.

Should Hobart have taken the post of commander with reduced power instead of Martel? Without Army Council status
we may doubt his chance of survival, although later Hobart
found, rather to his surprise, that he could serve the G.O.C.-in-
C. Home Forces, Brooke, without reservation. So with G.H.Q.

Home Forces, Hobart might have been in accord after a while. But at the beginning of 1941, within the War Office, Hobart's position could easily have been made untenable: there remained many who still abhorred him; indeed General Sir John Evetts (when Assistant Chief of the Imperial General Staff) remembers the buzz of ill-concealed pleasure that hummed round the corridors when, even as late as 1942, it seemed Hobart might have to be removed on the ground of ill-health.

Nevertheless, if Broad and Pile could not be made available, Hobart was the next most obvious choice for the post of C.R.A.C. and it is certainly arguable that misgivings should have been sunk and the chance taken. That it was not so is only further proof of the sincerely held belief of a man who, until then, had overcome every obstacle, had never refused an appointment and whose whole person was dedicated to armour, but honestly believed his enemies to be too strong. The sacrifice of lieutenant-general's rank in preference for the post of major-general in an armoured division, where age might soon make him obsolete, emphasises the depth of conviction and underlines that facet in Hobart's character which put strong personal ambition after the needs of the task.

However, by relegating himself to a junior position, under men of less experience and capacity than himself, he devised the ingredients of subsequent discord. By habit, Hobart was tuned to a pitch well above divisional level: in the realms of tactics he viewed the field from the standpoint of nothing less than a corps commander: as an organiser and administrator he commanded an understanding of problems at national level.

What he could not encompass at this moment was a technique whereby he could influence and create without coming into personal collision with the least compromising representatives of the opposition. Nor was his ego so strong that he felt enabled to turn to Mr. Churchill as protector whenever he ran into mortal trouble, despite the obvious display of patient patronage extended to him by the Prime Minister. Yet at this very moment in his career he was on the verge of utilising indirect contacts in such a way that, by the end of the war, they were to be the staple of his contribution.

10

THE BLACK BULL

General Wavell's victory in the desert at the beginning of December 1940, culminating in the *coup de grâce* at Beda Fomm in the first week of February 1941, did more than eliminate the Italian threat to Egypt and restore British spirits at the end of a year of defeat. It confirmed the British mode of desert warfare whereby it was thought right that infantry divisions accompanied by the heavy 'I' tanks should fight separately while the armoured divisions, in accordance with Hobart's ideas, operated as far out on the desert flank as they could against the enemy armour. But whereas Hobart had always envisaged the armoured brigades working concentrated in close co-operation with their pivot groups (as it had at war under his successor, Major-General Creagh), now they were being sent into battle farther apart from each other as well as from the Pivot Group. Paradoxically, despite the growls of General Wilson and others who decried All Tank methods, the drift to All Tank notions actually gathered momentum after Hobart had departed from the desert.

Pitted against the All Arms battle groups of the German Afrika Korps under General Erwin Rommel, after its arrival in Cyrenaica in March to restore the Italian position, the separated British groups failed to co-operate and were destroyed piecemeal. Moreover, the vehicles which had been superior to the Italians were now on the verge of being outclassed as German tanks armed with bigger guns began to make their appearance. But in early 1941 no British tank with a performance better than that of 1940 was in sight and the early American machines, although much more reliable than their British counterparts, offered no major improvements in battleworthiness.

The rush to accept whatever the factories could turn out during 1940 had not abated in 1941, generating a new imbalance. Because the emphasis in the late thirties had been in favour of the slow 'I' tanks these were being produced in greatest numbers, just when those most needed to fill the ranks of the new armoured divisions were faster, cruiser tanks. This manufacturing inequality was never corrected in Britain, and so it was that some of the new armoured divisions had to be equipped in 1941 and 1942 with 'I' tanks, and in subsequent years with American cruisers, since no cruisers of British origin could be obtained in sufficient number.

Meanwhile, the new British cruisers, Covenanters and Crusaders, coming off the factory lines, were the products of a crash programme and thoroughly unreliable in consequence. When tanks were in short supply, reliability became a crucial factor, so that when the day-by-day tank-battle strengths fluctuated wildly it was caused as often by wholesale breakdowns, rectified by frantic repairs, as by enemy action.

Unfortunately the situation seemed to be getting worse rather than better, both with regard to technique and tank technology. Martel as C.R.A.C. had to train the men, but could only advise on tactics and vehicle development—although his views naturally received considerable prominence and weight. But he could do nothing to co-ordinate the efforts of the War Office and the Ministry of Supply because they were not his concern, and so tanks increased dramatically in quantity but not in quality.

The foregoing is essential background to the development of Hobart's activities in the Second World War. Probably more clearly than anyone else he visualised the trends and the antidotes to be prescribed—and being Hobo, above all a Hobo without a future, he was fearless in saying and doing what he thought necessary to get things working along what he sensed were the right lines.

Fundamentally he believed the Armoured Division to be wrongly proportioned for its task. Its two armoured brigades, each of three armoured regiments and a battalion of motorised infantry, fielded three hundred and fifty tanks between them, but with an unarmoured support group of only a single lorry-borne battalion of infantry plus a towed regiment of field artillery and and an anti-tank regiment.

His concept of operations depended on the ability to move the armoured formations side by side at speed, with maximum surprise, to vital ground against which the enemy would be forced to counter-attack. Here he would establish his support groups in the midst of minefields, regroup his tanks behind an anti-tank-gun screen and deal with each enemy thrust as it developed, sallying forth from his defended locality once the enemy's cutting edge had been blunted. These were the tactics developed by the Germans after 1940 (and, not without significance, the tactics employed by Hobo's brother-in-law, General Montgomery, at Alamein). But they depended, in Hobart's view, upon possessing a support group sufficiently armoured and strong enough to reach and hold a viable defensive pivot : they would be enhanced if three, not two, armoured groups were provided to give the commander a mobile reserve; and they could best survive deep in the enemy rear if the supply 'tail' were cut to the minimum and given a comprehensive cross-country performance. These, after all, were the lessons taught by all the great commanders in the past.

Speed in action was related to size: not only would groups half the size of those planned be faster but twice as many could be formed, meeting his demand for three smaller armoured brigades in each division. Unfortunately, his was a division which could only be given 18 m.p.h. Valentine tanks instead of fast cruisers, so his discontent magnified. Then, having made his views known, he got on with starting 11th Armoured Division from nothing—a process at which he had no peer.

Let us now follow the first few months' training for war in time of war when time was already forfeit. Let us look over his shoulder and feel the division growing up.

His first day in the office, he wrote, was a strain, 'but the old brain seems to be getting back into gear again'; but the letter written to Dorrie on the 10th March, 'in pencil because there is no ink', sets the scene at his Div. H.Q. at Wormalds Green near Ripon:

We had a real Yorkshire welcome. Sleet driven by a NE wind for the last 100 miles of our journey. Seas of mud here. Everything is of course still in chaos—the 'state of becoming'. 30 or 40 odd men from various sources have arrived and the RSM of Div HQ (an old 2nd Battalion man—Pike) squelches round with them evolving order and decency. HQ is in a Red-brick Victorian 'manor' complete with tower, but with cold gaunt rooms—central heating obsolete and almost unworkable—and only two WCs. . . . Officers are billeted anything up to 7 miles away. An awful nuisance and handicap, especially when we all want to live together not only for work but to get to know one another . . . the various units of the Div have just, or are just on the point of arriving. Am starting to go round them to-day. Some are billeted 70 miles away. Transport very short. However—all will come right.

In next to no time everyone in the division knew it to be so, for not only was he seen by all within a few days (sometimes a few hours) of their arrival, but his drive to improve conditions imparted an unmistakable feeling that this general really cared. A week later, at his first conference of brigadiers and commanding officers, was repeated in terse detail his Training Instruction No. 1 issued in mid-March—a document which drew forth a mild rebuke from Martel.

GHQ Home Forces
22/3

Dear Hobo,
In your Training Instruction No. 1, which you rightly stress should be read by all officers, you say '11 Armd Div must be fully trained as soon as possible *enemy and higher formations* allowing'. I expect this just slipped in by mistake. We all agreed on the necessity for confidence in higher commanders, etc . . . so it is none too good spreading the opposite among junior officers. I know you only meant the War Office or something like that, but . . . etc etc.

A flood of instructions poured forth from Wormald Green,

followed in quick time by the general himself, making sure they were being obeyed. At his side Lieutenant-Colonel Harry Mackeson, his G.S.O. 1 (later to be M.P. for Hythe and a Conservative Whip), laboured with the desperate fury needed by all of Hobo's staff officers. By the end of March a Divisional School had been established at Leeds and Hobart's passion for training a formation centrally, guided by a display of coloured progress charts, first tried out on 8th Indian Brigade in Mesopotamia, took full rein in Yorkshire. To quote the Divisional History:

Those who were members of the division during . . . General Hobart's command will not readily agree that any formation ever trained more intensively. . . . Up hill and down dale, both literally and figuratively, he chased his men, from Brigadiers downwards; yet all respected his remarkable talents and the single-mindedness with which he used them.

They were terrified of him, at times shaken and depressed, but frequently inspired, while in the first week he expressed confidence to Dorrie:

I'm fairly pleased with my team. Some weak links in Div HQ, but on the whole what I expected. One (Cav) regt I saw to-day better, the other worse, than I expected. The Brig—may do. Met several old comrades in the ranks—now QMS etc etc, but all 'I was in 2nd Bn (or Tk Bde) with you, Sir, in . . .'. No Signals personnel—nor likely to be for 2–3 months.

Of some of the men he wrote: 'Disappointing lot. Mostly raw horsed cavalry straight from the horsed training regt.—and not even young, poor wretches', but of his first draft from a R.A.C. training regiment: 'High quality. Mostly 30–40 yrs of age. Poor devils, it's hard at that age after earning a decent income and being accustomed to home, wife and family, to be thrust into army life—blankets on bare boards, irritating routine, and complete lack of privacy.' He really understood them and cared, but as he said in his opening address: 'There are no short cuts to good tank maintenance. It depends on the knowledge and skill of every man in the crew.' As often as possible he talked to the soldiers, his eyes boring into theirs as, with short, clipped questions, he searched for the soul of each. Undoubtedly they were overawed at first, for Hobo's reputation flashed ahead of him like a warning beacon:

I asked one man if he were a family man. He replied nervously, 'Oh, no sir. I've only got one wife'. They are the most diverse assortment . . . the Butler to Lord X standing next to a Glasgow shop assistant on one side and to a Belfast butcher on the other . . . A few of the Cavalry regimental officers seem to have the experience or imagination to realise how different they are from their peace-time recruits. The cavalry are most charming fellows: and they really are working quite hard: but their standards are low, they are easily pleased: they always want to run before they can walk—or even stand. . . . It is very dangerous. I don't want to take the edge off their keenness: but presently it will be necessary to explode some of their complacency. The fact is that this is a professionals' fight and they are incurable amateurs.

It is part of the Hobo legend that he was anti-cavalry, but really it amounted to this: with standards so high and his determination that everybody should attain them, it didn't matter who they were, infantry, gunners, engineers, cavalry or tank regiment—they all had to be pushed well above normal—and if they failed had to go to make room for others.

The very moment of arrival in 11th Armoured Division was often a test in itself. When Major Rory O'Connor reported as G.S.O. 2, telling his predecessor he was a gunner, he received the earnest advice, 'Don't unpack.' A moment later, standing before the G.O.C. admitting he had never before served with armour, he was told, 'Well, you're of no use to me. You are a gunner, aren't you? I don't want a gunner as my G2.' At which O'Connor lost control and swung on his heel with, 'I'm extremely proud of being a gunner, sir.' By good fortune he had employed the formula best suited to deal with Hobo—meeting fire with fire, and in so doing founded a deep friendship. He remained!

Life on his staff was hazardous, casualties high, and in no department were they higher than that of A.D.C. These young men had to bear a heavy load, far greater than that normally imposed on officers of their tender years and experience: their place of torture more often than not was the front seat of the staff car (a vehicle called the Killing Bottle), from whence the A.D.C. was expected to read a map with accuracy, racing at high speed round the countryside engaging simultaneously in conversations of unexpected and limitless range. A.D.C.s, to Hobo, were expendable and only rarely could men be found to stand the pace. But one such as this was Lieutenant John Borthwick, a wartime commissioned officer of charm and marked ability who is now a director in a principal London firm of meat importers. Of his first meeting with Hobo he writes:

I was an amateur soldier straight from Eton and Oxford and with a healthy disrespect for authority. When I first heard Hobo speak it was in short staccato bursts but gloriously articulate. He was not an inspired orator but he did inspire curiosity and even admiration in the mind of a young subaltern, who hitherto had looked upon senior officers as a breed of middle-aged Scout Masters with bad manners.

Imagine my pride when I was invited to dinner during an attachment to Divisional Headquarters. The ordeal I expected turned to a heated argument about French Drama, in which he and I, the oldest and the youngest present, held the floor. It was thrilling. Here was a man bursting with power of leadership, and yet a scholar.

When I became his ADC—my predecessor said to me, 'this man is beyond me; we passed a train at speed with smoke pouring horizontally from the stack and the General asked, "Do you think that is beautiful?" '. But I knew at once that I, at any rate, could work for this man.

Borthwick recalls the enormous speed at which everything was done, almost as if Hobo was driving himself and everyone else beyond the bounds of reality. Partly this may have sprung from anxiety not to give anybody the slightest cause to suggest he was slowing down from advanced years: partly too it came from dedication and the determination not to emulate the failings of those senior officers he had served and criticised in the past: above all there was his patriotism and abiding understanding of the destiny of Britain, sharpened by a feeling for the brooding spirit of the man he took to be his ancestor—Oliver Cromwell. For the glories of England, her architecture, the grandeur of the countryside and her places of historical importance, Hobo always demanded time to pause and give thought. 'Just stop, John, take time, absorb it: understand what it means,' he would say. Writing to Dorrie on the 15th June 1941:

It was the 296th anniversary of the battle of Naseby—a critical event in the evolution of England—and as we passed within a few miles I turned aside to the field: and to think a little on that great honest man who stood there on that 14th June morning looking at the veteran host of the Royalist regulars, knowing full well the rawness and inefficiency of most of the Parliament levies, but still with high heart in his cause and confidence in the 'goodly company' of horse he had himself trained, so that in spite of his prayer for 'us poor ignorant men', he could face the battle with a quiet mind.

Amongst Hobo's first acts upon forming 11th Armoured Division was the submission to higher authority of a design for the divisional flash. Extracted from the family crest of the Blickling Hobarts, 'A bull sable, *passant, regardant*'—the Black Bull on a Yellow Field—and fully furnished, as the ladies of the Royal School of Needlework were requested to make it after their first design had been returned by Hobo with instructions that the outward signs of masculinity were not to be omitted. Consciously Hobart matched his own vigorous, uncompromising and impatient sense of urgency with the qualities of the great Ironside—drawing inspiration from an unproven claim to distinguished ancestry he saw his Black Bulls as a present-day company of Ironsides.

And just as Cromwell had need to struggle with his contemporaries, so did Hobart—and significantly it was in sympathy with Churchill that he did so. Defeat in Greece and, above all, defeat in the desert when, in April, Rommel erupted into Cyrenaica and practically destroyed all that remained of Wavell's victorious armoured force, drew forth a flood of criticism and discontent from Churchill aimed at Wavell in the Middle East and Dill in London.

A gulf of misunderstanding had been opening between the Prime Minister and the Army. Wavell, deeply conscious of his responsibilities as a commander and richly endowed with strategic insight, had failed to establish mutual confidence with the Prime Minister partly because of his own inarticulate inability to participate in debate and partly because of his distaste for the politicians' tricks of persuasion when they cut painfully across the cool, dignified manner of his own tutored reasoning. And Churchill, sensing Dill's support for Wavell's reticence, resenting a kind of pact designed to thwart his will, harried them with a barrage of questions designed to expose the facts he thought they were hiding. The failure of the British tank forces against Rommel in Cyrenaica drove the Prime Minister in search of answers to their technical failings and the causes of tactical failure. The generals were bombarded with questions, minutes and suggestions, some well informed and pertinent, others wide of the mark but tendentious—none of them bad so long as they could be channelled in the right direction (although Dill seems often to have failed in his efforts to do so), most of them multiplied if a reasoned solution were not quickly given. All of them were aimed at one goal—to shake out every last vestige of lethargy left over from the pre-war days.

On the 15th April the Prime Minister drew the attention of the C.I.G.S. to what appeared to be discrepancies in the issue of tanks to armoured divisions, pointing out:

By this return, which I study every week, you will see that you have 1,169 heavy tanks in this country in the hands of troops. The monthly production of over 200 is going to increase in the near future. If the training of the men has not kept pace with the already much retarded deliveries of the tanks, that is the responsibility of the War Office. I do not wonder that difficulties are encountered in Training when 238 cruiser tanks are given to one armoured division and only thirty-eight to another. Perhaps if the 11th Armoured Division had a few more 'I' tanks it would come along quicker.

Personally, I am not convinced that it is right to make each division entirely homogeneous. A judicious mixture of weapons, albeit of varied speeds, should be possible in the division. Moreover, some of these armoured vehicles ought to carry field artillery. . . .

At about this time Martel, in discussion with the Prime Minister, had been annoyed to have some of his arguments refuted by Churchill with, 'But General Hobart tells me differently', leading Martel to ask :

17th April

Dear Hobo,

It appears as though you have written to the PM. No doubt there was a good reason and he asked you to do so or something like that. Let me know because otherwise rumours get about. . . .

As ever,

Q

The reply, a frank denial, was of the sort that could only provoke further dissension.

Personal and strictly private

My dear Q.—you have asked me an extremely personal question about a private matter.

You are an old friend, and I trust you; I will therefore answer it for your personal information.

There has been correspondence between Winston Churchill and myself. But not since I accepted re-employment and returned to full pay.

As I have given you this information, I think you should now inform me what these rumours are of which you speak, and how they came to your ears.

I am well aware that I have few friends in high places in the Army. I know that some of these have not hesitated to do their utmost in order to damage me. I count on you not only as my immediate superior, but much more as an old and valued friend, to nail down such actions and to do your best to expose the perpetrations.

If you are not prepared to give me your full confidence it would be best for the public service for you to say so, and get rid of me. There would be no difficulty over this.

I will reply officially or D.O. to the other points of your letter.

Yours sincerely,

Hobo

It is more than likely that Mr. Churchill's original minute on the 15th stemmed, as he said, from reading the tank state. Moreover, his minute certainly did not represent Hobart's views on tank organisation (he would never wish to have 'I' tanks in his

A.C.—P

armoured division), and so it is much more likely that Churchill was thinking back to his talks with Hobart in 1940. Unfortunately Martel's reply was not reassuring to Hobart:

General Headquarters
Home Forces
21st April

Dear Hobo,

I was glad to get your note and assurance about private correspondence with Winston. You can rest assured that I will not allow any false accusations or rumours to spread, but I wanted to be sure that you had not corresponded recently. There was not the slightest reason why you should not correspond before you joined up again. I will tell you about this when next we meet.

Yours ever

Q

26th April

Personal & private

Dear Q—I have received yours of 21st. It does not answer the question I asked you.

I replied to your question, because you were an old friend, and for this reason only.

It rather appears now that you or your superiors, claim the right to forbid or control my private correspondence. I would be obliged if you could let me know if this is so.

Yours sincerely,

Hobo

The matter might have been settled had Martel told Hobart the cause of his original query, but this he did not do, thereby leaving Hobart under the impression that rumour and not a remark by the Prime Minister was at the root of the trouble.

Tuesday

Dear Hobo,

The position is just this. No one would dream of suggesting that your private correspondence should be controlled. If however we discuss some matter and come to a general agreement and then a senior officer writes to the PM and says he disagrees, that would obviously be disloyal. I never thought you had done anything like this but was naturally glad to get your statement so that I could correct any suggestion that might be made. Before you joined up you were naturally free to express any view you liked. Surely this is quite natural and clear. If we all collect for the tank parliament, everyone will be free to say what they like, because I will be there to refute any point I do not agree with; I am however having a preliminary meeting to exchange our views so as to get better value from the meeting.

Yours ever

Q

The whole incident was trivial and might have ended there and then had they not coincided with the subsequent meetings of Tank Parliaments and the manner in which they were arranged. On the 24th April the Prime Minister minuted the Secretary of State for War and the Minister of Supply:

I propose to hold periodical meetings to consider tank and anti-tank questions, the first of which will be at 10 Downing Street on Monday, May 5, at 11 a.m. These meetings would be attended by yourselves, accompanied by appropriate officers. From the War Office I would propose that the C.I.G.S., A.C.I.G.S., and General Pope should come, and General Martel and his Armoured Divisional Commanders should also be invited. On the Supply side I should like Mr. Bruton, Admiral Brown, and General Crawford to be present.

2. I am particularly anxious that all officers attending the meeting should be encouraged to send in their suggestions as to the points which should be discussed, and to express their individual views with complete freedom. I contemplate, in fact, a 'Tank Parliament'.

3. An agenda will be prepared for each meeting by my Defence Office, and it will include any points which you wish to place upon it, and any suggestions or questions which the Tank Commanders wish to put forward. I myself should like to discuss the organisation of armoured divisions, and the present state of their mechanical efficiency, as well as the larger questions which govern 1943.

These Parliaments were objectionable to Martel, as he says in his book:

During this time I held periodical conferences with the commanders of formations, so as to be sure that we were all thinking on the same lines. There was almost unanimous agreement on nearly every point, but General Hobart often held views which differed materially from all the others. He was still strongly imbued with the 'all armoured' idea and wanted the armoured division to be composed mainly of tank units. These views had reached the ear of the Prime Minister, Mr. Winston Churchill. In spite of all the great deeds performed by our war time Prime Minister, he was certainly very fond of listening to the views of critics. He had so often been repulsed himself when he had made proposals which had turned out later to be quite correct. He therefore initiated a series of meetings which he called by the name of 'tank parliaments'. . . . I did not feel very happy about these meetings. We were quite agreed in the Royal Armoured Corps as regards the right technique for armoured warfare, but I foresaw a danger that the Prime Minister might land us with a decision which some of his friends had suggested and which was not what we wanted. We were all for these meetings if he was going to give us more output or better men or something which could only be settled at that high level, but we did not want other people's views about organisation or technique. I therefore arranged for all the armoured divisional commanders to meet me just before the meeting at No. 10 and at that preliminary meeting we agreed as to what we would say if the Prime Minister descended to these detail matters. General Hobart did not usually join in our general agreement but all the other divisional commanders agreed to voice the same view if they were asked for their opinion. After all, the Prime Minister could not himself know anything about the technique of armoured warfare, and such matters were far best left to the Royal Armoured Corps to settle.

It is debatable that all the other commanders were as solid in agreement as Martel supposed. The variety of tactical handling in the desert and on exercises in England displayed no overwhelming uniformity—and rightly so, since evolution was continuous. Rightly or wrongly, Martel deliberately blocked the Prime Minister's desire for a free debate. In the strict sense, he was right to prevent his prerogative as commander from being converted into a forum for debate, but as one charged with the task of development he could be held wrong for not encouraging every possible avenue in the search for new ideas. In the eyes of the Prime Minister, who quickly perceived the nature of the

general's arrangements, Martel's position was indubitably damaged. Moreover, Alan Brooke, Martel's immediate superior, was
prepared to take part in free debate and was backed by the Prime
Minister.

To Hobart the whole business was repugnant. Tank Parliaments were a contribution to the drive to get ahead of the
Germans:

> We're a lap behind . . . we must find a short cut, new ideas, new
> methods, new applications. What we need more than anything else
> is a branch with scope and power to welcome, try out, experiment
> with new ideas (not only inventions, but tanks etc.).
> Yet when I write to urge this on Martel, he replies 'I think we
> have no time for research now'! ! !

In rejecting the request for research, Martel explained that,
of course, he was referring only to pure research—'seeking
knowledge without any particular aim', a strange statement from
a qualified engineer. Perhaps it was a coincidence that in September 1941 (three months later) the Ministry of Supply appointed
a Controller General of Research and Development to carry
out the very functions that Hobart knew were being omitted.
But at the end of June, when Hobart and Martel were arguing,
the breach between them yawned wide, when Tank Parliaments
were postponed because the generals did not voice their own
views.

Criticism of Churchill by the generals mounted in instinctive
reaction against his treatment of Wavell. The detailed tale of
the difficult relationship between Churchill and Dill and Wavell
(and later with Auchinleck), told with immense compassion and
scrupulous fairness by John Connell in his biographies of Wavell
and Auchinleck, evokes sympathy for the generals. But in
Auchinleck, p. 250, Churchill's treatment of his senior officers
is justly summarised:

> Had he been less impulsive he could have had his victories at far
> less terrible risk and cost. But had he been less ardent and less single
> minded, he might never have become Prime Minister, and Britain
> would have gone down in shame and surrender in 1940. In regard

to many episodes and many relationships in the Second World War, history, as it unfolds, may change the perspective; but the central fact that, but for Churchill's leadership in the first twelve months after he became Prime Minister, there would have been no survival and no victory is unshakable.

This Hobart saw at the time, and salted it with his own mistrust of the senior members of his profession and of Wavell in particular.

On the 25th June, a week after the failure of Operation 'Battleaxe' (Wavell's last attempt to destroy Rommel), and four days after Churchill had removed Wavell from command in the Middle East, Hobart wrote to Dorrie:

Every Exercise I go to fills me with more despair as to the training and handling of the Army. How can we hope to win the war on land? The carping and denigration of Churchill by the War Office and the senior generals on every possible occasion is growing louder and more venomous. I had to express myself very forcibly to Martel on this subject on Monday.

Hobart's vote was cast for Churchill and irrevocably against those in power at the War Office for personal and professional reasons. The belief that he was being intrigued against and the knowledge that poor use was being made of limited resources (illuminated by the flash-back of two disastrous failures in the desert) rankled and brought him again to the fringes of the political scene.

Lord Beaverbrook became Minister of State (with a seat in the War Cabinet) on 1st May 1941, relinquishing the post of Minister of Aircraft Production which he had filled so dynamically since May 1940. The post, one held only until 29th June, gave him freedom, under the Prime Minister, to investigate a variety of aspects of the nation's war effort, amongst them tank production. On the 17th May he rang up Hobart with an invitation to a talk. Hobart recorded:

I asked him to ask the War Office. I rang Alan Brooke and told him. He was not pleased. I said that if I went I could only say what I really thought: and if he didn't want me to do that, I'd rather be told not to go. He said he would consult the War Office. Later I got a wire 'no objection'.

He met the Beaver on the 19th, and in describing their talk to Dorrie, confined himself to essentials without mentioning his delight at the manner in which a coherent conversation was engineered in conjunction with the Beaver speaking explosively in turn into five different telephones:

He seemed a bit tired. . . . He was obviously not interested in the question of organisation of Armoured Forces which is disappointing as we can't make real progress till we get that right and a proper Vice-CIGS (Armoured Forces).[1] Beaver was entirely concerned with Tank Production and Design. However that is something. He realised his ignorance; asked sensible shrewd questions: and has his nose in the right direction. Anticipates 'having a row' but intends to get his way.

As a result of this talk he supplied Beaverbrook with a memorandum on tank supply.

Something certainly had to be done to rectify the parlous tank muddle if only to salve the nation's political conscience. So few British tanks were actually in action against the enemy in the Western Desert that the declining effect of the old and the nagging teething troubles of the new ones had not yet become so obvious as to be a scandal. But where waste took place in the public sector of the economy, the nose of the Parliamentary financial watch-dog was bound to get on the track. And when it became Government policy to send tanks to help the Russians resist the German invasion a pressing military need turned into the embryo of a first-class political issue. In conditions such as these nobody in the world of tank construction trusted anybody else: there were those in the War Ministry who felt the Ministry of Supply cared not one half-penny, and those in Supply who felt themselves greatly misunderstood as they laboured to make machines for soldiers who, they suspected, knew not how to use them.

1. However, shortly afterwards, Liddell Hart found Beaverbrook keenly aware of the subject, so Hobart had more impact than he realised.

The Select Committee on Expenditure under the chairmanship of Sir John Wardlaw-Milne formed sub-committees whose task it was to 'investigate' expenditure by different Ministries. As a member of the Supply Sub-Committee, and from a suggestion from one of Hobart's friends, Nesta Obermer, Miss Irene Ward, M.P., invited him to give evidence before this sub-committee. The letters between Miss Ward and Hobart make interesting reading in the light thrown on the Army political scene and the influence Mrs. Hobart had on her husband's actions in those difficult days. At the time he was recovering from pneumonia but still commanding 11th Armoured Division from a hospital bed.

Ladies' Carlton Club,
5, Grosvenor Place,
Hyde Park Corner S.W.1.
5th August 1941.

Dear General Hobart,

I've got to write you a very frank letter, which is somewhat disconcerting as I don't know you, but I'm sure you'll understand.

With regard to the Select Committee, the machinery about your visit was put in motion. As it was the Ministry of Supply Sub-Committee (which deals with Tank production etc.) who wanted you to come, the proper procedure as you are a serving soldier was, as a matter of courtesy, to ask the chairman of our Army Sub-Committee Sir Ralph Glyn, whether he had any objection. His Committee deals with the War Office in the same way as we deal with the Ministry of Supply. Sir Ralph, Sir John Wardlaw-Milne (our Chairman of the whole Committee) and our Clerk to the Committee were very anxious your future should not in any way be prejudiced. They said the War Office is very frightened of you and what you know and would hate to think your knowledge would be given to us.

As you probably know you are protected and your evidence is privileged and even the Prime Minister cannot ask to see it and the members of the Committee are bound by the provisions of the Official Secrets Act. There is no disclosure that you have been called to give evidence, but it was felt you would run a risk of it being somehow known that you had been sent for.

Of course officially you could not be victimised but, to be quite frank, we all know that however strong the protection, it is very difficult to afford protection against some methods which can so easily be applied, and victimisation is the most difficult thing in the world to prove. Anyhow I promised to write as I'd raised the matter with the Committee. Nesta Obermer seemed to think you would like to talk to a responsible Committee and of course suggested it to me and urged me to ask for you, but she is so nice I doubt whether she knows how foul the machine can be. Now I've put the whole position I must say I'd like to hear your evidence and so would my Colleagues, but we are all agreed the decision as to whether we send for you must be made by you. You *must* consider your *future* and how far the national interest will be served (though it undoubtedly might be) by your telling the unvarnished truth, as against your own interest.

I've put the case as best I can. I just don't know how anxious you are for your evidence to be given. If you *don't* want to give it we shall understand. It's frightful isn't it that one should have to write like this when we're fighting for our lives?

Yours sincerely,

Irene Ward

Headquarters
11th Armoured Division
Home Forces.
9.8.41.

Dear Miss Ward—First of all, may I apologise if I am addressing you incorrectly, and it should be Mrs. Soldiers are ignorant folk—as you know—and I have no book of reference here.

May I say that I much appreciate your letter and the thought which prompted it. But I am a man without a future : and the military authorities have already done all in their power to discredit and disgrace me. But, in any case, I do not think that personal considerations should be allowed to stand in the way of national interest. If it is considered that my evidence may be of value, it appears to me it should be demanded. But it should be demanded openly through my superiors viz The Army Council.

My views are well known to them. I have never concealed them. I do not wish to go behind their backs.

They threw me out. But as I have accepted re-employment at the personal request of the C.I.G.S. I am again 'set under authority', and I feel that it is for the Army authorities to give me permission to wait on your Select Committee; or to object.

Not for me to do so.

If I am permitted to appear before the Select Committee you need not fear that I shall hesitate to express my own opinions, whether on oath or not!

Yours sincerely,
P. C. Hobart.

Letter from Mrs. Hobart to General Hobart:

Leadenporch,
Deddington,
Oxfordshire.
August 13th.

My beloved. A golden morning of rain—that was because no less than 3 letters from you arrived. One (7th Aug) had missed me at Harlech—but I hadn't missed it—as you'd been a darling and sent one here too the same day. It was the one about Hull. It does touch the emotion to think of the heroism there is in such places—and how a word to or from the King and Queen is of such great price to the people living in circumstances so bad that they might almost resent the contrast of the King and Queen's prosperity.

Now—yours of the 9th and Irene Ward's (she *is* a spinster) letter. Very interesting from several points of view:

1. The purely female political—No man would or could write a letter like that. A man would leave out, hardly think of, all the threads of implication and would never give you so much space, time, or thought—Perhaps women will never be greatly in evidence politically because they are too sensitive and too thorough—No human mechanism can perhaps stand so great a strain—Anyhow no man would have used so many words!

2. Is this our British form of Gestapo. Big ideas etc.

3. If you REALLY are dissatisfied with the Tank under production, with the Policy and Training of the R.A.C.

If you consider them disastrous—and not likely to be able to fulfil their urgent conditions—

THEN
THIS IS YOUR CHANCE

at a cost to make your supreme effort to get this put right.

What I do not understand is the Power this Committee has to put things right—Is it merely a sub-semi-public-parliamentarian committee—to air dissatisfaction or has it the ultimate object of helping the P.M. or of putting him wrong?

It seems to me that your answer was the right one—RIGHT—that sort of right—perhaps more high-minded than theirs—the W.O. etc—deserve—or will ever give you credit for—I wonder if anything more will come of it. Is Irene Ward strong minded enough or determined enough to push on with the project of getting all the low down. I shall praise her highly if she is. . . .

He was never called to give evidence and perhaps it was as well, for the strain increased upon him that autumn as other outside pressures accrued. Pneumonia took its toll but was not crippling. At the hospital bedside his staff gathered to receive a steady flow of directives, for he believed that once he gave up the reins they would be given to another for ever and, in fact, a suggestion that he was too old to command a field formation was made and given momentum by those who resented volatile methods and those who feared for their jobs. It might have been more apt to echo General Martel's complaint concerning the succession of postings to replace the multitudes Hobo found unsatisfactory (on Hobo's own calculation a thousand officers and men had been weeded out, from brigadier to trooper), for this lack of security in office in 11th Armoured Division was something foreign to the conservative, military way of life.

Yet Martel had not thrown Hobo over and there is no reason to believe that he was at the root of a move to rid himself of the turbulent priest in August 1941. He asked Hobart's advice on his proposal whereby the armoured divisions should be formed into groups—a proposal dear to Martel, favoured by Hobart (who did not care what they were called so long as they were realistically balanced), but rejected by Dill and Brooke neither of whom believed that the Royal Armoured Corps should be allowed to develop into a private army. Indeed, Martel's self-avowed intent to make the R.A.C. omnipotent in the manner of Hobart's original proposals caused War Office opinion to swing decisively towards integrating armoured troops with conventional formations—thereby underlining the rising power of Brooke and the decline of whatever influence Martel possessed. In a letter to Dorrie on 2nd September Hobart analysed his relationship with Martel and the problem facing those wishing to make rapid advances:

He is a good chap, keen and conscientious: and able—but he lacks the ultimate strength of character. Curious in so brave a man, who is a good boxer and fundamentally upright. But he'll never fight for anything—I mean never fight his superiors.

He argues, 'it's no good, you see your objective and go straight for it, in a bee-line, through every obstacle, wire entanglement etc. And in the end those pull you down. You haven't reached your objective: and you've done yourself in the process. If my seniors are opposing my ideas, I drop it: and continue to work round to my objective by outflanking.' Well, that's a good soldier's analogy: it's specious anyway.

But if the need is great, if the urgency seems vital and there isn't the time for all the elaborate manœuvre and sublety?

Of course there's a lot in what he says. But, *au fond*, he shrinks from unpopularity, 'doesn't want to have a row'. Of course, I know well I'm too much the other way: too confident: too opinionated.

*   *   *   *   *

To test some of the new armoured divisions a number of large-scale exercises were run that autumn. The principal one, called 'Bumper' and run by Brooke, had as its chief umpire Lieutenant-General Bernard Montgomery. These were the tests Hobo hoped would demonstrate 11th Armoured Division's superiority over its contemporaries, and, as he told Dorrie:

The things I enjoy about soldiering are dealing with men direct—personally, and the tactical handling, by personal judgement and decision (in Armoured Formations actually by one's own voice over the wireless) in the field. I have in the last 6 months, with the help of a few good chaps like Mac and George, built up this Dvn from nothing into the beginnings of something that may prove formidable in due course if given equipment, instructed direction, and strict control. . . . I don't for a moment think I have their affections, but I do believe I have their confidence. And I know they are developing a spirit of their own: a good confidence in themselves (at present really not warranted!): and the sort of grouching grinning abuse of the Dvn which is how the English cover up their real pride in what they are proud to belong to. This is the third new Armoured Formation I have formed and built up. No one else in the world has done this. Ever. Three times lucky? It bears on its helm and sleeves the

crest of my family. It is my own creation in a way that neither the
1st Tank Bde nor the 7th Armoured Div were. These were built of
made bricks: mostly good bricks (Some required a good deal of
knocking into shape, it is true!). But this Division has been built literally from zero: from a bucketful of men pulled out of civilian life.

All this is sentiment? Yes. But sentiment backed by and founded
on reason. And isn't this just the very stuff of which all the best and
most worth-while things in life are made? My feelings for you, for
instance.

There is also the hard-headed 'practical' side. Here I deal almost
entirely with men under my own command: 99% of my time. Only
about 1% with those above me. Now I'm damned bad with my
superiors. Here I deal very largely with practical definite soldiering
problems. A large proportion of them even actually on the ground.
Where I can make definite immediate decisions—'Round that hill.
Behind that ridge. Over that stream. Right. Left. Fire. Stop.' That
sort of thing. Where a decision is demonstrably—optically!—right
or wrong.

Or at any rate the results of a move will be shown within a few
hours to have been false or true.

This is the sort of thing I believe myself to be some good at.
Though, God knows, I am fully conscious of the overwhelming im-
ponderables and uncertainties of war. And of how every decision is
really a guess, made on inadequate and largely inaccurate intelligence. One is dealing with men: morale. That fascinating imponderable, incalculable thing that cannot be described, that is not wholly
reasonable—that may achieve the impossible, triumph over overwhelming odds; or may crack and collapse for no lawyer's reason.

But 11th Armoured Division, the last to be formed and the
least well equipped, had to continue training and at the same
time provide umpires for 'Bumper' (its senior staff officer as
Montgomery's R.A.C. adviser, and its general as a senior observer): its own exercises would follow, meanwhile its leaders
would have the chance to assess the other armoured units in Britain, giving Hobart direct access to Montgomery.

As September and October went by, exercise after exercise and
conference after conference, Hobart's letters pick out two issues
dominating his thoughts—the startling demonstration by his
division that it had become a better tempered instrument than

even he had thought, and the depressing sensation that those in authority were closing in upon him again. An investigation by a Committee into Tank Organisation prompted Martel to organise, once again, a unified R.A.C. opinion which drove another wedge between Hobart and himself. Hobart made it clear that '. . . if I give evidence I must say what I really thought'—and he was not prepared 'to be a mere gramophone of his [Martel's] own complacent views'; and noting how furious Martel had been about the Committee being held at all because it was by direct order of the Prime Minister, quoting Martel saying, 'What does he want to butt in for. Everything is perfectly satisfactory etc. etc.'

Minor intrigues grew and festered in a body whose directing brain had become tired from overwork. For eighteen months Dill had led the British Army through one of the most testing periods in its history; a time overlain by defeat and disappointment and only mottled by success and encouragement; exhausting months spent in rebuilding as he thought right while striving to guide the throbbing inspiration of the Prime Minister into safe, practical channels. Now Dill was exhausted and in urgent need of a successor, just when the results of Brooke's 'Bumper' exercises had shown by natural selection who amongst the aspiring commanders were worthy of further advancement, and just as the Prime Minister, testing each candidate in turn by speech, deed and reaction, was making up his mind who should be the new C.I.G.S. There were many contenders but when Lieutenant-General Nye, asked by Churchill who he thought should be C.I.G.S., replied, 'There is only one conceivable choice—Brooke'; the Prime Minister commented : 'Yes, everyone thinks so.'

Amidst this jockeying there grew an ever closer understanding between Brooke, Montgomery and Hobart. Montgomery had always been a protégé of Brooke, sharing his views on the organisation of tank formations. Hobart, on the other hand, had fostered an aura of professional superiority over Brooke derived from his infinitely greater experience with tanks; and soured by his mistrust of Brooke's motives in arranging appointments in 1938 in particular and his opposition to an Armoured Army in general. Although not in agreement with Brooke's con-

tention that armoured divisions should take their place as part
of conventional formations, Hobart's criticisms of the performance by the armour during 'Bumper' are almost carbon copies
of Brooke's diary note for 2nd October :

I am delighted with the way Armoured Divisions have come on,
but very disappointed at the way Higher Commanders are handling
them : they have all got a great deal to learn, and the sooner they
learn the better.

Hobart's letters continue to refer to petty intrigues, emphasising an accusation that he had shown bias against the commander of his Support Group (rejected by the G.O.C.-in-C. of
Northern Command). In discussion Martel said reports had been
reaching Brooke that 11th Armoured Division was unhappy and
on edge : and that Hobart was never satisfied. As Hobart himself
wrote to Dorrie :

The latter statement is correct . . . as regards my Support Group—
the Commander of this I have never been satisfied with and I have
had to be constantly drawing his attention to shortcomings, not
only in discipline and administration, but also in gunnery.

Still there was no indication that a crisis had been reached, and
at the start of an R.A.C. conference at Sandhurst he told Dorrie
on the 4th November : 'Brooke has been friendly. Martel less
so, in fact I think he has not supported me, but it'll be O.K.'
And then, in the same letter :

All plans just changed. Special officer arrived with message from
P.M. that he'd like to visit 11th Arm Div on Thurs. Day after to-
morrow. All my Key Officers are down here. I've got NO Signals.
But—we'll tee something up somehow. And I'm darn pleased. Not
one of my Army superiors has given us one word of encouragement.
This will please the men. I fancy many of them would rather it was
Winston than the King.

Nigel Duncan who was there when the message came through
said it was fascinating to see the way Hobart and his staff reacted
to the need for speedy improvisation to overcome appalling obstacles. A concentration by units spread from Wales to Scotland

had to be made in less than two days on the Yorkshire moors in time for a three-hour inspection of the entire division, including a demonstration of tactics by Brigadier Charles Keightley's 30th Armoured Brigade. Walking alone with Keightley to watch the demonstration, Churchill asked about 'the enthusiasm interest and morale' of the division. Keightley wrote next day to Hobart. 'I gave them to him in no uncertain terms! But I certainly gathered someone must have given him the idea.' The men, wild with enthusiasm when Churchill spoke to them, confirmed Keightley's opinion. Then Hobart travelled for three hours in the special train talking about tanks to the Prime Minister. Describing their meeting to Dorrie, Hobart wrote:

PMs visit went well, in spite of weather. He isn't happy about Army matters, I gather . . . I can't tell you much now: but it unfortunately looks as if I had again become a bone of contention—or rather a symbol for a policy—between W.O. and Govt.
Rather as it was in 1937.
The men were delighted to see Winston. And I must say it was damn good of him to come. He said to me once, during the cheering 'It's very touching . . . the confidence of the people.'

As he left, the Prime Minister dictated a signal. 'To all ranks 11th Armoured Division I am very glad to have seen this grand division which General Hobart has trained so well. I hope a chance will come for it to play a glorious part in the destruction of a hateful enemy. Friday will be a whole holiday. Winston S. Churchill.'
As Hobart wrote to Dorrie on the 18th November:

We are fully assured that the W.O. and Martel and all have been doing their best to keep me out, and since 'forced by the politicians' to take me back are more determined than ever now to get rid of me at the first opportunity. All the more since I am now 'obviously' hanging on to Winston's coat tails: and him too they hate and plot against. But *at the moment* they can hardly 'laugh off' his visit and subsequent message to me.

A letter followed on the next day with cheerful comments

on the replacement of Dill by Brooke as C.I.G.S., and Brooke by Lieutenant-General Sir Bernard Paget.

This morning's news re Dill etc.

Brooke is the best soldier we have. He is a commander. I don't know anyone else who would command Exp Force as well. He will be a good C.I.G.S. too, I think : but others might have done that equally well.

I am not an admirer of Paget : but Home Forces is decreasing in importance, and *if* they form a new C-in-C Expy Force parallel to Home Forces, it may be O.K.

Monty deserves promotion to a Command.

It will be interesting to see what changes AB brings in.

Up to date he has gathered all power into Home Forces and opposed successfully any extension of W.O. control.

When he goes to W.O. things may well swing the other way. And this may lead to a proper organisation of Armoured Forces which Brooke has always opposed so far (partly, at any rate I think, because he wanted to keep Comds RAC in his own pocket).

The clouds were clearing away, so it seemed, with the arrival in power of men with fresh ideas. A last back lash from the November turbulence took place in the Cumberland Hotel, where Martel sought out Hobart and upbraided him for speaking freely to the Prime Minister : and the hot rejoinder did nothing to seal a gaping breach which was never repaired. The generals who were to lead the Army for the rest of the war were taking their predestined places. It was not a moment too soon.

In Russia the Germans were completing the conquest of the Ukraine, hammering at the gates of Leningrad and beginning a last abortive offensive to take Moscow. In the Far East the Japanese moved stealthily up the trail to war. In the Western Desert Auchinleck's offensive against Rommel's Afrika Korps started an armoured battle (the greatest yet fought by British tanks) which exposed, once again, faulty British generalship and the combat deficiencies of the tanks themselves.

Martel's influence was on the wane—to such an extent that by June 1942 he asked Brooke to let him control the procurement of new tanks since the raising and training of new armoured

A.C.—Q

formations was fully launched. The proposal was rejected—but that did not resolve the dilemma of British tank production.

The next cruiser tank, Cromwell, was nowhere near ready, although it should have entered service in 1942. Moreover, only three hundred of the six-pounder guns with which it was to be armed had been delivered by December 1941, despite the fact that the gun had been designed in 1938, passed its tests in July 1940 and the first production order given for five hundred in December 1940. In December 1941 a satisfactory mounting had still not been evolved, largely, to quote the report of the Select Parliamentary Committee under Sir John Wardlaw-Milne, because: 'The Army Authorities apparently were still not clear as to how many were required for tanks and field mounting respectively'—leaving the Ministry of Supply to make up its own mind as to the number that should be made of each. All too late, for the day of the six pounder (not in service until mid-1942) was passing: within a year a still larger gun—the seventeen-pounder—could alone outgun the Germans, but for technical reasons could not be fitted to the Cromwell because it was too small to mount such a big weapon. In this way the compass of disenchantment swung indecisively from side to side between the War Office and the Ministry of Supply with neither strong enough to bring it to rest pointing in the right direction.

In this uncertain state, with a new C.I.G.S. entering office on the eve of a crushing defeat in the Far East, fearful uncertainty in Russia and a fierce grapple in the Mediterranean, the British Army squared up to 1942, unconvinced as yet of its ultimate destiny.

II

THE BEST OF THE BLACK BULL

The privilege of spending week-ends away from Army routine has always been highly prized by soldiers, and those who served under Hobart approved the way he shared their delight at being home with the family. Here the cloak of responsibility would fall and those who saw only the austere, unbending side of the General might have wondered at the sight of him walking round the garden, revelling in the flowers, and playing with his boisterous young daughter, allowing her to take flying leaps on to his stomach. Never were the stresses and strains of work allowed to interfere with his home life: indeed it was not until many years later that his daughter became aware of her father's part in the war.

John Borthwick recalls spending a week-end at Deddington in the course of his duties as A.D.C. and (a most unusual thing) being asked to have his wife stay there at the same time. He recalls how happy was the atmosphere:

We fed the ducks. Hobo liked ducks because he thought they smiled, that they had a sense of humour and they waggled their tails. In the morning the General came in bearing early morning tea and removed my shoes and cleaned them. This was an act of humility and of kindness which impressed me pretty deeply. It was one of those little things that made the man : he was frightfully thoughtful and kind, and had enormous charm—and he was fun.

At home a great tranquillity engulfed him, for as he wrote to Dorrie in March 1942, at a highly critical moment in his career :

How darn lucky *we* are.

I've just been looking through the Compassionate file for Feb. Dozens of cases of pitiful trouble. Officers and men. Dependent invalid mothers : ruined small businesses : arrears of rent : bombed homes : sick wives and families with no home : hopeless loads of overdue instalments for rent or furniture on the instalment system : divorces : unfaithfulness : wife and children gone and not known where etc etc.

One knows these things : one realises with one's mind how exceptionally blessed one is and yet this contemptible creature sometimes (? often) allows himself to get depressed, disagreeable, cross and cantankerous.

Towards the end of February his appendix had to come out— leaving him strong enough to retain control of the division from the hospital bed, but not so strong that he could hope to deceive the Medical Board looking into his fitness for further service. Once again the spectre of redundancy arose : absence of more than three weeks could be legal reason to replace him in command. The peril was checked by his wife writing without his knowledge to Nesta Obermer (that gregarious lady who had already drawn Irene Ward's attention to Hobart), and she, in turn, wrote to a friend who passed the news to Mr. Churchill. Whether this had effect is unknown—as it turned out the Medical Board found Hobart unfit for active service for two months, but, notwithstanding, permitted him to resume command of 11th Armoured Division on 6th April.

The tide now ran strongly in his favour, though truculently against Britain. In the Western Desert Auchinleck's hard-bought success in Operation 'Crusader', in turning the Axis out of

Cyrenaica, had once again been reduced almost to nought by Rommel's spirited counter-stroke. The British were back licking their wounds in the Gazala Line. It had taken Auchinleck's personal intervention, coupled with the removal of the commander of the Eighth Army at the height of the battle, to save 'Crusader' from failure; there had been serious shortcomings in the handling of the British armour, mostly traceable to faulty organisation aggravated by the rising technical superiority of the German tanks.

Almost *ad nauseam*, because he believed it to be fundamental, Hobart bemoaned the quality of the key men at the War Office, their lack of 'stern determination', as he phrased it, and the general lack of confidence. Of Brooke's power to infuse he remained to be convinced, but towards his brother-in-law, Lieutenant-General Montgomery, the commander of the South Eastern Army, he directed new interest. John Borthwick remembers Hobart giving vent to a somewhat disparaging thumbnail sketch of Montgomery when they went to see him at Reigate, but driving back afterwards admitting that the meeting had been pleasant and not as acrimonious as expected. Monty appeared to him to be 'growing up and looking towards greater horizons'. 11th Armoured Division was now under Montgomery's command, so they met frequently. On the 19th February:

I saw Monty yesterday. Was bidden to accompany him in his car for ½ hour. I think that success has suited him and really improved him. He is less bumptious: and I suppose his inferiority complex is now assuaged. He looked well and fit: gave his orders out well and briefly.

And on the 17th June—by which time Hobart had taken part in Exercise 'Tiger' (one of Montgomery's major exercises in which a new organisation for armoured divisions had been tried out):

Monty spent day, so I was in car with him a good deal of the time. Quite affable. Shrewd and basically sound soldier, as I know. He does not understand armour or mobility as well as he thinks he does, but he is the only Lt Gen or above whom I know who understands it at all!

He seems inclined to give me a pretty free hand: but he may of course be merely lying low. . . . He is at any rate a good soldier; he knows his own mind: he is determined: and he will not let us into disaster through ignorance, stupidity, or vacillation. He is the only Army Comdr at present of whom I can say that.

The new organisation of the Armoured Division tried out during exercise 'Tiger' was not all to Hobart's liking. An armoured brigade had been taken from each division and replaced by a brigade of infantry mounted in unarmoured lorries: the artillery had been strengthened, but reconnaissance had still to be carried out by an armoured car regiment. In fact this was almost the copy of a German reorganisation of a year before designed to double the number of divisions available for the Russian campaign; moreover, the German infantry rode in vehicles with a better cross-country performance and more protection than the British, and so the tactical applications were found to be of a different nature across different country against a different class of enemy. Where Hobart wanted three armoured brigades there was now only one; instead of greater mobility many more vehicles were wheeled instead of tracked, and vulnerable because only the tanks and a proportion of the artillery were armoured. Yet he was not blind to the virtues of the new arrangement, admitting that the increase in the proportion of infantry had its advantages because it re-created the old Pivot Group. An extract from a letter after Exercise 'Tiger' gives us not only his opinion of the organisation and the outcome of this most ambitious exercise run by Montgomery but also the endurance of this man of fifty-six only two months after a major abdominal operation.

30th May 42

7.30 p.m. We've just ceased fire. 12 days. Have had 7 hours sleep in the last 64 hours—only one hour last night. We've really had good weather. A bit of rain. Sometimes high wind. But only once both together. And on the whole not too warm for marching (the infantry) by day or too cold for sleeping at night. And of course the country at its best. Even the beanfields in full scent.

The Div handles quite well, and the spirit and keenness are good. Of course I think the organisation half-boiled and in fact all wrong. But in the actual jobs we had (we never had to meet another armoured div and the country is the closest and most unsuitable for mobile tank work that you could find) it worked all right. I'm now writing to you as we creep slowly along to harbour, every road jammed tight with vehicles of every arm and division—the manœuvres ended in a proper tangle of the opposing sides. One's transport may with luck reach us in 2 or 3 hours and with luck we'll be asleep by midnight.

The Divisional Headquarters staff arrived home, dirty and exhausted, flinging themselves down in the mess for a drink and a meal, talking in monosyllables through the thick haze of fatigue, all satisfied with their efforts but longing for sleep, with one exception—Hobo. No sooner fed and relaxed, he was up and saying to his G.S.O. 1: 'All right now let's go through all the points we've learnt.' The man was indefatigable.

Nor was he any less fearless than the same man who had been twice decorated for bravery in the First World War. Brigadier Keightley, standing beside him in the spectator stand amongst a galaxy of senior officers watching a demonstration by a pair of artillery regiments, was dismayed when an unchecked switch of target brought the full force of the guns to bear on their hillside. Shells whizzed all over the place, killing six people, but, throughout, Hobo remained upright while others flung themselves to the ground, so Keightley, much against his inclinations, followed the example of his G.O.C., and was rewarded for this staunch discipline by a typical Hobart aside as the last shells fell: 'More of that, Charles, and there'll be a better liquidation of generals than Hitler ever thought of.'

*   *   *   *   *

June 1942 was the nadir of Allied fortunes. The overrunning by the Japanese of the Far Eastern theatre, coupled with the initial success of the German drive to the Caucasus and the headlong retreat of the Eighth Army from Gazala to El Alamein, drew a net around the Middle East. Almost everywhere the Axis

Powers had the initiative; nearly three years on the defensive was beginning to bear down on the morale of the British people. Yet by the end of July, amidst disquieting news from Russia as the Germans drove east to the Volga and south-east towards the Caucasian oilfields, the moves designed to reverse the tide of defeat were being prepared. Auchinleck stopped Rommel at El Alamein and by the middle of July felt strong enough to take the offensive himself—a bold stroke coming so near to throwing Rommel back whence he came.

On the Home Front grew a nagging movement to persuade the Government into launching an invasion of France that year, a shallow, public cry for a Second Front in 1942, with the well-meant purpose of relieving the Russians, which ignored reality: there just were not the resources available to carry out so vast a project as that. All that could be done was intensify the raids which had started in 1940 and were to reach a crescendo when, on 19th August, Canadian troops, with Commandos, landed at Dieppe and fought a bloody battle against a strong section of Hitler's so-called Atlantic Wall. Because only a few objectives were reached the raid was classified as a failure: in the event, however, there now stood revealed most of the problems inherent in this sort of operation; talking points for the armchair critics, but essential data for those whose job it was to plan for the day when the real Second Front could be launched. Dieppe was expensive capital investment in the development of amphibious warfare, immediately prior to the first large-scale project when failure could not be admitted at any price.

On the 24th July an Anglo-American decision was taken to land on the North African coast from Casablanca to Bone in November: this was Operation 'Torch'. Automatically this postponed 'Sledgehammer', an American proposal to land in Europe in strength in 1942, and allowed more time for dissemination of the lessons learnt on the beaches at Dieppe. Brooke had worked with consummate patience to win acceptance of 'Torch' in place of 'Sledgehammer', channelling limited resources into fields where success seemed likely and avoiding the sort of setback inherent in an inadequately prepared Second Front. Now, in person, he could interweave the threads of 'Torch' with those of the next desert offensive from El Alamein: in so doing he could investigate the affairs of the British Army in Egypt. For at that moment neither he nor Churchill had confidence in Auchinleck or some who served under him. However, Brooke desired most to go to Egypt and make decisions—above all on his own— at the end of July, so it was not to his liking when, at the last moment, Churchill decided to come as well.

Shortly before they set out the instructions for 'Torch' appointed Lieutenant-General Alexander to command the British component—First Army—the chance of glory for the man who had weathered disaster in France in 1940 and Burma in 1942. But Auchinleck, who had weathered disaster as well and just before Churchill arrived in Cairo had fought Rommel to a standstill, was to be denied his laurels. Churchill was determined on a change in the Middle East and on a new commander for the Eighth Army, which since late June had been led by Auchinleck in addition to his other tasks in the Middle East. The first choice for the Middle East Command fell on Brooke, with Montgomery at the head of Eighth Army, but Brooke, much as he prized an opportunity to command in the field, declined. After nine months' intensive practice he had learnt how to co-operate with the Prime Minister and control his impetuosity: this was not the moment to make a change. Proposals and counter-proposals abounded, resolving at last in the decision to cut Middle East Command in two, one half consisting of Persia and Iraq only, to be placed under Auchinleck, and the other, a new Near East Command responsible for Egypt, Palestine and Syria, becoming Alexander's (his place in command of 'Torch' to be given to Montgomery). To Hobart's one-time G.S.O. 1 in the Armoured Division, Strafer Gott, they gave command of Eighth Army, until fate imposed the final decision, killing Gott when his aircraft was shot down, with the result that at Brooke's instigation the Prime Minister called for Montgomery to command the Eighth instead of First Army.

Thus Montgomery and Hobart were parted just as their collaboration reached an unprecedented cordiality, and concurrent with the mobilisation of the formations selected to comprise First Army. Hobart's first intimation that his division was amongst them is reflected in his letter to Dorrie on 16th August:

> Certain orders have reached this Div. which completely change future prospects. We are v. busy. I shall get some leave during the next fortnight, but cannot now say when, or how many days. When I do come I shall want to get everything settled that I can; so if there's any business about insurance, G., Springfield etc. that you want my help over, let's be ready to talk it over.
> I'll be bringing back all redundant belongings.

Feel the note of vibrant excitement, like that of a schoolboy who, having been picked as a reserve for the School 1st XI, has been told that he is to take the place of an opening batsman. That the Commander of 9th Corps, under whom he was to work, was Lieutenant-General John Crocker—one who had once been his own staff officer—was a reason for joy, not bitterness, and Hobart seems to have written a letter of great charm and dignity to which Crocker, a sensitive but undemonstrative person, replied.

> HQ 9 Corps
> 18.9.42
>
> My dear Patrick,
>   . . . Thank you for the note I found waiting for me when I returned here last night. I have always hoped that we might renew our partnership again. It is a queer twist of fate that this hope should be allowed to come true with our proper roles reversed. You know that this is none of my seeking. I wish we could change places. I am deeply appreciative and am moved to intense admiration at the graceful way you have accepted the situation. As you know I am not very good at saying things, but I'd like you to know how I feel about this.
> Yours ever,
> John Crocker

At last he was to lead his Black Bulls in battle to prove his theories and the thoroughness of his methods; better still, under a man he had trained himself and trusted. Alas! The very order for mobilisation was the warrant for a change of command for 11th Armoured Division. To go on active service a man must be fit and this no Medical Board would pronounce for Hobo. So it was that Major-General Jack Evetts, who had just arrived at the War Office, to become A.C.I.G.S., heard the smug jubilation rustle round the corridors when those who least liked Hobart sensed that this time the rules would be too strong.

Again Mr. Churchill got to hear and intervened.

4 Sept 42

Prime Minister to Secretary of State for War

I see nothing in these reports [of the Medical Board report on General Hobart] which would justify removing this officer from the command of his division on its proceeding on active service.

General Hobart bears a very high reputation, not only in the Service, but in wide circles outside. He is a man of quite exceptional mental attainments, with great strength of character, and although he does not work easily with others it is a great pity we have not more of his like in the Service. I have been shocked at the persecution to which he has been subjected.

I am quite sure that if, when I had him transferred from a corporal in the Home Guard to the command of one of the new armoured divisions, I had instead insisted upon his controlling the whole of the tank developments, with a seat on the Army Council, many of the grievous errors from which we have suffered would not have been committed. The High Commands of the Army are not a club. It is my duty and that of His Majesty's Government to make sure that exceptionally able men, even though not popular with their military contemporaries, should not be prevented from giving their services to the Crown.

This time not even an eloquent Churchillian minute sufficed, although it is possible that knowledge of the Prime Minister's personal interest deterred those who considered retiring Hobart for good. Instead there was a plan to form two new armoured divisions, although it seemed unlikely that sufficient resources to do so could be found. In the event only one, the 79th, was made and given to Hobart—the fourth formation of its kind that he was to raise. Saying farewell to a military organisation you have built yourself with loving care is never easy: Hobo always found it hard and probably never more so than with 11th Armoured Division. It was entirely his own creation and he loved it dearly.

It would have been easy to be bitter in sorrow—but instead only the sadness is there. To Dorrie on 15th October 1942,

> HQ 11th Armoured Division,
> Home Forces.

Just a line—for the last time with this heading.

I spent Tues. aft. and all yesterday going round my units. Visited them all, shook hands with every officer, and walked round the ranks and then spoke to every man in the Div. except those on duty.

Reception varied. From awkward silence—to a spontaneous '3 cheers for the Hobo!' in one unit. Mostly they listened intently, and gave three regulation cheers.

(I was struck with the large proportion of eyes that are grey, blue or hazel: and the comparative rareness of brown. Yet this colour is said to be dominant.)

I couldn't help feeling keenly 'Morituri te salutant' (Those about to die salute you). These are my chaps: in six months a lot of them will be dead. . . .

> Love Patrick

They 'dined me out' last night. All COs and Brigs were here as well as the seniors of Div HQ Staff who of course had arranged it. V good dinner (oysters) and Liebfraumilch. Can't think how they raised it.

This morning is really the worst part, in some way. Waiting to hand over to Brocas.

Fortunately the next command was ready at once so he could switch his mind to it when its principal administrative staff officer (A.A. & Q.M.G.) Lieutenant-Colonel Charles Humphreys arrived to drive him away. That night he sketched the divisional flash—a bull's head staring at its beholder in angry defiance with a note alongside: 'Advise me about Divl Sign. I thought about having the Bull's head alone—Is this too too symbolical!!!' It was to be the 'best of the Black Bull.'

He never forgot the Black Bull and his Black Bulls never forgot him. Extracts from the many letters received as he left 11th Armoured Division aptly describe Hobo's impact. From the C.O. of 27th Lancers, Lieutenant-Colonel Andrew Horsbrugh Porter:

Dear General,

Savill told me today that you were changing your command.

It is most distressing news for everyone and although my first thought is for your feelings, my second is for my own regiment. . . .

All my officers and NCO's looked forward to fighting under you and their loyalty and confidence will not be easily transferred. . . .

We shall miss you in every way. Personally, I have learnt my job from you—as far as I have learnt it!—and I shall be always grateful to have had nearly 2 years under your command. I sincerely hope the occasion will arise again.

One thing is dead certain—that the Bull sign is peculiarly yours—and wherever the Black Bull goes it will carry your name with it.

Again Sir, I should like to say how deeply I sympathise with what must be a grievous disappointment to you, but I have learnt from you that personal feelings don't count so long as there are live Germans in the Field. . . .

And from Lieutenant-Colonel Rory O'Connor, his late G.S.O.1—the gunner who had once been so roughly welcomed.

My dear General,

I am naturally bad at verbal expression and I was quite unable to express to you, before you left, the very deep feelings in my mind.

Having had the honour of serving you as G2 and then G1 for just over a year, I felt that I had really reached the goal of complete mutual confidence.

I felt that I was able to say exactly what was in my mind and at the same time to know and understand your views and methods.

I liked to feel that I enjoyed your confidence too and I am sure that feeling was justified from the way you always discussed both personal and training matters with me.

This mutual confidence, together with the very sincerest respect and affection which I always felt towards you, engendered a friendship which meant a very great deal to me and of which I shall always be proud.

Your leaving then was first and foremost, the loss of a great personal friend; that in itself was sufficient of a blow but taken in conjunction with the irreparable loss to the Division of the Commander who had raised it from birth, it was a blow which I found exceedingly hard to bear.

Knowing you as well as I did, I appreciated so deeply the feelings which you must have suffered. No words of mine can soften that wound, but you have the satisfaction of a job well done and a knowledge that every officer and man in this Division appreciates full well the debt we all owe you.

I shall try to carry on the traditions you gave us and I will serve your successor as loyally and whole-heartedly as I served you.

I shall always be grateful for the immense amount I learnt while on your staff and I shall try to acquire that tremendous sense of duty and that moral courage which you portrayed in a measure that I have never met before. . . .

A few weeks later was published a little book entitled *Tanks and Tank Folk* containing Eric Kennington pastels showing the G.O.C. and some of the officers and men of 11th Armoured Division. It is a dramatic memorial depicting the inner confidence of men who knew their job with certainty. The two portraits of Hobart, entitled 'ACV-1' and 'GOC', are not the best of Kennington ('ACV-1' is almost a caricature), but both illustrate the intense concentration of the man and his unmistakable sympathy with machines.

And from their General leaps forth the vibrant enthusiasm of 11th Armoured, so aptly caught by a poet in the division when, at about this time, he wrote:

> And now the time, the longed for moment nears,
> The dreaded moment, too, our hopes and fears
> Have centred on, the chance to prove our worth,
> The chance to earn our right to this dear earth,
> Which now may see us die, which gave us birth.
> At last the moment's here, at last the chance :
> 'Start up!' 'Stand by' 'Be ready to advance'.

*   *   *   *   *

The new 79th Armoured Division, unlike the 11th, came into being from an amalgamation of pieces taken from older formations, but, as of old, their G.O.C. flung himself with irresistible zest into the process of meeting them, explaining his aims and welding them into a solid unity. A soldier of the division, given a lift in Liddell Hart's car ten days after Hobo had arrived, already knew not just the name but also the impact of his General —if for no other reason than he 'made the officers hop'. But although the fires burnt bright, some of their heat had been drawn by familiarity with the task and the incontrovertible feeling that he was not to be allowed to command in battle. His letters lack the rapturous descriptions of each visit or of people: with more time to think, because so much of the work is routine, he ponders profounder matters with Dorrie as he once did with Betty in 1917 and 1918 after he had mastered the art of brigade major.

He who could be so charming or so outrageously rude by choice or by omission, now found time to debate 'charm':

You pose an intriguing speculation. Is charm a dangerous virtue—or vice?

I should say unhesitatingly a virtue. What tremendous pleasure it gives: and how widespread—aye, there's the rub. It is so—public: so much common property, so to speak. Like a public woman. Think of the most frequent exponents—actresses.

And why not? Why exclusiveness, what virtue is there in selfish possessiveness? The sun shines, the birds sing, the lilac throws its scent for all.

Yes—but in fact when it comes to people there is a value in discrimination, in some sense of fastidiousness.

A woman may be a prostitute, and be a darn fine woman all the same.

But broadly speaking, it isn't the case. The very fact of being able (assume that she is not driven by desperate economic or financial necessity) to give herself to all and sundry, to simulate the last delights of intimacy, to be able not only to tolerate but to seem to enjoy with anyone what is fundamentally, essentially a communion of two.—This is surely the real stigma of wantonness, the real corruption: NOT the mere sexual union of bodies.

But to come back to charm. It *is* a great virtue because it soothes, flatters of course, and in fact exhilarates us. It makes us feel better: have life more abundantly. But it is terribly dangerous—to its possessor. It slips so easily into insincerity, habitual insincerity to others and then—to oneself.

I can speak as an unbiased observer, as no one has ever accused me of charm! But I do believe that unless it is based on very great and unusual virtues and strength of character, it often becomes pretty fatal. To the possessor. . . .

You've got it: but quite in different quality, because in you it's an outward shining of real inward grace. . . . Nesta has something: but it isn't really charm—charm is magic—it's virtue with her. . . .

Men—Andrew Porter, Brocas Burrows, Horrocks, Mac., [his late GSO 1]. . . Anthony Eden, Justice Tilly, Strafer Gott, . . . Gort. All had some degree. In about half these cases it was the shining forth of real inward quality: in the others, to my judgement, a purely superficial quality—as is indeed most visual beauty (flowers, landscape, skin, sky etc.). Guess which of them I mean.

His new G.S.O. 1 would have been astonished had he known of that letter. Lieutenant-Colonel A. W. Brown, R.T.R., had spent the war in rather out-of-the-way places—in Poland, Norway, and Canada—interspersed with periods as a staff officer or instructor with armoured forces. He has said:

This was my first actual meeting with Hobo face to face, and . . . it was with mixed feelings. . . . The HQ was in a very old fashioned, stone Yorkshire type house at Rawdon near Leeds: rather dark, very cold and not particularly comfortable. I was taken in to see Hobo, we had a short discussion and he then said, 'Well, I will now show you your room'. He went out into a long dark passage. At the far end of this passage, against a lighted doorway, a rather elderly shuffling figure could be seen. It looked as though he was about a mile away. Hobo took one look up the passage, seized me by the arm in an enormous grip and said with a hoarse chuckle in my ear, 'Do you see that? Who do you think it is?'. I said, 'Well, I really don't know, sir.' He said, 'That's the doctor—poor old man.'

There were, of course, the characteristic alterations to staff (it was rumoured that the small wicket-type turnstile gate leading out of Rawdon Railway Station never stopped clicking while 79th Armoured Division was being formed), yet the principal staff officers suffered very few casualties. Charles Humphreys, the A.A. & Q.M.G., and Alan Brown, the G.S.O. 1, stayed as long as they wished and only departed when Hobart thought they were forfeiting promotion by remaining too long away from troops. The junior staff changed more frequently, but even with them stability began to be achieved as, gradually, men of higher intellectuality and robust spirit entered. The post of A.D.C. was as difficult to fill as ever. John Borthwick had been sent to attend the Staff College course in the summer of 1942 and on its conclusion came back as G.S.O.3(Ops). His progress was in strict accordance with Hobart's views on A.D.C.s, as he told Dorrie:

The fact is that anyone with personality and brains enough to hold down job of A.D.C. in an Armoured Div (as I run it) is good enough to be a Staff Officer, if not a Squadron-leader.

The standard of officers continues to drop, although we are very short in numbers also. The fact is, I suppose—probably more apparent to you than to me—that however much one may consciously guard against it, subconsciously one wants the type of chap who's pleasant socially, speaks the same language, has conventional table manners, and doesn't want to spend his spare time in a pub or a cinema. And I fancy that's where we go wrong.

I understand that in the German Army all that has been revolutionised, and that there is complete fraternisation between junior officers anyway and other ranks. With us Regular Officers set the tone. We have the conception of the Army as a Social institution, a class business, a buttress of the existing financial (i.e. social) order. And that is not only uneradicable in our class, but must have strong national roots as it is so easily and quickly inoculated into newcomers, temporary officers, *and* the normal N.C.O. type also—probably they are its staunchest upholders.

Because they were aware of their General's reputation the division weathered the storms of enthusiasm and practised energy, no matter if in early 1943 they felt hard pressed. In any case, elsewhere on the battlefronts and at the conference table events were turning to bring forth pressures of undreamt magnitude.

* * * * *

Montgomery's victory at El Alamein added to the success of 'Torch' and began the purge of German influence along the length of the North African shore. By the end of January 1943

A.C.—R

only the stretch from Tunisia to Tripoli remained unconquered: by then, too, the Germans had almost been ejected from the Caucasus and their besieged army in Stalingrad was at its last gasp. With the dawn of 1943 came a clearer vision of an end to the war: lit by success, the men who had wrought the change outshone those who had struggled before in adversity. The outlay of three years' indomitable struggle by Churchill was being repaid, the scheming of Brooke bearing fruit and new commanders Eisenhower, Alexander and Montgomery making reputations that were to dominate beyond the day of final victory.

With the tang of success in their nostrils the Allied leaders met at Casablanca at the end of January 1943 to lay plans for the next year's operations. In confirming a resolve to knock Germany out of the war prior to Japan, the bulk of the land forces were committed to Europe. But when the Americans finally agreed to Churchill's and Brooke's contention that the major effort in 1943 should concentrate on clearing the North African coast as a prelude to striking into Europe through Sicily and Italy, they delayed most unwillingly an earnest conviction that the final decisive blow could only be achieved against Germany through France and Belgium: to them the limited, peripheral, indirect strategy of Britain missed the enemy heart. Getting their own way was a major diplomatic triumph for the British leaders, but it was bought in the knowledge that, come 1944, American determination to stage a major invasion of Western Europe could no longer be resisted. By then the American share of the Allied effort would be preponderant, their desire to fight a full-scale continental campaign irresistible.

Churchill, deriving from the failure of his foray at Gallipoli a fear and distaste of assaulting heavily defended shores, dreaded the invasion of France. Brooke, a witness of the slaughter of infantry in the First World War, with first-hand knowledge of the abundant difficulties in operating across open shores at Dunkirk, had imbibed a healthy respect for the power of German coastal defences revealed during the raid on Dieppe in August 1942. But whereas Churchill's mind seems never to have been quiet concerning the decision to invade France, perhaps because he still did not fully evaluate armoured fire power, Brooke told the Americans that the Allies could definitely count on invading France in 1944—and said so in the belief that it was a feasible operation of war.

Once the basic decisions for action in 1943, the appointments of commanders and the allocation of resources had been made, Brooke turned to design and prepare a spearhead to pierce the German Atlantic Wall in 1944. There was still a shortage of almost every commodity. Nothing was shorter in supply than manpower—a compulsive factor in Brooke's desire to channel Allied efforts against the more remote and weaker parts of southern Europe in 1943, instead of the stronger and easily reinforced territories of France and the Low Countries. The Anglo-American planners under General Morgan had concluded that five divisions would be needed in the first assault on France in order to establish a beach-head of sufficient width and depth to withstand the preliminary counter-stroke mounted against it. Morgan planned on the assumption that enough landing craft for five divisions would be available, but in 1943 it actually looked as if there might be only enough in the spring of 1944 for three, let alone five—a state of affairs provoking Brooke's comment to Morgan, 'Well, there it is. It won't work, but you must bloody well make it!'

Even if enough landing craft could be made available, it was still highly improbable that a stretch of beach uncluttered by mines and obstacles and undefended by direct enemy fire could be found. Arrangements to clear the obstacles and minefields (which every day were being laid in greater profusion) and then move rapidly inland, over the sea-walls and anti-tank ditches, to assail the enemy fortresses guarding the approaches to each port and route centre were in their infancy. There was a dire need for the modern equivalent of the old-time siege-train to breach the ramparts of the Atlantic Wall. In the distant past siege operations had been protracted and formal, and only rarely launched from the sea; something slow and similar to siege warfare had taken place in the First World War at enormous cost in lives; now the utmost speed was needed to drive several lanes through the defences of each beach with minimum loss as a prelude to the commitment of the orthodox mobile arms,

intact, to the decisive battle of manœuvre. The essential requirements were control, speed and economy of lives—conflicting
demands all too rarely accommodated at once in the past, but
now essential in order to match the rate of German retaliation.

It was obvious that the greatest economy in lives and the
highest speed in operation could be attained by using armoured,
mechanical devices in the forefront of the assault—even ahead
of the leading men on their feet. This understanding became
less comforting in face of the fact that neither the equipment, the
men to work it nor the techniques to do so were available in
quantity. Truly there was a nightmare selection of experimental
devices under various stages of development by a number of
different specialist organisations, in different theatres of war. But
central direction was remote and there was nothing in existence
to select and train a special large-scale force capable of getting
men from the water's edge through a defended belt to the open
ground beyond at high speed and low cost.

Then Brooke had what he later called 'a happy brain-wave'—
to charge 79th Armoured Division with the task of developing
and training the armoured formations that would lead the assault
on D-Day. In fact, the choice was inevitable since the resources
to maintain every existing armoured division were already failing: one had to go, so 79th, the last to arrive, was first to go.
Nevertheless Brooke had need of a ruthless man of immense
experience with the development of armour and the ability to
push unconventional ideas into practice. Martel's engineering
experience made him a candidate, but six months before Brooke
had sent him to India on a tour of inspection and abolished the
post of C.R.A.C. in his absence.

On the 10th March Hobart was acting as Chief Umpire on
'Spartan', a large-scale exercise in the South of England in which
the Canadian Army played a considerable part, commenting with
typical freedom on the failings he discovered:

Summing up my impressions, I would say that the performance of
the actual units engaged, and the standard attained in what one
may call the 'mechanism' of tactics, had markedly improved since
the 'Bumper' exercise in September 1941. But on the higher levels

there was little sign of improvement—and the performance there was not merely disappointing but ominous.

Apart from these failures in direction, there was also evidence of defects in our tactical organisation. A particularly depressing feature was the time consumed in getting orders down to the troops which had to carry them out. In a number of cases, something like 36 hours passed between the time that the commander-in-chief decided on a move, and the time when the troops were actually on the move.

In this connection, I was interested to find that three senior officers to whom I had shown my December memorandum on 'The Problem of Quickening Manœuvre'[1] remarked to me that the exercise had convinced them of the necessity of eliminating links in the chain of command, particularly the Corps, if the tempo of operations was to be accelerated.

That day Brooke called him to London to break the news about 79th Armoured Division and then outline the new task— the development of amphibious, minesweeping, obstacle-clearing and night-fighting tanks for the invasion in 1944. Hobart asked if the job would be operational or merely training and experiment—would he go overseas 'which you seem so anxious to prevent me doing'. Brooke took it well and smiled and said that when the new devices came to be used in the field it would be natural for Hobart to supervise their handling. It is a sad but inevitable commentary on Hobart's lack of confidence in those above him that he interpreted the request as another attempt to 'side-track' by removing him from the mainstream of armoured thought, relegating him to training and debarring his chance of going to war. But he asked for time to consider and used it to consult Pile and Liddell Hart, neither of whom hesitated in agreeing with Brooke. It was a superb opportunity and there was not another general in the British Army capable then of its fulfilment. Liddell Hart remembers Hobo arriving at Stoke Hammond on a wet, miserable day, and urging him to accept

1. There is no trace of this document, although its purport, the need to reduce the number of Formation H.Q.s in the Chain of Command to enable the least number of minds to affect Command, is clearly visible in a letter written in amplification to Liddell Hart in January 1943. It seems likely that Hobart sent out an original paper by Liddell Hart under his, Hobart's, name in order to disguise its origins and deflect a certain type of personal criticism.

because 'it would mean that he would have the direction of tactical experiments that might count for most in the coming phase of the war'. There ensued a protracted and exhaustive argument while they paced up and down on the terrace outside, watched by those indoors, their noses pressed to the panes in the fear that, from the vehemence and gesticulation, a breach of the peace was imminent.

Sometime then Hobo reached his decision, still expressing sadness that he would no longer have an influence on armoured tactics and the pleasure of commanding a mobile formation, but taking consolation in the thought that by applying himself to a solution of the problem of clearing minefields, the choking of movement on the battlefield might be averted. It was characteristic that, at once, he wished to share the decision with his staff. Alan Brown, who in the absence of his G.O.C. on 'Spartan', had looked forward to a few days with his feet up at Rawdon, found the peace shattered after only twenty-four hours by a peremptory call to join Hobart immediately in East Anglia. Here they walked in the grounds of the house where the General had his field headquarters, while the new plot was revealed. Brown recalls how, after Hobo had finished, he turned in a sort of dramatic gesture and said, 'Well, what do you think?', and his reply, 'Well, sir, I think we can do it and I think we should.' Hobo looked at his G.S.O. 1 for a moment—'It seemed', says Brown, 'a very long moment before he spoke again', and then said, 'Right! We will.'

And they did.

12

THE 'FUNNIES'

Progress remains the hand-maiden of necessity; the origin of the tank followed by the attachment of ancilliary devices to tanks during the First World War was merely the adaptation of a new weapon system to the changing environment it had, itself, thrust upon the battlefield. To overcome the natural and artificial obstacles placed in their way by the enemy, tanks had to acquire special fittings. Bundles of chestnut palings called 'fascines' were carried to fill crossing places in anti-tank ditches: bridges suspended on the tanks were developed to enable them to cross wider gaps such as canals and streams: there was a floating tank of robust but elephantine construction, a model equipped with flame-throwing equipment; and to transport infantry as close as possible to their objective, infantry carriers, modern Trojan horses capable of transporting thirty armed men under armour, were constructed. And, as might be expected from a race with maritime traditions, there was an early attempt to make possible the landing of tanks from the sea and, by giving them special tracks, assisting in the crossing of beaches and the sea-walls beyond.

Experiments with ancilliary equipment for tanks between the

wars became starved of funds since the limited finance allotted to the R.T.C. in the 1930s had to be spent in urgent priority on battle tanks. In any case, field engineer equipment fell within the province of the Royal Engineers and they could only afford to spend small sums to help a sister corps whose existence continually remained in jeopardy. Invariably, many armoured exercises began with the assumption that devices to enable tanks to cross obstacles were available, when, in fact, none existed.

In other directions a few experiments took place with amphibious tanks and, to help movement and shooting by night, searchlights were acquired and fitted on light tanks; but nothing was on a large scale.

When the purse strings loosened in 1937, research work on specialised armoured devices began again in response to Hobart's spur as D.D.S.D.(A.F.V). The main effort turned towards increasing battlefield mobility by improving obstacle crossing devices and investigating means to destroy minefields. By the outbreak of the war, mine detonating roller devices pushed ahead of tanks, bridging and a few light swimming tanks were under development, while a large number of small armoured infantry carriers (the successors to Wavell's half successful experiments) had actually come into the hands of the troops. Of other important experiments a very bright searchlight of original design which could be mounted behind armour took pride of place: bought from a French syndicate this device was the forerunner of an effective tank-mounted searchlight, later called C.D.L. (Canal Defence Light).

However, when Research and Development almost came to a halt after Dunkirk, only the most obvious and urgent specialised equipments continued to prosper so that by the summer of 1942, minesweeping, C.D.L. and bridging tanks alone had made significant progress. As a minesweeper, the roller had lost favour, its place, usurped by the flail, a drum with chains attached which when rotated in front of the tank, beat the ground and set off the mines. First proposed by a Major Galpin and then a Mr. Sutton, this idea had been suggested to and rejected by the War Office early in the war: not until the pressing need to conquer mines arose in the desert was the matter raised again, and then the efforts of Auchinleck and a Major du Toit actually improvised an operational machine which first showed its value at El Alamein.

A revolutionary swimming tank, invented by Mr. Nicholas Straussler, floated within collapsible screens attached to the tank's hull with the object of displacing sufficient water to give buoyancy while propellers, driven by its own engine, pushed the tank through the water: on reaching the shore the screen could be collapsed and the tank brought into action. This came to be called the Duplex Drive tank—the D.D. It looked like a small boat, took up little more room than that required by the tank itself, and was so simple that Hobo cried he could have kicked himself for not thinking of it many years before. Nevertheless the War Office, on Admiralty advice (sought, no doubt, in the spirit of their guarded mistrust of the Ministry of Supply) at first resisted the enthusiasm of the Ministry of Supply for Straussler's invention, suggesting it was unseaworthy.

At Dieppe, Churchill tanks had landed early in the assault, but lacking means to break through the enemy concrete emplacements became separated from the infantry and also from the engineers whose task it was to destroy obstacles. Afterwards, appropriately enough, a Canadian, Lieutenant J. G. Denovan, suggested that a conventional tank should be modified to carry engineers and their equipment into the forefront of the battle under armour, the genesis of the first Armoured Vehicle Royal Engineers (A.V.R.E.) produced, as were so many special vehicles, by private enterprise out of official sources.

Practically without exception each special device suffered from major shortcomings in addition to the myriad of defects associated with all new equipment: most had to be mounted on obsolete tanks because these alone could be supplied in quantity. The Baron flail (a very unreliable device) and the first C.D.L. were carried on the Matilda at the expense of its main armament: the first production D.D. was built around the Valentine and even the A.V.R.E., adapted from an early mark of Churchill tank, was entering upon obsolescence.

Not one of the first tanks equipped for a specialised role could fight in any other capacity. The flail and C.D.L. only had machine guns; the under-armoured D.D. Valentine, after it had succeeded in swimming ashore, was unlikely to have much influence on the battle because it lacked a gun capable of firing high explosive; alone, the Churchill A.V.R.E. packed a punch in the Spigot Mortar firing a twenty-five-pound explosive charge, called the Petard (better known as the Flying Dustbin), a distance of eighty yards—but this missile was really only for use against concrete obstacles and emplacements at short range and would be helpless in a long-range encounter with enemy tanks or anti-tank guns.

These were the machines handed to Hobart for conversion to battle. In theory it should have been only necessary for him to assess the capabilities of each, train their crews, devise the best means of employment in conjunction with each other and then, as if he were a young squire, hand the sharpened sword to his knight, the assault commander, to do battle as best he could. But in medieval days weapons and tactics evolved slowly and were well understood from frequent use; only rarely were revolutionary secret weapons introduced. Now in the Twentieth Century a host of new devices had to be explained in haste to many commanders to enable them to make best use of an enormous and complex armoury—and industry had to be persuaded or bludgeoned into making, at great haste, fantastic novelties foreign to their previous experience. To Hobart, the problem of adapting men to machines, and machines to overcome the German defences, almost took second place in educating the senior, orthodox Army Commanders and the Captains of Industry to the demands of specialised armour.

Concurrently the selection of units and men, the making of contact with the designers and manufacturers of equipment, the acquisition of secret areas where experiments and training could go on unobserved from outside, and the winning of support from those in authority to put urgent work in hand regardless of the time-honoured procedures of orderly bureaucracy, had to go ahead with typhonic violence.

The units selected for specialised training had long been in existence and were trained to some standard or another. Hobart's decision to convert the 27th Armoured Brigade, from 79th

Armoured Division, to man the swimming D.D. tanks, meant that crews already efficient in cruiser techniques had to learn to work even more closely with infantry and, above all, how to operate the D.D. Valentine tanks. Deliberately he retained a brigade already used to his methods rather than an unknown tank brigade—the 36th—which already had experience with D.D. Valentines: wisely he put people first by backing the men he knew and who knew him.

The historian of the 4/7 Dragoon Guards, one of the regiments in 27th Brigade, sums up their feelings on the day Hobo told them of their new task:

This was a tremendous day. Up to now we had been pushing forward blindly . . . life appeared to have no particular object. We hoped that one day the war would end, but it was difficult when one looked at the map or read the newspapers to see how this was going to happen. Now, in a flash, our eyes were opened. We had a goal . . . one that it would take us all our efforts to attain.

At the same time the 35th Tank Brigade, which for the past year had been trained with C.D.L. at Penrith in Cumberland, came into the division as the only formation which, at that time, had deeply studied its special role.

To man the A.V.R.E.s some frustrated squadrons of Royal Engineers joined in May. Up to then they had been trained to handle poison gas and were afflicted by a deep mistrust of their task and whether they would ever be given the opportunity to practise it in earnest: in the spring of 1943, according to one of their commanders, their morale had sunk to its lowest ebb. Nor was their induction into 79th Armoured Division calculated to be happy, for their new equipment looked as improbable as that which had just been taken away, while the fire of their new commander was forbidding. To Hobo this new role for the Sappers assumed a peculiar importance: he rejoiced at the opportunity to convert his old corps to an armoured mobile task which, to him, seemed to have been disastrously forsaken by the Royal Engineers for far too long. It rapidly struck the officers and men of 5th and 6th Assault Regiments R.E. that they were commanded by a man whose determination to train them for one of the most exacting tasks of the war went hand-in-hand with an evangelical reforming zeal.

Until November 1943, 27th and 35th Tank Brigades with 1st Assault Brigade R.E. were the only combat elements in 79th Armoured Division, but there was also a foundation of components without which nothing could function—the workshops of the Royal Electrical and Mechanical Engineers. It was their primary task to repair the vehicles of the brigades, but it was from their limited manufacturing capability that there frequently came feats of improvisation far in advance of their original purpose—for where industry failed the R.E.M.E. were often driven to succeed.

The demand for specialised armour on a large scale had only been conceived by Alan Brooke at the beginning of March and was not confirmed until 1st April. By then Hobart had formulated his own ideas on a charter and widened its original scope to include, with Brooke's agreement, the development of flame-throwing tanks. Brooke, laughing at Hobart's eagerness, also agreed to a clause which ran on the lines: 'Your formation will be trained primarily in their special roles and secondly as normal tank formations. Your headquarters must be capable of functioning operationally.' The new mandate triggered a flurry of enquiries long before their portent had been digested in Whitehall at 'working level', so for about six weeks Hobo struggled against a stonewall frustration which only began to evaporate as channels of communication became established and, with it, knowledge that the C.I.G.S. was fully behind the demands of the G.O.C. 79th Armoured Division. Not until the end of April did Hobart suggest to Dorrie that things seemed to be making progress, but this was a gross understatement, for already the foundations of success had been laid. In his first instruction to 27th Armoured Brigade can be detected the moving spirit of his policy:

Confronting us is the problem of getting ashore on a defended coast line—success of the operation depends on element of surprise caused by new equipments. . . . Suggestions from all ranks for improvements in equipment to be encouraged . . . to assist secrecy considered preferable all ranks have direct access to CO for putting forward ideas.

This sense of sharing was vital in a community dedicated to hard work and invention for its future survival: it can safely be said that the secret of 79th Armoured Division's success lay in its habit of drawing ideas from all levels and rejecting nothing without investigation no matter how fantastic it appeared.

There ensued an exhaustive search for suitable training areas. Quite a number in connection with D.D. amphibious work were already in being at Narborough and in the Kyles of Bute, and the C.D.L. School was well established at Lowther Castle: but none of these simulated the sort of defences to be overcome on the coasts of France and the Low Countries. However, at Orford Peninsula in Suffolk there existed a battle-training area ideal for secret training, but whose civilian population in consequence would have to leave—a heart-rending process taken by many with extraordinary equanimity after they had been told that vital work was to be done on their land. Here were built reproductions of every known obstacle to be found in the Germans' Atlantic Wall—great concrete walls, deep ditches, minefields, steel barricades and a host of other novelties to represent the worst the enemy could make.

Next, Fritton Decoy, a secluded inland lake, was requisitioned to train the D.D. units. The Decoy had been used for pleasure boating before the war, besides being a highly developed duck shoot the banks sloped gently in places and precipitously in others: it was surrounded by trees. But in obtaining the consent of its owner, an Admiral with a considerable local reputation, permission had to be obtained along with the warning that the water from the lake supplying his house might be contaminated by fuel oils. Fortunately the Admiral was not the least concerned about letting the Army use his lake and, as for the water, 'Water's for washing. I drink port', and Hobo, recalling a visit to the redoubtable sailor, wrote: 'And I should say that was true', before launching forth into a description of the Admiral's home, a little gem of close observation and reporting:

He has a fairly noble stone XVII Century house in the Vanbrugh Style. The door was opened to me by a scullery wench—I fancy the only servitor and we were shown through a mantle hall piled with cases of empty bottles, fishing gear, golf clubs, poultry food etc. into a fine drawing room of good Queen Anne proportions : pillared : and the big panels on the walls completely filled with oil frescoes (not at all bad—'school of' Titian etc) of more than life size Satyrs, nymphs etc. The room looked like a jumble-sale otherwise. Floor, tables, chairs heaped with carpenters tools, accounts, writing materials, letter cases, gun implements etc. etc. A green parrot on a mid-Victorian perch in the middle, and an affable elderly woman in early-20th Century tweeds, *and* the most nondescript hat (*really* Gert & Daisy) you ever saw. The mistress of the house. A nice completely unselfconscious, kindly, busy, fairly competent dowdy country county woman (e.g. her first two subjects were the value of silage as a milk-yielding feed, and the Hobarts of Blickling).

At Fritton there sprouted a D.D. School including dummy ramps of a landing craft and, later, cisterns in which crews learnt escape drills from submerged tanks as if they were trapped submariners. Finally there was the need for an area where all the specialised devices could train as teams and fire their main armaments. At Linney Head in Pembrokeshire a well-developed tank range with the sea on two sides looked just right, but unfortunately the Royal Air Force kept a small radar station there and were not prepared to give it up. The struggle to obtain uninterrupted use of Linney Head in August and September 1943 was protracted and at times, it seems, almost bloody, but in the end Hobo had his way. It was essential that he should, for in a year's time the men of 79th Armoured Division were meant to be operating with perfection in the vanguard of an assault on the most heavily guarded shoreline in the world, knowing how to overcome a series of technical and psychological problems unlike any faced by tank crews before. If they were not allowed to recognise failure, nor could their leader, and it was this which drove him on until there came a time when 79th Armoured Division ceased to question the feasibility of miracles.

Hobo attended whenever something new or of importance was taking place. He missed nothing. When a particularly dangerous trial had been ordered he was there: hold-ups in production or procrastination by any one of the organisations involving the division (be it the War Office or any one of a dozen army head-quarters) would be the signal for his arrival to blast opposition aside. He travelled about a thousand miles each week either in his staff car—the Killing Bottle—or by air, taking travelling companions who lived in an agony of apprehension. The car journeys were as nearly non-stop as the human organs would permit with meals taken as they went. Therefore Charles Humphrey, the A.A. & Q.M.G., dreaded every journey, for the only nourishment provided, apart from continuous conversation, was sandwiches—which he loathed. By air they often flew in an Anson piloted by a white-haired Frenchman nicknamed 'The White Haired Coon', with whom Hobo used to converse until the Coon had to gesticulate and let go of the controls, with the result that each flight became punctuated by a succession of minor, random aerobatics.

Almost from the start Hobo practically ceased to believe that the Director of Research, his official contact in the Ministry of Supply, was capable of producing all the devices needed in time for 1944. Not everybody could be convinced of the need for each item (and it only required one Doubting Thomas or low-grade designer to put a whole project back at its starting point), the processes of procurement were clumsy, industrial capacity at a premium and nearly everything needed for the invasion seemed to acquire a compelling priority of its own. Therefore some special items requiring only a small production run which did not have overwhelming support from above were liable to go to the bottom of the priority list or disappear altogether.

Having lost faith in the Directorate of Research after two or three months' frustrating liaison, to quote Hobart:

. . . we ceased altogether to deal with that Directorate which had no executive power whatever—dealt solely with ACIGS(W)[General Evetts] who happened at that time to be an officer who did everything in his power to 'chase' Directorates, Ministries etc and was, in consequence, of great assistance to 79th Armd. Div.

General Evetts himself recalls with relish the visits paid to him at frequent intervals by Hobo. Then he could be sure that an invitation to lunch, preceded by a ride in the Killing Bottle, was to be the occasion for some high-pressure arguments designed to squeeze new concessions from the Ministries or from industry. This Evetts did not mind, although he knew many who resented Hobo's short circuiting of the channels of command and so-called interference. To Evetts (a man who never failed 79th Armoured Division), as to so many others, Hobo acted as an inspiration, bubbling over with ideas ranging far beyond specialised armour. For those who wished to foster progress a talk with Hobo was a tonic in itself.

Industry reacted in the same way as the Ministries, since factory managers whose production had failed to meet the requirements resented Hobo's efforts to discover why they were not up to schedule. But a leading industrialist, Sir Miles Thomas of the Nuffield Organisation, has this to say:

It was after a game of croquet, which he played with saturnine fierceness, that he first mentioned to me . . . a 'jumping' tank. His idea was that if you had a rocket pointing downwards at each corner of a tank or transport vehicle and touched them off simultaneously the vehicle would jump, and if the rockets were mounted on swivels the vehicle could be conveniently steered. . . .

He was never short of ideas.

It is sometimes said of inventors that they don't *have* to be mad to create ideas—but it does help. I wouldn't accuse Hobo of any form of madness, but he certainly had tremendous applied ingenuity. . . .

When some of his dreams had to be translated into hard metal on the drawing board the stress merchants who had to work out the design requirements sometimes found themselves up against an apparently insoluble problem. I know of several highly qualified designers who were not ashamed to go to Hobo and to admit that one particular approach to his problem did not seem to be working out and would he, Hobo, be helpful in thinking of another approach. . . .

In short, he not only thought up original ideas but he helped considerably in their realisation—and this frequently in the face of discouraging criticism in that ice-cold core of depressions that I suppose I had better just call 'The Ministry'.

It was Hobo's impression that if he did not go to meet the men actually producing his new devices nothing would be ready in time. In July 1943 not even enough Baron or Scorpion (Valentine) flails nor Valentine D.D.s were ready to train the troops: with the range at Linney Head available only from August to October the time about to be lost could be crippling. He wrote to the War Office specifically concerning the delay in deciding to adopt the Sherman tank as a flail, but also on matters in general.

There seems to be in some quarters a frigid attitude as regards mechanical matters. I believe this is due largely to inadequate co-ordination of the activities of designers, producers and users and insufficient drive behind design and production. In any case, the need is so acute that we cannot afford either to neglect or drop any possible method of dealing with minefields. . . . Owing to the delay in producing equipment for my formations to try out it seems evident that intensive training with mine clearing forces will have to take place during late Autumn or more probably during the Winter and Spring.

Delivery of the Valentine D.D.s to the operational regiments of 27th Brigade began as late as the end of July, and flails did not appear in quantity until the autumn so that only then was it worth converting one of the original armoured brigades—the 30th—from Hobart's old 11th Armoured Division, to learn the minesweeping craft they would employ against the enemy the following spring. Small wonder that his letters reflected despair and the fear that the siege train would not be ready in time, or even that an invasion could take place at all.

At this time Hobart's correspondence underwent a fascinating change. Official letters lost none of their bite—but now acquired a greater authority founded in the awakening knowledge that Brooke was backing him to the hilt. Brooke himself wrote on 15th July, after a day spent at Fritton when he was taken sailing in a D.D.: 'Most interesting and inspiring to see old Hobo so happy and so well employed.' As earnest of his faith he gave approval for five hundred Shermans to be converted to D.D. directly overriding the Deputy C.I.G.S., Lieutenant-General

A.C.—S

Weeks, who held the Valentine D.D. good enough for the job. In June, after a visit by Brooke, he had written to Dorrie:

> . . . he said he had only asked me to come and see him in order to hear how I was getting on.
> Well . . . I wonder.
> He was extremely affable. Talked of 'old times' when 'you and I' etc. And when I left told me to drop in and see him whenever I could. Well, well.

But after the 15th July both Alan Brown and Alan Jolly (who took over as G.S.O. 1 in August) record that Brooke was the only man from whom Hobart would accept an adverse decision without argument. The conversion was complete.

Letters to Dorrie, for obvious reasons of security, told nothing about the experiments and, as it happened, she appears to have been visited by an 'agent' trying to discover if her husband talked about his work. In June a new contentment enters the theme of his writings, caused partly by the sheer joy of creative work, partly in the knowledge of full support from above, but not least because in the Birthday Honours List he had been created a Knight. The hand of the Prime Minister is clearly discernible —the timing of the Honour showed that it rewarded the services of a decade and could have nothing to do with specialised armour. A wire from Churchill just back from a visit to the triumphant British Armies in Tunisia:

> On my return to England I send you my warmest congratulations on the honour so richly deserved which has been recently bestowed upon you.
>   Winston S. Churchill

drew forth a song of adulation:

> That—from him. Handsome. I don't know which has given me most gratification—that wire, ex-RQMS Tom Coomb's wire [one of his old RTC soldiers]or Erskine's letter from 7th Armd Div.

The knighthood was an expression of complete justification and approval. He could echo the remark of his eldest brother

Charles who, when honoured shortly before (and belatedly too) by the award of the C.I.E., said the letters stood for 'Charles' Indiscretions Excused'.

*   *   *   *   *

In mid-1943 General Morgan, Chief of Staff to the Supreme Allied Commander (Designate) (C.O.S.S.A.C.), was drawing up the plans for an invasion of France in 1944, as the last offensive by German Panzer armies in Russia beat itself to death on the Kursk Salient and the Allied armies in the Mediterranean prepared their first large-scale seaborne landing upon Europe against Sicily. No obstacles such as confronted an invader of the Atlantic seaboard lay across the shores of Sicily or, for that matter, any part of what Mr. Churchill aptly called the 'soft underbelly of Europe'. Therefore none of the sophisticated machines being prepared by 79th Armoured Division were urgently needed even had they been available. Their secrets remained carefully guarded.

In Sicily, and later in Italy, the assaulting infantry led the way ashore under the cover of heavy aerial bombardment and naval gun-fire, followed by waterproofed tanks wading from their landing craft. Because beach defences were not highly developed, it was possible for the troops to land and consolidate a deep beach-head at speed with relative ease before the full force of the enemy counter-stroke from inland could be gathered and thrown against them. However, wherever an invasion could be launched within range of protective fighter aircraft from England, the European coastlines were so heavily fortified and mined that it was certain the Germans intended to fight for the beaches while preparing an immediate armoured counter-stroke to intervene at the height of the battle. Therefore it was desirable for armoured troops to be ashore first and having got there to be followed by infantry; if this process could be carried out by night as well as by day, so much the better.

The simple fact that 79th Armoured Division's devices were specialised implied they could not work independently. Naturally the need to co-operate closely with the Navy until they hit the beach was mandatory: but once ashore they must combine amongst themselves and, later still, with the other arms as they landed. It was Hobart's impression that the Navy looked somewhat askance at his swimming tanks. Vice-Admiral Lord Louis Mountbatten's Combined Operations Organisation, which had led the way in developing the techniques for operations from ship to shore, left the staff and members of 79th Armoured Division with the feeling that sailors looked on D.D.s as unseaworthy craft (which in many ways they were), while their G.O.C. found Mountbatten personally most elusive, and his landing craft, at first, hard to come by. As is typical of trials' work on unproven equipment, there are always groups whose natural scepticism, not infrequently mated to the advocacy of a rival, sponsored system, is quick to seize upon early failure as a reason for premature rejection. Thus, when the first Sherman D.D. sank in full view of a senior member of Mountbatten's staff, that officer returned to Combined Operations and said the idea was no good—forgetting that for his benefit it had been launched in totally unsuitable conditions. These were early days. Neither the Navy nor 79th Armoured Division had learnt to appreciate each other's problems, but after protracted negotiations for permission to carry out sea launchings at Stokes Bay off the Isle of Wight matters began to improve, even if occasionally in a hesitant manner.

Nigel Duncan, by this time a colonel, had the task of running the first launchings from L.C.T.s under the auspices of the Sea Wing—a typical Hobart centralised school of instruction. Formidable difficulties intervened, for not only were unknown aspects being investigated, but the demands of secrecy became totally prohibitive when a nearby beach at Stokes Bay suddenly swarmed with hordes of workmen, constructing strange caissons (parts for the great artificial harbour called Mulberry). Until a new secluded beach could be found, G.H.Q. Home Forces forbade launchings. The D.D. instructors were Canadians—men of sterling qualities but fretting under the restrictions imposed by secrecy—and some there were whose experience in inland waters inhibited them against the perils of the sea.

Anyway, no launchings had taken place before Hobo came

down to see for himself, and Duncan, backed by a wealth of experience of his General, philosophically rode out the passing storm. At dinner that night Hobart concentrated his attentions on the Chief Trials Officer and the naval officer in command of the L.C.T.s. By 1 a.m. as Hobo recalled, 'after dint of drinking too much spirits', everybody had been persuaded and he called down the table, 'Nigel—we launch tomorrow.'

Next morning an L.C.T., with seven Valentine D.D.s on board, breasted a six-inch sea to the accompaniment of warnings by the trials officer that the conditions bid fair to lead to fatalities. At last, the first tank drove down the ramp, cocked its tail in the air and slid into the water—then drifted helplessly when the driver found it impossible to engage the propeller. In next to no time a naval launch secured a towing line but, taking up the slack with a jerk, pulled the D.D. on to its beam and sent her to the bottom, fortunately leaving the crew swimming on the surface.

The next launch proved successful but was followed in quick succession by two more partial failures and then a total stoppage when the fifth tank jammed in the door of the L.C.T. So far Hobo had viewed the trial with objective interest, although clearly not pleased, but chatting with the crew of the sunken tank his patience ran out.

Hobo: 'What member of the crew were you?'

Soldier: 'The driver, sir.'

Hobo: 'Did you have any difficulty getting out?'

Soldier: 'Oh, no, sir, none.'

Hobo: 'Did your escape apparatus work all right?'

Soldier: 'I don't really know, sir. You see the oxygen bottle was empty.'

Duncan says that by the time they reached shore he felt depressed and shaken. They lunched unhappily and then out of the blue, as he got into his car, Hobo remarked, 'Well, I'm sure it will go all right. Now look, you've got thirty chaps there and each has got to do six launches as a commander and six as a driver and he has got to do it by day and night as well.'

Duncan reckoned this at about three thousand launches and, remembering the speed of launch for only five tanks in the morning, said. 'I don't honestly think we can do that.' Then quite suddenly the whole aspect changed as Hobo patted Duncan on the shoulder saying, 'Of course you will—you'll find it will work out all right.' A month later D.D. tanks were leaving the L.C.T.s at one very fifteen seconds.

The resolution of a practical relationship between the Navy and the D.D. crews came at the lowest working level—the crews of the craft concerned: a passage from the History of the 4/7 D.G. describing their first sea training in December 1943 brings it into perspective:

As was to be expected, we found that there were a great many complications; we now had not only ourselves to consider, but the Navy who had always to think of winds and tides and currents. They too had big problems to master in launching several Squadrons from numerous craft in such a way that they could all link up together and arrive on the beach simultaneously. This was no easy matter with clumsy vessels like DD tanks, which were little better than rectangular blocks in shape, only capable of four knots and therefore unable to catch up if once they got left behind; and in fact, if it was against a current, they had to go flat out in order not to go backwards; and both we and the Naval craft commanders had much to learn before we became proficient.

The essentials of the D.D. technique had been mastered by the end of 1943, and units began to work with the formations they were to support in the invasion while training and training again to become perfectly expert. Given the chance, tanks would be able to land from the sea on their own in the van of the invasion and shoot from close range at the enemy coastal positions prior to moving inland to engage the enemy armoured counter attack.

The future of the C.D.L. tanks was more obscure. The beam of light, projected through a slot two inches wide by twenty-four inches long, generated by a carbon arc lamp estimated at thirteen million candle-power, could be spread to cover a frontage of three hundred and fifty yards at one thousand yards range. This enabled aimed fire to be delivered at about one thousand yards range; beyond this out to four thousand yards away there was ample illumination for movement. However, C.D.L. was also capable of blinding the enemy with a flicker induced by the automatic movement of a shutter across the light aperture, and this facility, it was claimed, raised the weapon system above a mere battlefield aid by transforming it, in the minds of its keenest advocates, into a battle-winning weapon in its own right. The cloak of secrecy smothered the C.D.L. School at Lowther Castle, where a great many equipments were made ready with the intention that they should be used all at once, in mass, as the decisive element in their first battle. For the parents of the C.D.L. had learnt from the disappointment of the fathers of the tank and were not going to expose their masterpiece prematurely.

In the depths of the secrecy hid the fate of the C.D.L. Because experiments with bright lights (clearly visible to the local inhabitants around Penrith who could read newspapers in the street when the black-out was defiled night after night) had to be confined to a relatively small training area, the frontages under consideration had to be relatively narrow : very few people outside Lowther Castle could be let into the secret and therefore the commanders of operational formations usually did not even know of the existence of C.D.L., let alone its scope and how to employ it. Therefore, for a long time the claims of the chief designer, Mr. Mitsakis, and his military collaborators, went unchallenged by soldiers with combat experience. In October 1942 a C.D.L. School was set up in the Middle East to continue the training of 1st Tank Brigade, but by the time they were ready the Battle of El Alamein had been won and the war had moved away to Tunisia, so no experience from battle could be acquired in 1943.

Hobo had to adapt C.D.L. to the sort of battle to be envisaged in Europe. In fairness to most protagonists of C.D.L., they never claimed that the C.D.L. was a panacea to night operations— saying no more than 'it is a very important and valuable adjunct'. With this Hobo agreed, for the highly realistic and imaginative battlefield trials he devised at Linney Head in September 1943 fully confirmed the claim that C.D.L. was an invaluable shooting aid, but showed that the light, even when mounted on the same tank as the gun, was best used in co-operation with guns firing from other tanks. It was shown that, although the lights had a blinding effect from straight ahead, the C.D.L.s stood out clearly from the flanks and were vulnerable to aimed anti-tank fire: furthermore dust and smoke (well simulated during the trial) seriously degraded the illuminant. Hobo also demonstrated that the rigid formations devised by the C.D.L. School to keep a phalanx of moving C.D.L.s perfectly co-ordinated behind its wall of light, was not a practical operation of war. Amongst the dust, smoke and shock of battle, human beings are more prone than usual to error and even when the battleground is as smooth as a billiard table, there will be deviation and the demand for manœuvre: a rigid formation could then disintegrate.

Far from discarding C.D.L. as a result of the Linney Head experiment, Hobo sought to propagate it as the logical successor to his own experiments with spotlights mounted on light tanks in 1935. He did not enthuse over C.D.L., but continued planning to integrate them with seaborne assault teams as the only means of guiding them if the landings took place in the dark. Meanwhile he kept the devices in the minds of the G.O.C., Home Forces, General Paget and later, with more significant consequences, to others.

In the autumn of 1943, even with the help of C.D.L. and naval searchlights, the technique of night fighting was so retarded that a landing from the sea amongst the forest of obstacles and minefields shielding every yard of the French shoreline could not be considered feasible in the dark. Only by daylight could demolition squads find their way ashore to open narrow lanes for the first assault waves—and only by daylight could exits from the beaches be opened up at sufficient speed to permit the rapid 'pegging out of claims' inland.

The Germans had built a strong crust of concrete emplacements (some of them ten feet thick) giving shelter to men and guns of all calibres. There were anti-tank ditches and walls, minefields and wire, and on the beaches rows of gate-like metal barriers (called Element 'C') and ramps with mines attached. Each artificial obstruction was integrated with permanent obstacles, such as cliffs and sea-walls, and every barrier covered by fire. Each type of obstacle required a special antidote and with the exception of minefields (to which the flail was usually the best answer), most were tackled by the A.V.R.E.s mounting one or more special appliances. The basic Churchill A.V.R.E. armed with the Petard, crewed by five men, of whom the driver was usually a member of the Royal Armoured Corps and the remainder Royal Engineers, in a neat way symbolised Hobo's career—the original Royal Engineer propelled into action in a tank by an R.A.C. soldier. With a detachable Small Box Girder Bridge pivoted on its horns, the A.V.R.E. could bridge ditches, craters and mount sea-walls: with great fascines (bundles of wood) it could fill holes and ditches in one slick motion. Once rid of bridge or fascine, the A.V.R.E. commander was free to fire the Petard against strong points, Element 'C' or any other barrier; or if the Petard on its own was found insufficiently powerful, much larger, hand-placed charges could be used by manœuvring the A.V.R.E. as a shield for the dismounted crew against enemy fire while they tackled their objective with General Wade or Beehive shaped charges.

Every conceivable method of tackling every known German defence was worked out on the full-scale models at Orford. Some kinds of sea-wall were found to be too big for the S.B.G. Bridge—so to cross these a Churchill tank with its turret removed and a bridge carried on its back was constructed and called the 'Ark'. When it was discovered that minesweeping tanks bogged while flailing in soft ground, such as the foreshore of a beach, a large plough (called the Bullshorn Plough) was built on to the front of the A.V.R.E. to furrow eighteen inches deep and cast the mines out on either side of the tracks. Both the Ark and the Bullshorn Plough were designed and manufactured in prototype by 79th Armoured Division's own workshops—typical examples of the manner in which, when faced with the need for a quick solution to a new problem, Hobo used his own resources rather than wallow in the troughs of official procurement procedures.

Sometimes the blast from a Petard would open pathways through minefields, but the process was slow and unwieldy. Yet the flails, Barons and Scorpions, besides being unreliable, could flail at only a half-mile an hour and were simply tank hulls with the flail device and its special engine mounted; they had no combat capability—a state of affairs contrary to 79th Armoured Division's charter and their commander's inclinations.

Since the destruction of mines was the responsibility of the Royal Engineers, the Engineer-in-Chief, in conjunction with the Department of Tank Design in the Ministry of Supply, were deeply involved with flails before Hobo's advent. However, general agreement on the need to incorporate a flail with the Sherman tank broke down when the E.-in-C. supported a somewhat Heath Robinson adaptation, all wheels, cogs and chains, instead of a simpler, more robust device devised by a Mr. Rackham. Hobo supported Rackham's solution, called Crab, and had his way (as he usually did).

The decision to take Crab came in June 1943, but production had to be arranged and started, leaving, in the meantime, only a few Barons and Scorpions available for tactical trials; but much was learnt. At El Alamein flails had been used singly to cut only a narrow lane: thus a single mechanical breakdown or battle casualty could close the gap indefinitely. 79th Armoured Division gave each troop five flails with a view to opening a lane three flails wide while keeping a reserve of two for emergencies. When the drum rotated and flung the chains against the ground a terrific cloud of dust and mud arose through which the crew could barely see at all, preventing the gunner from aiming his main armament and raising difficulties in station keeping. Practice alone solved these difficulties.

The essence of a breaching operation was precise timing and speed under constant control. Each element in the assault force had to be landed to a timetable so that its limited repertoire could be fitted to the activities of a team and the supporting bombardment. First, D.D. tanks had to land, lowering their flotation screens once grounded in shallow water in order to bring their guns into action against the enemy positions which had survived the bombardment.

Then, while the D.D.s sought to dominate the beaches, Hobart envisaged C.D.L.s (if it were at night), A.V.R.E.s and flails being brought ashore in landing craft to tackle the first of the obstacles. In every place the order of landing had to be adjusted to match the layout of the defences, but from the beginning it was assumed that mines would be met on the beaches, interspersed by barricades, sea-walls and ditches further inland. Hence the early trials provided for landing craft disgorging flails first, to beat their way up the beach, followed by a C.D.L. to illuminate the scene if the landing was in the dark and then A.V.R.E.s carrying bridges, fascines or whatever equipment was deemed appropriate. Each team was composed of all the devices essential to breach one gap plus a reserve afloat in case of local failure. Armoured vehicles dominated the leading echelons of the invasion : only after armour had conquered the defences were infantry to be exposed.

The intensive programme of experiment and training at Linney Head left not a spare moment and envisaged every imaginable type of assault operation. Starting from first principles the whole process progressed to a design which enlightened everyone including Hobart himself. The first simple but perilous exercises aimed at practising the D.D. crews in driving over the rocks on the sea-shore and then, with their backs to the sea, shooting at targets on the cliffs. Then came the dissection in discussion of operations by C.D.L.s, flails and A.V.R.E.s in breaching a minefield, followed by drill movements by day, and then full-scale exercises against a simulated minefield by day and night. There ensued, step by step, discussions and exercises to discover the best ways to overcome a wide variety of defensive systems, practice of massed attacks by tanks and infantry with C.D.L., and the assault of inland fortified zones or the rearward defences of ports. Each exercise, framed with maximum realism, imparted a lasting enthusiasm and confidence as the lessons were hammered home.

At a staggering rate a mass of new knowledge was acquired, absorbed and disseminated throughout the division. Fresh ideas poured in, were turned over by Hobo and his advisers, rejected or, if sound, tried out and incorporated in the general scheme. A standardised and simple modern system of control for siege warfare evolved from practice. Radio networks linked every unit in each assault team and radiated back through lane commanders to breach commanders, becoming in the process integrated with every element in the assault—sailors, tankmen, infantrymen and gunners. A host of wireless sets acted as the membrane of an infinite variety of organisational and assault permutations, arrived at after exhaustive and searching investigation and trial in the face of every possible realistic distraction.

In the midst of this torrent of thought and experiment it became essential to save the good from being masked by the bad, and to prevent too many projects running at once. Hobo certainly tended to try too much at once, his thoughts were constantly in motion and he did not always frame his newest ideas clearly: without staff officers who could understand and interpret he was wasted, but in this respect he picked well. Both Alan Brown and his successor as G.S.O. 1, Lieutenant-Colonel Alan Jolly,[1] much younger men than their commander, had the facility of reading his intentions clearly, mixing it with strong nerves in survival—and there were several more who learnt to live with Hobo and have since risen high in their respective professions.

It was the measure of Hobo's foresight that he grasped the need to study and practise attacks on the type of enemy defensive positions which would be met inland, and the hallmark of his workmanship that nearly every drill evolved at Linney Head found service in action. His vast imagination and unceasing, provocative zest for inquiry unearthed in minute detail from every possible source a fantastic number of new ideas. Night Direction Keeping devices ranging from flares, lights, Bofors guns firing tracer ammunition and radio beacons were all asked for and tried out. A highly successful escape apparatus for D.D. crews designed by a commander in the Royal Navy, after dealing direct with Hobo, went into production under naval arrangements when the speed of progress by the War Office appeared too slow. To speed up acceptance of the Crab Flail, its acceptance trials were carried out by 79th Armoured Division in August 1943 and not by D.T.D. who had sponsored its com-

1. Now General Sir Alan Jolly, K.C.B., C.B.E., D.S.O., Quarter-Master-General to the Army.

petitor. One suspects Hobo's determination that D.T.D. should not have an opportunity to disapprove.

No sooner were the assault techniques solved in so far as possible in September 1943, than Hobo set about educating the senior officers destined to command his weapons in action. Elaborate demonstrations arranged at Linney Head for the C.I.G.S., for General Paget, the C.-in-C. Home Forces, for General Morgan of C.O.S.S.A.C. and as many as possible of those who would plan or execute the invasion, injected a genuine understanding at the higher levels of the potentialities of each 'Funny', as the siege train's pieces came to be known. It is clear that the D.D.s and C.D.L.s made the greatest impression: but perhaps it was the vast increase of fire-power 79th Armoured Division added to the assault which raised the hopes. For the C.I.G.S. it was a glorious vindication of his own judgement in selecting Hobart for the task: to Generals charged with the command of assault formations (such as Crocker, now Commander of 1st Corps, or Graham, the Commander of 50th Division), the sight of each weapon acted as an essential introduction to their coming task. The D.D.s, the A.V.R.E.s and the flails won unqualified approval: the C.D.L.s an admiration mixed with reservations. Perhaps, if the C.D.L.s could have been shown as integral parts of conventional tank units, melding their lights with the gunfire of ordinary tanks, they might have won general acceptance: as a solo weapon they were not so convincing. Therefore, so long as the possibility remained of the invasion taking place in the dark, C.D.L.s would have to be in the first flight of the invasion fleet. Otherwise, they would be relegated to the bottom of the priority list. In the autumn of 1943 nothing was settled, and afterwards Hobart was never able to describe how each piece of equipment came to be selected since the plan evolved at the whims of a changing cast of personalities, both Allied and German.

*   *   *   *   *

In a way it was changing personalities who caused the greatest rub. C.O.S.S.A.C.'s Chief of Staff, General Morgan had, perforce, to compose the invasion plan from limited resources on behalf of a non-existent Supreme Allied Commander. By the end of September 1943 the embryo plans had indicated the Normandy coastline in the area of Caen as the best place for the landing since here the defences were weaker and, in their rear, the terrain such that action by the German mobile, armoured reserves would take longest to develop. In October, General Eisenhower, the C.-in-C. Mediterranean, saw the C.O.S.S.A.C. plan and commented that it would have to be launched 'in greater weight and on a wider front'. He did not know then that it would be his destiny to put the plan into operation as Supreme Commander Allied Expeditionary Force and unfortunately, in a way, it was not until the first week in December 1943 that the job became his.

Once revealed, the division of command under Eisenhower appeared nicely balanced in relation to the initial forces allotted by Britain and America. On D-Day, when the landings first took place, each nation's effort would be roughly equal and the total forces committed no more than that of an army group. Logically, only one man could command the invasion as a whole and continue to conduct the land battle until two army groups, one British and one American, came to be formed in France. Then Eisenhower would take overall command of the operations. Operational command of the British 21st Army Group, and with it the invasion, went to General Sir Bernard Montgomery: later the 12th United States Army Group would be commanded by Lieutenant-General Omar Bradley, who, until then, would lead the American element in the invasion (under Montgomery), as Commanding General 1st U.S. Army.

These were the men for whom Hobart was to work after they arrived from their posts in the Mediterranean. However, until they made up their minds about General Morgan's plan, a mild state of suspense ensued, although the struggle to train and equip went on unremittingly. Here, during the pause, an opportunity occurred for Hobo to turn his mind to the wider, national scene and indulge in random speculation. The year gone by had been one of personal glory and justification, ending with

a sense of satisfaction as he surveyed the products of his labours
—the papers setting out invasion drills, the expanding number
of battleworthy D.D.s, C.D.L.s, Crabs and a meccano-like assembly of attachments on the A.V.R.E.s. Once again his formulation
of a doctrine upon which a nationally important undertaking
depended for success had resulted in his dictating an original
method of assault, cutting the pattern of a hundred land battles
to come. Safe in the approval of the Prime Minister and the
C.I.G.S., his personal influence rode high. Thus having driven
himself to such a pitch, he felt flat when, for a while, only individual projects required 'chasing' and no more progress could
be made with the Grand Design.

Possibly out of boredom, maybe as self stimulation, he turned
to consider the social scene and the way it might alter as the war
ended and peace wrought its changes, his letters to Dorrie im-
parting the full radical transposition from the unorthodox military field, matched with disillusionment with some sections of
British Industry, to a left of centre stance in the world of politics.
In September he wrote:

I remarked once . . . that I thought a really witty and subtle Socialist could produce a very telling indictment of the rich not for
acquiring riches, but for their manifest incapacity for knowing how
to spend money sensibly. Let them go on making money, but some
one else must spend it for them as they so obviously don't know
how to.

He sensed the swing to Socialism in an incredibly penetrating
passage from a letter written on 24th September 1943:

I have a feeling that Winston's complete domination of the H of C,
the overwhelming surge and tide of his speeches, the very masterli-
ness of his management which seems to leave critics speechless, may
have the effect of producing in many quite honest people uneasiness,
a feeling that they haven't been able to express *their* apprehensions
and that these have been swept aside, ignored, rather than met:
and so a faint, and probably unconscious resentment. But one that
may grow considerably under the surface, and burst out surprisingly
strongly at an awkward moment.

As it did in the General Election of July 1945! And on 29th September:

The financiers and industrialists naturally want cheap labour: and contend that we can't compete in World-markets without. Not under existing conditions (un-mechanised collieries: badly-planned old fashioned factories: unscientific management etc in many cases). But does not Dagenham where the minimum wage pre-war was £5 show what can be done when technical and managerial efficiency is combined with modern lay-out and British workmen.

I have unhappy suspicions, largely strengthened by my visits to various factories during this war, that our industry is about as modern and up-to-date in its outlook and methods as was our Army Council in 1939—and the worst of the senior officers.

In 1940, while he was in the Home Guard, a friendship had grown up with Frank Pakenham,[2] the private secretary to William Beveridge, the future author of the Government-sponsored report on post-war social security—the charter of the Welfare State. The Beveridge Report fascinated Hobo and on 3rd January 1944 Pakenham came to his H.Q. to talk about it to the men. To Dorrie he wrote of the points which impressed him most:

Frank P's idea about ensuring employment after the war is, in essence, the necessity for Govt to influence the *total* national expenditure in such a way as to ensure that there is sufficient purchasing power to absorb what is produced.

We already have a Central Statistical Bureau: and for the last 3 years the Treasury Annual budget White Paper has given the figures of total national income and expenditure, as well as those of course of total Govt income and expenditure.

It would mean Govt control over imports, exports, and some administrative device for quickly altering taxation.

We shall certainly have to have the two former anyway, whatever happens, it seems to me: if we are to have any economic future vis-a-vis U.S.A. and U.S.S.R. He says that Unemployment averaged $12\frac{1}{2}\%$ during the inter-war years. It ought to be possible to keep it steady round 5%.

2. Now Lord Longford.

Frank P's lecture went down well. He is not a good speaker in the sense of being an orator, or even having a good delivery but he has a very lucid brain and can put complex things simply. The men were enthralled of course, and I had to stop the questions and shut down after $1\frac{1}{2}$ hours or they would have gone on all day.

This was the people's retort to Churchillian dominance, the early warning, for those who could sense it, of the political change to come. Undoubtedly Hobart sympathised with the yearnings of those searching for a readjustment of the structure of power, a reaction contrary to the traditional allegiance of army officers and probably prompted partly by pique at his own fate. Nevertheless his overriding emotion was an immense admiration and understanding of the people.

Of course, he was an idealist; somewhat naive and, in the process of resolving his opinions, subject to swings and contradictions any one of which might lead to misrepresentation. He hated waste and believed the profit motive inadmissable in wartime. With the leadership and love of the cause essential in drawing forth the best from the people, he knew there had to be compassion of the sort he found on a visit to a firm in Cardiff making flail equipment.

The head of the firm (whose father started the works in a very small way) a man of my age who only occasionally dropped an 'h' struck me as a fine type (and he was very fair about the workpeople : though I tried him in 2 or 3 ways). Much better than the next 'public school generation'. His brother had a shock of white hair and a most attractive soft voice almost like S of Ireland but actually made me realise where the fascination of Welsh revivalism and preaching might be.

I purposely remarked at lunch about those unhappy coal stoppages.

One of my officers instanced indignantly the colliery where 900 had come out because one lad of 17 ordered down the mine, refused to go. The 'Daniel' at the end of the table spoke up. 'Do you know that that lad's father and his father's brother had both been killed underground in that very mine. What good do you suppose would be done by a lad like that scared stiff underground?'

A.C.—T

Unhappily, possibly as a result of this introspection, he became engulfed by one of his blackest depressions, its evil contents spilling out on those close to him—in particular on Dorrie. To her he wrote:

Is it senility: a basic fault of character in me: or an essential mental frivolity that I find with . . . so many others that much as I respect them and like working with them have a deep regard for their characters, sound judgement and knowledge—yet, unless we're engaged in strictly professional matters, I don't find them or their company amusing—or even interesting. It's no good saying all the fault lies in them: because this feeling is definitely increasing in me. I'm glad of the excuse of office-work for something to get away from them: when we're not discussing actual immediate problems of my work: and I find their company at meals dull.

Probably this was a by-product of staleness which a good spell of leave might have dispelled, but he was also worried. Once again he had forged a weapon. In the New Year the Captains of the Invasion would arrive fresh from their triumphs in the Mediterranean. They might cast him aside: on the other hand he might be propelled into even more violent activity.

Waiting is never easy, even when you are 'a man without a future'.

13

INVASION

Stopping off at Marrakesh to see Churchill, while on the way back to London, General Montgomery saw the C.O.S.S.A.C. Plan on the New Year's Eve of 1944, and next day gave Churchill his reactions. Expanding on Eisenhower's opinion that the frontage of the assault was too narrow, Montgomery envisaged a cramping of subsequent operations to the detriment of the break-out from the beach-head. To match the greatest concentration the enemy could gather against the beach-head, an equal and preferably greater rate of landings would have to be made simultaneously behind the actual assault by the Allies. Moreover, if the beach-head started off cramped, there would not be room to receive reinforcements after D-Day, the selection of points through which to break-out would be curtailed, and a sort of stagnation might well ensue.

Montgomery came to London on the 2nd January with instructions to revise the plan in conjunction with Eisenhower's Chief of Staff, Lieutenant-General Walter Bedell Smith, Admiral Sir Bertram Ramsay the C.-in-C. of the Naval Forces, and Air Chief Marshal Sir Trafford Leigh-Mallory, the C.-in-C. of the Air Forces, and after a fortnight's intensive study and discussion, reached conclusions on the extent of the strength needed to widen the frontage of the initial landings. The most far-reaching effect of this expansion arose from the need for greater numbers of landing craft: as a result the invasion date had to be put back by at least one month to gain time in which to acquire this extra shipping. Amongst the many other additional demands to be met, the provision of more specialised armour to support the increased number of assault formations was a prime consideration.

Only three days after Montgomery returned home Hobart wrote to Dorrie:

I've just been summoned by the Great Man Monty for 11 a.m. on Sat. Bowler-Hat? He doesn't like 'old' men, nor has he ever liked me.[1] (However I think that the W.O. would want to keep me on in a new job which they are being forced into making, and for which they can't think of anyone with the particular experience.)

His fears concerning the future relationship with Montgomery were groundless, and unjustified, for in Montgomery's opinion Hobo was 'brilliant'—and he had fully concurred with Brooke's decision in 1943 to get Hobo to develop the specialised armour. As it happened, Montgomery brought with him, as armoured adviser, Major-General G. W. Richards (who, it will be remembered, had served with Hobart in the 4th R.T.C. in 1928), but Martel suggested that perhaps he should take Richard's post, and was very angry to be turned down by Montgomery on the ground that he did not have the qualifications for the job—'he had only commanded a few tanks in action south of Arras in 1940'. Montgomery did not want to be told how to *handle* armour in battle, because he confidently thought he knew all about that, but he did want to be told what went on inside tanks and this was partly Richards's task. However, he also wanted somebody else within 21st Army Group to command a specialised set up such as 79th Armoured Division. Montgomery appointed Hobart to act as his Specialised Armour Adviser, settling the question of whether H.Q. 79th Armoured Division should

1. Here is his familiar technique of warning Dorrie of impending disappointment on the eve of an important change in state.

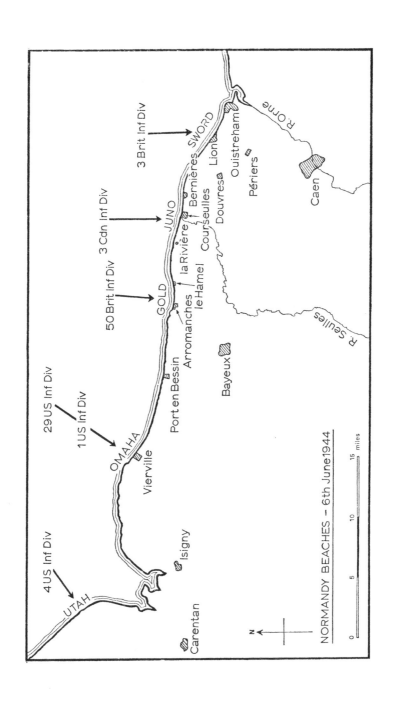

4 US Inf Div

UTAH

Carentan

Isigny

29 US Inf Div

1 US Inf Div

OMAHA

Vierville

Port en Bessin

Arromanches

le Hamel

Bayeux

50 Brit Inf Div

GOLD

la Rivière

3 Cdn Inf Div

JUNO

Bernières

Courseulles

Douvres

3 Brit Inf Div

SWORD

Lion

Ouistreham

Périers

Caen

R. Orne

R. Seulles

N

0   5   10   15 miles

NORMANDY BEACHES – 6th June 1944

go to France behind its special armour—and thereby giving Hobo his chance to go to war at last.

It is significant that from the time of their meeting on the 12th nothing is to be found in writing concerning this special relationship. Hobart is not even mentioned in Montgomery's 'Memoirs', although he received special copies of a number of key papers emanating from H.Q. 21st Army Group. To all intents and purposes Hobart ceased to criticise Montgomery and at once accorded him the same willing loyalty he had given Brooke.

A small 79th Armoured Division 'cell' attached to H.Q. 21st Army Group at St. Paul's School, Hammersmith, and manned by John Borthwick, now G.S.O. 2 (Ops), began to feed in Hobart's ideas through the Chief of Staff, Major-General Francis de Guingand, and the B.G.S., Brigadier H. E. Pyman. Borthwick, reflecting on the kindness accorded to him by so many senior officers when he himself was a mere armed civilian of twenty-six years of age, found that they listened most attentively to him, the more so when, to emphasise a point, he added, 'My G.O.C. said . . .' Moreover, Borthwick noticed the significant manner in which Hobart's ideas often foreshadowed much of what came to pass, for it seemed to him that Hobart's appreciation of the manner in which the battle should be managed in Normandy was perfectly in tune and sometimes ahead of the Commander-in-Chief's own pronouncements. Either they read each other's minds with fluent accuracy or they discussed matters with unrestrained frankness. There are very few records of what transpired between Montgomery and Hobart whenever they met in private, but it is inconceivable that a very considerable exchange of ideas by direct or indirect means did not take place. Clearly Montgomery sought advice and Hobart, we know, was the last man in the world to withhold it.

De Guingand has this to say of Hobart's impact on 21st Army Group:

Some of the staff under me would become terrified when they knew General Hobo was about. He was such a go-getter that they never really knew until he had left what new commitment they had been persuaded to accept. I found his visits acted as a tonic, for his enthusiastic and confident nature would never consider failure. An answer *would* be found—and it usually was.

During a period of four weeks a series of demonstrations showing the entire menagerie of 'Funnies' were put on by 79th Armoured Division for the benefit of Eisenhower, Brooke, Montgomery, their senior commanders and staff. There was only one serious omission—Montgomery's failure to see the C.D.L.s. According to Hobart it occurred from a shortage of time, but the outcome generated a loss of co-ordinated opinion amongst the top commanders, for Eisenhower, on seeing the C.D.L.s, became so enthusiastic that he insisted they should not be used until the Americans had them and could use them in force at the same time as the British, while Montgomery, with his mind concentrated on landing in France by daylight, had no need for C.D.L. in the initial assault. The C.D.L.s never recovered from this set-back, but the other devices were more fortunate.

De Guingand tells us that after a demonstration of D.D. tanks at Studland Bay, Montgomery held a conference in his train from which evolved the decision to land D.D.s first in the assault. After that the arrival of the other specialised armour would not be controlled by any fixed rules—'a "menu" would be selected to suit the problem presented by the particular beach in question'. These fundamental resolutions opened the way to a resumption of detailed planning of the specialised armoured assault technique in a thoroughly realistic setting, and also illustrated Montgomery's understanding of the value of Hobart's work.

Montgomery's immediate grasp of the value of each 'Funny' impressed Hobart enormously, as he told Liddell Hart, 'Very quick to understand—said Americans must have a fair share of everything.' But Ike, according to Hobart, was 'not so discerning', although clearly swept away by the D.D. Harry Butcher, Eisenhower's naval aide, not present in person at a demonstration on the 27th January, tells us in his book that to his chief the D.D. was far away the most exciting gadget he had seen. He heard that Eisenhower had gone for a ride in one and had actually steered it during its amphibious run. The upshot of

Eisenhower's visit on the 27th was a firm order for D.D. tanks for the American assault divisions, followed by the use of C.D.L.s after the assault at an appropriate moment in the subsequent battles.

Perhaps because the other devices had not struck his imagination, Eisenhower left the final decision on American participation with flails and A.V.R.E.s to Bradley, and the latter, in turn, passed the problem to his staff. There might have been difficulties (none of them insurmountable) in training American crews to handle the Churchill A.V.R.E.: in any case, had they wished it, British A.V.R.E. units could have been attached to the Americans for the assault. Ostensibly, the Americans rejected the A.V.R.E. and Crab because of difficulties in training, despite the fact that the Crab was mounted on the American-built Sherman tank. That the Americans appreciated the difficulties of overcoming obstacles is shown by their attempts to develop a super rocket Petard of their own: demonstrated in front of Corps and Divisional Commanders at Slapton Sands, it performed with miserably poor results, appearing to threaten friend before foe. It is with relief that the historian of the 70th U.S. Tank Battalion records the discarding of this rocket launcher in favour of tank guns. Having failed with their own weapon, the Americans rejected all else and continued to rely on conventional weapons without further investigation of the problem. Perhaps a strain of national pride ran through their consideration, but an apparent failure on the part of Bradley to command, and of his staff to study the obstacle problem objectively, lay at the back of Hobart's mind when he wrote about American officers to Liddell Hart on the 3rd March:

. . . those I have met with the brilliant exceptions of Eisenhower, Bedell Smith and Rose have not been impressive.

This may be due to a certain shyness or closeness. But when asked for opinions, they appear to me to hand out a string of platitudes . . .

On the other hand, the Other Ranks, some of whom I have trained, are thorough, reliable and keen. It is the officer class that seems so weak.

Yet when it came to acquiring D.D.s, Eisenhower tackled the matter in a wholly characteristic manner. The D.D., as Hobart wrote, 'was the one thing we could not provide, as we had great struggles over its production for the Sherman and endless obstruction and were doubtful if we would get even the minimum requirement by D-Day ourselves. I told Ike this and asked if he could get it made in U.S.A. The upshot was that I got all the blueprints plus the best one of my experts from Birmingham the same day and they were flown to U.S.A. in a special plane next day. The first 100 D.D. Shermans were delivered from U.S.A. at Liverpool within 6 weeks'.

The final allocations of specialised armour to the assault were confirmed on the 10th February, the scene dramatically described by Hobart in a letter to Dorrie.

Biting wind and slurries of sleet. Not the best conditions for demonstrating things to senior officers. However—they paid attention. I brought them in here and gave them a mug of mulligatawny soup each. And the results were satisfactory.

Today were the important ones. Who made decisions. Monty's CGS and Brig S.D. and Chief Engr; 2nd Br Army Comdr; Comdr U.S.A. Army Group and his Chief of Staff and an Arm Div Comdr; Engineer in Chief, and DCIGS.

I shut everyone out of the room when we got back—to our mulligatawny—and as we munched sandwiches, in 40 min, got definite decisions on a whole number of points that have been hanging fire for months.

There followed an interesting assessment of the respective commanders of the British 2nd Army and the American 1st U.S. Army.

At dinner here last night I had Bimbo Dempsey on one side, Bradley on the other.

On these two men the success or failure of our invasion will depend. During the radio news—with its stuff about the Anzio landing—which presents a pretty grim outlook to a soldier who understands the situation—it was almost theatrical. In a few months' time. I think they are both good chaps. Straight, honest and capable.

The third of the trio, Freddy de Guingand, Monty's C of S, is much cleverer and quicker than either: and younger. But—he has not the responsibility.

Now the complete bill for specialised armour in the invasion could be presented, and the exact number of equipments with the men to crew them calculated. Now too the assault techniques could be thrashed out and settled in detail. For the Americans, three battalions' worth of D.D.s had to be trained, the 70th, 741st and 743rd U.S. Tank Battalions: time was short but they started on Valentines at Fritton on the 2nd February—only a week after Eisenhower's decision. The 3rd Canadian Division, due to take part in the assault as part of Crocker's 1st Corps, already had two armoured regiments, the Fort Garry Horse and the 1st Hussars, in training on D.D.s in December.

In November a third assault regiment R.E.—the 42nd—had been converted to A.V.R.E.s and started to learn about the growing miscellany of devices which experience and intense experiments showed could be tacked on to their strange vehicle. The Crab flails were beginning to arrive at a depressingly slow rate with 30th Armoured Brigade, soon to be under the command of Brigadier Nigel Duncan, allowing a start to be made with the complete Lane Gapping Teams planned for D-Day.

As C.D.L. went out of the assault there appeared in its place a new 'Funny'—the Churchill Crocodile flame-throwing tank, which had been 'born' later than its sister 'Funnies' and weaned by the Petroleum Warfare Department in conjunction with the firm of Lagonda. In fact a number of different experimental flame-throwing tanks had been made earlier in the war and one called O.K.E. went, but unhappily sank, with the Canadians at Dieppe. Not until 1943 did the idea really catch on and only then after Hobart had seen it at Orford, and personally buttonholed Sir Graham Cunningham of the Ministry of Supply to get him to underwrite the production of the Crocodile prior to persuading Brooke to include flame-throwers in his charter. Even so, not until the end of March 1944 were sixty production versions of the gun and its ancilliary trailer ready for the first Crocodile regiment—the 141st Regiment R.A.C. (The Buffs). Like so many other special equipments, this one suffered from the ignorance engendered by close secrecy and the resultant misunderstanding of its characteristics and functions. Nevertheless they were ready just in time for D-Day, only because Hobart had given a hearty push to the scheme a year before and then maintained pressure all along the line of development and production, chiefly through the medium of his one-time adjutant—Brigadier Yeo.

Systematically the plan of invasion took shape, each stage enlivened by the discovery of unforeseen problems. By mid-February it became apparent that there must be a senior member of 79th Armoured Division present at every level of command down to Division to advise commanders and their staffs on the best way to use specialised armour. As a start, command of all 79th Armoured Division troops in the assault was given to Brigadier Duncan. A protracted debate revolved round acceptance of the final loading tables for each of the tank landing craft (L.C.T.s) and eventually something like eleven different permutations to suit two different classes of L.C.T. were devised in close consultation with the Navy—all the old hesitations having totally dissolved to be replaced by real mutual understanding.

Frequently some new problem raised alarms and temporary despondency leading to a redrafting of plans: often the trouble had some natural phenomenon at bottom or the enemy had disclosed a new type of defence to which no antidote had been prescribed. The case of the blue clay was the most dramatic of the 'unforeseen natural discoveries'. Geologists had hinted for some time that some beaches contained strips of a peculiar soft blue clay (the last traces of ancient forests) saying that vehicles would bog in it. A daring reconnaissance on the Normandy beaches brought back samples of blue clay and confirmed the geologists' estimates. Montgomery told Hobart to devise equipment able to cross the soft patches and to integrate it with the assault teams. Hobo formed a special Trials Wing under Major Drew in less than thirty-six hours at Brancaster in Norfolk where an example of blue clay was to be found. Lorries rushed all over England 'raiding' ordnance depots for every imaginable appliance which might help solve the problem, while the R.E.M.E. workshops, working round the clock under their commander, Charles King, began manufacturing a weird collection of medieval looking contraptions.

Of the more improbable devices, a huge rocket-driven carpet-laying wheel was rejected, although some sort of carpet offered the best solution. Earlier in the war a roll of chespaling and hessian had been mounted on the front of the light Bren-gun carrier to lay a path over barbed wire obstacles for infantry to cross on foot. An enormous carpet made of coir and tubular scaffolding rolled on a drum rotating on the front horns of an A.V.R.E. produced a device which worked. The designs were sealed, and the workshops started to turn out a typical 79th Armoured Division improvisation which worked just well enough to do its job.

In mid-March somebody suggested D.D. tanks would be highly vulnerable if the Germans set fire to the sea in the approaches to the beaches as the British had planned to do in the face of the German invasion threat in 1940. So a D.D., manned by a volunteer crew, sailed into a patch of flaming fuel thrown on the water to put it to the test. To the watchers this was one of the more spectacular trials and everybody, Hobo amongst them, heaved a sigh of relief as the D.D. emerged from the smoke and flames, its canvas sides steaming but intact.

Many a trial and every exercise rushed by urgency became fraught with danger, yet sound management, aided by good fortune, kept the casualties remarkably low. Then on one night in April the D.D. crews of the 4/7DG suffered their most harrowing experience as told by their historian :

Shortly after the launch had taken place—it was just at dawn— the weather underwent a change for the worse. The wind increased, the waves grew bigger, and the tanks began to get into difficulties. Heavy waves beat against the screens and sloshed over into the tanks, which never seemed to rise high enough to breast the swell. The effect of shipping water was cumulative, as the clearing pumps were not big enough to deal with water in this quantity, and so the more they shipped the lower they sank and the more they shipped.

Finally they reached the point at which the weight of water shipped was too great, and one after another tanks began to plunge to the bottom like stones.

Bravery amounting to heroism was shown everywhere that morning. One cannot praise too much the drivers who remained in their seats, in water up to the waist, but knowing that the tank must be kept going at all costs. When conditions got too bad and the drivers were half submerged, most commanders brought them on deck and managed by opening the engine covers to keep the engine going by remote control.

When a screen collapses, as it is almost bound to do if the tank sinks, it collapses inwards and the great danger is that it will trap the crew who are standing on deck. This did happen in several cases.

Six tanks sank and six men were drowned that time, but their loss was not without its reward, for it led to further investigation of the D.D.; shortly before D-Day the discovery of a weakness in the front top rail of the screen showed why it bent under heavy pounding, and immediate steps were taken to strengthen the weak member. There is never an end to rectifications of this sort, but the hallmark of 79th Armoured Division's trials combined a sense of urgency, speed and thoroughness suited to the excitement and drama of the occasion such as normal peacetime research cannot match.

As the great day approached and the troops finished their training, moved into their concentration areas to waterproof their vehicles for the last time, checked over every detail of their equipment, then to have their part in the invasion explained to them, chance alone threatened preparedness. For the fighting men purposeful toil never ended, but for the planners there came the time, a few days before the sailing, when only routine matters remained, along with the agony of waiting—and the overriding uncertainty of the weather. Training, planning, and equipment were good—all could be set to naught by chance.

*   *   *   *   *

On 7th April General Montgomery had given out his orders with supreme confidence. His first aim, 'the establishment of a firm base from which to peg out claims forward', the keynote 'deep penetration with armour early'. Already a paper he had circulated in March had gone into greater detail on lines that could not fail to meet with Hobart's approval. 'The tank is initially the best supporting weapon. But the infantry must marry-up with their own supporting weapons early, and release the tanks for

offensive action. . . .' Dealing with the composition of breaching
parties with flails and A.V.R.E.s: 'Each breaching party, or forward body, must have its own commander . . . the [infantry]
battalion commander must be . . . well forward in front of his
battalion so that he can take charge of the battle on the beach
at the earliest moment. . . . The Bn Commander should be in a
tank.' For Hobart these were the fruits not just of a year's work
with specialised armour, but of two decades of scheming, teaching, pleading and bullying.

The story of D-Day, the awful pause when the worsening
weather brought about a twenty-four-hour postponement and
threatened the entire plan, the picture of the armada closing the
Norman coastline, the sight of the airborne forces, the rever-
beration of the bombardment and the ordered sequence of the
craft riding up the beaches to disgorge their contents against the
Atlantic Wall—all have been described before in minutest detail
and will not be repeated here.

Hobo was in England close to Montgomery's Tactical H.Q.
on D-Day, standing the night before outside the doors behind
which Eisenhower made his gallant, lonely decision to 'go' despite the hazards of the weather. He asked Admiral Ramsay, as he
came forth from the room, what the chances were. 'He was evidently gravely concerned. He said, "We've made the decision.
We are going. It will be finally confirmed at midnight. The gale
is bad but Meteor hold out hopes that there will be a lull for some
hours from midnight. Anyway we are going." '

Hobart and all of those who had staked their endeavours on
armour in the forefront of the invasion, focussed their attention
on two critical aspects of the landing. They wanted to know
how each device had stood up to its first full-blast operation
against the enemy and, concurrently, the manner in which the
crews, the majority of whom had never seen action before, had
coped under fire. Nobody doubted that all would be well, for the
confidence that had grown up during training could not be gain-
said—the height of satisfaction would come from the magnitude of success, but this was directly related to the second of
the vital questions—the comparison of performance between
those beaches where specialised armour had been used in full,

those where it came only fragmentarily into action and those where it was almost totally absent.

Naturally, an exact comparison could not be made in respect of performance on different beaches. The experience of the combatants varied widely—some, like those in the 50th British Division and the 1st U.S. Infantry Division, were veterans of the campaigns in North Africa and Sicily: 3rd British Division, on the other hand, had not experienced action since it had been evacuated from Dunkirk but had spent the past three years doing little else but rehearse the invasion: others, like the 3rd Canadian and 29th U.S. Division, were meeting the enemy face to face for the first time. The opposition varied too: only on Utah, the most westerly beach, was it intermittent; elsewhere resistance mounted a uniform pattern, except on the beach to the east of Utah—the one called Omaha—where it was fierce and unyielding. In some sectors the bombardment hit all its targets, in others it missed, but nowhere did it subjugate the defence entirely and everywhere tanks and infantry were beset with the problem of fighting on the shore and for every bound they took inland. A common denominator was the foul weather and rough seas which deluded the German High Command into believing that no landing could take place (and therefore slowed their reactions because it caught them psychologically unprepared) but it tested the skill of the assailants to the utmost and, inevitably, imposed exacting problems of seamanship on the sailors and the crews of the D.D. tanks, as well as a severe strain on the internal organs of the soldiers themselves. Not on one single beach could the original plan be carried through unmodified, and invariably the weather dictated the changes.

Another critical imponderable was the strength of each beach linked to the state of its obstacles and minefields and the nature of the routes leading inland. Utah beach, smooth and shallow and undominated by any natural feature, suffered constriction inland from extensive inundations, so amongst its narrow exits, with the assistance of airborne troops dropped beforehand, the severest fighting could be expected. Omaha beach, totally different again, was dominated by high ground intersected by several pronounced natural exits or 'draws' up which an assault might easily be channelled. The ground beyond grew close, ideally suited to defence and not in the least conducive to mobile, offensive action with armoured forces.

To the east of Utah and Omaha (the objectives allotted to the U.S. 1st Army) stretched the British sector from Arromanches to Ouistreham, where the beaches were smooth and gently sloping, but where the blue clay patches which had given rise to the need for the A.V.R.E. carpet were to be found. The natural exits from these beaches were not dominated by terrain, but were cluttered instead by seaside villas, little towns and ports, and thickly sown minefields. Further inland more open ground than elsewhere in the whole of the Allied assault front invited intervention by the enemy Panzer divisions, grouped in depth from Caen to the hinterland of Metropolitan France. Only close to the pivot of Caen could the clash of armoured forces take place at once and, therefore, here it was essential to seize a deep bridgehead at once to act as a cushion to the turbulence of a mobile encounter.

As was the intention on every other beach, the British aimed to land at half-tide when the obstacles on the beach would be above water and most easily negotiated and neutralised. This meant that the advance from the water's edge to the sea-wall had to cross some two hundred yards of open beach, a fearful prospect had it been the intention to lead with infantry on their own. It was only with specialised armour available that the adoption of this course could be contemplated because the tanks in the van of the assault, aiming their guns point-blank through the slits of the pill-boxes, gave the infantry a chance to cross the open strands largely unmolested.

Unfortunately, on the front of 50th Division on the western flank of the British landing opposite Le Hamel and La Rivière, the roughness of the sea forbade the launching of the 4th/7th Dragoon Guard's D.D.s, which fell behind and eventually waded ashore from their L.C.T.s after the infantry. Therefore the L.C.T.s carrying Crabs and A.V.R.E.s found themselves ashore first and were forced to carry out the dual task of subduing the defences while clearing paths through the minefields, over the soft clay, and opening routes inland. On 50th Division beaches, out of twelve lanes attempted, five failed, the highest rate of failure on any part of the British front. The choice of the Crab and A.V.R.E. commanders between the need to 'gap', the necessity to fight for their own survival and the desire to support the infantry as they landed in the next wave, was hard; and the extent of their sacrifice in giving priority to the first and third choices to the exclusion of the natural inclination of self-protection can be measured by the speed with which 50th Division crossed the beaches, the way the enemy defences were overcome and the depth of six or seven miles' penetration achieved by nightfall, costed against the loss of nine Crabs and six A.V.R.E.s from various causes. Nowhere did the plan work to perfection and mostly success came from improvisation and the availability of sufficient armour for use as a contingency reserve. Time and again the ability of Crabs and A.V.R.E.s to 'fight' as well as 'breach' was decisive—they even found themselves leading the D.D.s, after the latter had landed, on the advance inland towards Bayeux.

The 7th Canadian Brigade came ashore to the east of 50th Division on either side of the estuary of the River Seulles at Courseulles. Conditions here were the reverse of 50th Division's because eight D.D. tanks from A Squadron 1st Canadian Hussars, on swimming in from only eight hundred yards out, found themselves supporting the infantry alone because the L.C.T.s carrying Crabs and A.V.R.E.s were thirty-five minutes late. Nevertheless, fire from the D.D. tanks at the water's edge temporarily silenced the immediate coastal defences but, as at Dieppe in 1942, neither tanks nor infantry could get far beyond the sea-wall until the obstacles had been destroyed. To the east of the estuary a similar situation arose where fourteen D.D.s got ashore against light enemy resistance, but where the Crabs, flailing up and off the beach, struck mines as they turned, and a third Crab 'flogging' round them, became bogged near a crater and a demolished culvert. Then an A.V.R.E. trying to fill the crater with its fascine became bogged too, and the gap had to be completed by bulldozing a second fascine into the hole before laying a S.B.G. Bridge from yet another A.V.R.E. over the culvert. This all took place under heavy fire, at a cost of three lives, a price

A.C.—U

which would have been multiplied manifold and might still have been unrewarded had armoured vehicles not been there. But because of delays in gapping, exploitation from this beach slowed down, causing succeeding waves of the assault to pile up on the foreshore. The impetus of the assault came here from the Canadian infantry, who, once clear of the beaches, marched inland practically on their own, but with failing momentum in the absence of the armour held back at the choked exits.

At Bernières, where 8th Canadian Brigade landed, the roughness of the sea caused an inadvertent reversal of the timetable. Since the D.D.s of the Fort Garry Horse were never launched and did not land until an hour after the infantry, and L.C.T.s carrying Crabs and A.V.R.E.s were delayed, the infantry were left to face every element of disaster. Indeed, one company of the Queen's Own Rifles landed square in the beaten zone of a German strongpoint and lost half its complement as it ran across one hundred yards of beach. Here the fighting spirit of the Canadians was extraordinary, as unassisted and as if inspired by the misfortunes of the shattered timetable, they cleared the beach at the double ahead of the Crabs and A.V.R.E.s coming ashore to set about four copy-book Lane Clearance operations under fire. Then, once gaps were cleared, the crew commanders turned their weapons on the enemy positions remaining in action, although in places the surging enthusiasm of the Canadians impeded the firing of Petards because their men had pressed too close to lucrative targets. On this beach it was a free-for-all; a Bridge A.V.R.E., knocked out as it disembarked by a 50 mm anti-tank gun, was avenged by a sister A.V.R.E. dumping a Flying Dustbin on to the gun position : Element 'C', blocking one ramp off the beach, was demolished by Petard fire, the ramp flailed clear and the barbed wire wrapped round the flail drum freed; then an A.V.R.E. with a fascine filled a ditch beyond, finally opening the way for 9th Canadian Brigade, with tanks, to come through on their way to the deepest penetration of the day—right to the outskirts of Caen.

To 3rd British Division fell the most important task on D-Day, that of linking up with the 6th Airborne Division holding the eastern front and driving in a deep thrust to seize Caen.

In front of the seaside resort of Lion-sur-Mer, 8th Infantry Brigade, the spearhead of 3rd British Division, was assisted by the full menu of specialised armoured support. Thirty-four D.D.s of 13/18th Hussars were launched a full five thousand yards from the shore and thirty-one, by superb feats of seamanship, reached the water's edge and opened fire on the enemy. Notwithstanding the accurate shooting of the D.D.s, the Crabs and A.V.R.E.s still sustained losses from constant fire, as they worked their way up the beaches and through the rows of villas. Bullshorn Ploughs were employed here and several crews from disabled A.V.R.E.s came into action on foot. One Crab flailed up the beach and straight over a troublesome German gunpit, followed by an A.V.R.E. laying its bridge across the wreckage. Close on their heels came a battalion of infantry to join with the 13/18th Hussars in a drive for the Périers Ridge and the first brush with German tanks.

The beach at La Breche, one of the few British beaches subject to observed fire from inland, was thought to be the toughest nut of all to crack. It was tough, and had not the 13/18th Hussars arrived in so timely a manner the fate of the Crabs and A.V.R.E.s might have been sealed, for the leading vehicles came ashore under fire and the beach remained a most unhealthy place until late in the afternoon. Every lane was driven through with a singularly devoted persistence; as one Crab or A.V.R.E. after another was hit and stopped, others moved forward from their L.C.T.s to take over and complete the task. When a badly laid S.B.G. bridge blocked a lane, a fresh one was painstakingly driven past it. Where another S.B.G. was put down askew, A.V.R.E. crews dismounted under small arms fire and placed charges by hand against the dunes to blast through a gap: in this lane all the Crabs and A.V.R.E.s were knocked out. In another, where all the Crabs stopped, disabled, the task of locating and disarming the mines was completed by hand. The single-minded determination of the 79th Armoured Division crews in hacking their way through regardless of cost did more than guarantee a clear run for the follow up—they literally dominated the show in the midst of a furious battle. And when, later, 185th Infantry Brigade (which, it happened, was at one time the lorried infantry formation in 79th Armoured Division) came ashore to strike for Caen, Crabs went with it and the D.D.s helped the infantry clean out the strongpoints which still directed fire on to the beaches from further inland.

The 4th Commando belonging to the 1st Special Services Brigade led the advance from La Breche to Ouistreham in the van of the rest of the brigade, its task to link up with 6th Airborne Division, cross the River Orne and exploit eastwards. But although specialised armour had not been intended to take part, events and chance decided otherwise. When 4th Commando became held up in Ouistreham, with their C.O. severely wounded, the A.V.R.E.s of 79th Squadron were called from reserve after completing their original task on the beaches. The bald statements in the squadron log outline the manner in which they dominated the subsequent proceedings:

1500 hours Commanding Officer 4 Commando reports to Squadron Leader that lock gates and bridge at Ouistreham held by enemy. Ask Squadron Leader for assistance. Squadron Leader promises to take over since Commanding Officer is badly wounded. Squadron Leader asks for infantry and gets none.

1530 hours Squadron Leader moves off with 10 AVREs. Enemy is surprised and West bank taken, but enemy blew East span of bridge.

1630 hours After intense Besa and Petard fire, enemy surrenders. 6 officers and 51 other ranks taken prisoner with 3 anti-tank guns and equipment.

Squadron deploys and takes up position on West bank with Bren posts on East bank. Locks and remainder of bridges inspected for demolition charges and are made safe.

2000 hours Four AVREs move off to support 2 Royal Ulster Rifles at Benouville. Remainder hold lock gates until relieved by infantry the following morning.

And a troop of 13/18th Hussars D.D.s, whose duty it was to remain with its squadron to assist in the subjugation of the last beach defences, on leaving the beaches, to quote the regiment's history:

... turned left and disappeared towards Ouistreham, where it became involved with the Commandos under Lord Lovat. All efforts to recall it failed. It eventually reached the bridge over the Orne and was not rallied till the evening.

In war the reasons for success are multifarious and often fortuitous. Luck plays a leading, and sometimes, sinister part, but it can be mitigated by sound, detailed foresight and planning and by the sort of meticulous training which takes into account every conceivable occurrence and implants in the minds of officers and men much more than mere method and technique. The best training is psychologically aimed at building up superb morale even without the existence of previous experience in the subjects taught. This kind of morale, the sort admitting no defeat, was the kind of spirit inspiring the crews of the specialised armour on the 6th June 1944.

The success of each landing resolved generally in proportion to the success of specialised armour, and on the British sector one sort or another of it had been landed in the van of the assault on every beach but one. On that one beach, where the infantry had been compelled to lead, the casualties in men were disproportionately high compared with all the other beaches. Where D.D.s found themselves on their own and the gapping devices were late or severely hampered, the subsequent infantry casualties mounted somewhat high (notably in 3rd British Division's sector) and deployment inland became difficult to achieve at speed. But on those beaches where the gapping devices led and the D.D.s arrived late, encouraging results were achieved at a high price in Crabs and A.V.R.E.s, although low cost in lives. The proof of the vital part played by Hobart's men on the 6th June is strikingly illuminated by results: British casualties were remarkably light, yet across the entire front penetrations of from six to nine miles inland took place. It was shown that the failure of one or more elements from a varied mass of armoured devices did not presage total failure since other types automatically made good the deficiency—but always the factor of protection given by armour ensured economy in lives and, above all, decision.

Similar conclusions could be drawn from the American Sector when, at Utah Beach, thirty-two D.D. tanks of the 70th U.S. Tank Battalion launched two miles instead of four miles out as originally intended. There is a divergence of opinion as to whether or not they reached the beach before or after the first wave of infantry. The Campaign Study by the Historical Division of the U.S. Army, repeated by their Official History, says they beached 'approximately 15 minutes after the first assault wave'. Chester Wilmot in his *The Struggle for Europe* quotes the commander of the leading American regiment (Colonel J. S. Van Fleet) and prisoners' reports as saying the tanks arrived first. Undoubtedly the surprising conversion to tanks on the water-front of what had appeared, to the Germans, as small infantry landing craft, came as a terrible shock. Direct opposition collapsed immediately with the result that heavy shell-fire from inland and the perils of the minefields alone restricted work on the beach. The mines were dealt with by teams of demolition squads who waded ashore pushing rafts and carrying sixty pounds of equipment each, but because A.V.R.E.s and Crabs had been rejected, the only specialised armour used, apart from D.D.s, was armoured bulldozers. The extent of the obstacles at Utah hindered in no way like those at Omaha or on the British beaches, yet the laborious manual clearance of this one beach under shell-fire cost forty-five casualties and compared most unfavourably with the one hundred and sixty-nine lost by 79th Armoured Division on three, more heavily defended beaches throughout the *whole* of D-Day in the face of every conceivable opposition.

At Utah the clearance of the beach was simplified by the dominance of the D.D.s, but at Omaha only two D.D.s arrived and everything else went wrong from the outset. Regardless of the turbulence of the sea, twenty-nine D.D.s from 741st U.S. Tank Battalion launched from six thousand yards and, of these, twenty-seven foundered. Engines were swamped, the bilge pumps could not cope with the inrush of water, and in several cases the struts supporting the canvas screens failed. There are recorded instances on D-Day of crews shoring up the screens by bracing their shoulders against the weakened points. Later three more of 741st Battalion's D.D.s waded direct from L.C.T.s and on their right the 743rd Tank Battalion had all its tanks brought in in this way. The Americans have been self-critical about the state of the training and maintenance of their D.D.s at this beach, but a heavy burden of responsibility must fall on those who made the decision to launch so far out to sea.

Having reached the beach, there the assault stuck. The enemy position was powerful, manned by a good division in strong-points which had missed the heart of the bombardment, over-looking a mass of obstacles and minefields. In most cases the infantry became pinned to the beach, while the handful of tanks could shoot only from the water's edge since no lanes could be cleared up to and over the dunes and sea-walls. The fate of the heavily laden beach clearance teams coming ashore with their thinly armoured bulldozers is told in the U.S. Army Historical Division's account:

The Army-Navy Special Engineer Task Force had one of the most important and difficult missions of the landing. Their chances of clearing gaps through the obstacles in the half-hour allotted were lessened by accidents on the approach to the beach. Delays in load-ing from LCTs to LCMs and in finding their way to the beaches re-sulted in half of the 16 assault teams reaching shore 10 minutes or more late. Only five teams hit their appointed sector, most of them being carried eastward with the result that Dog Beach (the 116th RCT zone) received much less than the effort scheduled. As a fur-ther effect of mislandings, at least three teams came in where no infantry or tanks were present to give protective fire.

Men burdened with equipment and explosives were excellent tar-gets for enemy fire as they unloaded in water often several feet deep. Of 16 dozers only 6 got to the beach in working condition ,and 3 of these were immediately disabled by artillery hits. Much equip-ment, including nearly all buoys and poles for marking lanes, was lost or destroyed before it could be used. Eight navy personnel of Team 11 were dragging the preloaded rubber boat off their LCM when an artillery shell burst just above the load of explosives and set off the primacord. One of the eight survived. Another shell hit the LCM of Team 14, detonating explosives on the deck and killing all navy personnel. Team 15 was pulling in its rubber boat through the surf when a mortar scored a direct hit and touched off the explosives, killing three men and wounding four. Support Team F came in about 0700. A first shell hit the ramp, throwing three men into the water. As the vessel drifted off out of control, another hit squarely on the bow, killing 15 of the team. Only five army personnel from this craft reached shore.

Despite such disasters and under continued intense fire, the engineers got to work on obstacles wherever they landed and with whatever equipment and explosives they could salvage. Some of the teams arriving a few minutes late found the rapidly advancing tide already into the lower obstacles. Infantry units landing behind schedule or delayed in starting up the beach came through the demolition parties as they worked, and thereby impeded their progress. One of the three dozers left in operation was prevented from manoeuvering freely by riflemen who tried to find shelter behind it from the intense fire. As a final handicap, there were instances where teams had fixed their charges, were ready to blow their lane, and were prevented by the fact that infantry were passing through or were taking cover in the obstacles. When Team 7 was set to fire, an LCVP came crashing into the obstacles, smashed through the timbers, and set off seven mines; the charge could not be blown. In another case, vehicles passed through the prepared area and caused misfire by cutting the primacord fuse linking the charges. A naval officer, about to pull the twin-junction igniters to explode his charge, was hit by a piece of shrapnel that cut off his finger and the two fuses. The charge laid by Team 12 went off but at heavy cost. Their preparations completed for a 30-yard gap, the team was just leaving the area to take cover when a mortar shell struck the primacord. The premature explosion killed and wounded 19 engineers and some infantry nearby.

In net result, the demolition task force blew six complete gaps through all bands of obstacles, and three partial gaps. Of the six, only two were in the 116th's half of the beach, and four were on Easy Red . . ., a fact which may have influenced later landing chances. Owing to the loss of equipment, only one of the gaps could be marked, and this diminished their value under high-water conditions. Their first effort made, the demolition teams joined the other assault forces on the shingle or sea wall and waited for the next low tide to resume their work. Casualties for the Special Engineer Task Force, including navy personnel, ran to 41 per cent for D-Day, most of them suffered in the first half-hour.

On Utah Beach the presence of D.D.s helped persuade a rather feeble enemy to collapse at the outset. The infantry and engineers were lucky here in that their opponents were not as determined and well organised as at Omaha. But deliberate assaults planned over a long period should be capable of circumventing the pitfalls of misfortune. On Omaha, where everything went awry, there was no reserve to supplement the supreme courage of the American soldier. That day a nation which rightly prides itself on its whole-hearted use of machines to reduce labour, put machines aside and thrust men, well nigh unprotected, into the teeth of a deadly fire. Had A.V.R.E.s and Crabs been present at Omaha it is almost certain that men's lives would have been saved and more progress made at far less effort. As it was the Americans were, at best, only five hundred yards inland by nightfall and in the exits from the beaches work still went on to clear minefields which had already exacted a fearful toll. Chester Wilmot has advanced the opinion that:

At Bradley's HQ . . . Montgomery's plan for armoured assault was regarded as just another example of British under-confidence and over-insurance. . . .

This may have been so—it is an important characteristic of any fighting organisation that it should have confidence in its own methods and experience. Americans are rarely slow to adopt new ideas when they are shown to be advantageous, but they had not experienced the defences of Dieppe and none of their landings in North Africa or southern Europe had been heavily opposed. So it seems much more likely that when Bradley's staff came to study the problem of clearing the beaches they failed, from lack of experience, to evaluate the real strength of the defences to be overcome and the multitude of snags which could arise if there was a deterioration in any one phase of the plan. They had a justifiable faith in the pugnacious ability of their own soldiers and in the event, at a high price, that ability made up for the miscalculation of commanders and staff.

It was as well that the Germans were unable to launch a heavy counter-attack at Omaha when the initial assault faltered on the sands. In the British sector a diluted armoured counter-stroke actually reached the coast between the 3rd Canadian and 3rd British Divisions on the evening of D-Day. Its weak composition and late arrival happened only partially as the result of Allied counter-action : fundamentally the fault lay with the slowness with which the German High Command made up its mind and ordered the counter-attack. If for lack of A.V.R.E.s and Crabs the set-back at Omaha had been repeated on the British Sector, as well it might have been on the front of 50th Division and part of the front of 3rd Canadian Division where D.D.s failed to land on time, and if the Germans had launched their Panzer Divisions from Caen promptly, the outcome of the invasion might have been poised on disaster. Undoubtedly, in those circumstances, even if a foothold had been retained, there would have been many more at home to mourn its achievement, and the task of breaking out made many times more difficult to accomplish.

Universal credit has been given by historians to the part specialised armour played in ensuring the success of the invasion at an astonishingly low cost—and Hobart has received his share of the praise. It should be remembered that the invasion would have taken place in June no matter how much specialised armour was ready for action by then—every other conventional weapon was to hand and every seaborne assault up to then had been of the conventional pattern. Only because Hobart pressed so hard and often took the law into his own hands did it become possible to throw *a mass* of specialised armour with a high, orthodox fighting capability ashore—without his drive and determination it might only have been a dribble of semi-effective machines treated as a bonus, supplement to orthodox assault. He was not there to witness the victory—but a great share belonged to him all the same.

*   *   *   *   *

The first British Armoured Division to land in Normandy after the sea assault was the 7th—the Desert Rats—followed seven days later (on the 13th) by the 11th—the Black Bulls.

A proud Hobart set sail for Normandy on the 8th June to visit the beaches, to assess the state of his own men and machines and see for himself, on the 13th, all his creations at the front together. Getting there so early was, in itself, a triumph of determination and subterfuge. His Tactical H.Q. had been refused shipping space, but persistent badgering at last extracted a slot for one vehicle which Hobo promptly said would be a D.U.K.W. (a very large amphibious vehicle) and filled with a jeep, a motor-cycle, quite extensive radio equipment and skeleton staff.

Not everything gave him complete satisfaction, for the magic of success of the specialised devices had begun to recoil to their disadvantage. From the beginning specialised armour had been in short supply and on D-Day the losses in machines heavy. Twelve out of fifty Crabs and twenty-two out of 120 A.V.R.E.s had been destroyed. Many others had received damage capable of repair in due course, but avoidable wastage exceeded replacement. A.V.R.E.s were in great demand in the van of the attack both against the remaining fortress positions as well as conventional field works, but Hobart noted how commanders forgot how short was the range of the Petard and that:

The Infantry are apt to claim that its mere presence has a moral effect on the enemy and, therefore, expose AVREs to fire which cannot be returned.

In the same way he found Crabs sometimes being used to flail when lifting of the mines by hand could be achieved more economically. Returning to England a few days later with a sheaf of notes containing information from which action in improving equipment could be started, he brought, too, a resolve to become firmly established in Normandy himself as soon as possible in order to exert pressure to prevent the misuse and wastage of specialised armour. At the same time he schemed to widen its scope while, in the meantime, Brigadier Duncan remained in charge of Crabs, A.V.R.E.s and Crocodiles doing the best he could to ensure their correct application until his Divisional Commander came to stay.

Not until the 22nd July was Hobart's Main H.Q. finally set up in Normandy, although in the intervening weeks he alternated between England and his Tactical H.Q. located as close as possible to Montgomery's H.Q. In England he harried the authorities, the factories and his other units to adopt and absorb the lessons from the battlefield: in France he branched out in other directions, for it was here that he could employ his experience in close proximity to the battle and, at the same time, indulge a fancy for action under fire.

By mid-July Hobart and Duncan between them had begun to establish a working arrangement with the field formations in regard to the employment of specialised armour in a variety of situations. When it came to assaulting fortifications associated with the Atlantic Wall from the landward side, the techniques developed for the beach assault were easily adaptable, its classic application being the final reduction on the 17th June of the heavily defended casemates protecting a radar station isolated and besieged at Douvres. The 79th Armoured Division History describes the meticulous planning of this operation—a masterpiece of combined distraction, concentration and thorough execution:

The position consisted of two strong-points, deep underground with strong reinforced concrete above, the whole surrounded by mines and wire in a 40-yard-deep belt. The defences included five 50 mm anti-tank guns, numerous 20 mm and light automatics and 'Tobruk' shelters with twin Spandaus. The garrison consisted of 5 officers and 200 men, most of whom were air force personnel.

An assault force of 26 Assault Squadron RE and 'B' Squadron, 22 Dragoons, was supported by Royal Marine Commandos. Diversions and covering troops were found by 77 Assault Squadron RE and operated from the South and West. Four assault teams (each two Crabs and one troop AVREs) attacked under covering fire from the remaining Crabs and after an initial bombardment from heavy artillery. The Crabs flailed, AVREs petarded shelters and emplacements, dismounted crews placed 70 lb. 'Beehive' charges under smoke protection, the infantry went in and the garrison surrendered.

22 Dragoons lost 4 or 5 Crabs on mines; these were all recoverable and no personnel casualties suffered. 5 Assault Regiment RE had four AVREs written off and three more damaged by mines; 3 other

ranks were killed and 7 wounded. The infantry had no serious casualty.

In the thick hedgerows of the bocage it became more than ever essential to use the specialised armour with discretion, and each new field formation arriving from England had to be taught its characteristics. By now the veterans of D-Day knew a great deal themselves and could play an authoritative role down to quite a low level in shaping minor tactical plans to suit their own limitations, but it was less easy for newly arrived crews, such as those of the flame-throwing Crocodiles, to speak with the same authority. Only one troop had seen action on D-Day and the whole flame-throwing project was so secret that as much as a month after D-Day several less essential members of the unit, 141st R.A.C., had not even seen a Crocodile.

It was scant wonder that, at first, some infantry commanders failed to integrate the Crocodiles properly with the battle, but, instead, called on them after all else had failed. The experience of one troop leader, invited to take his Crocodiles alone and un-supported into an enemy-held village to salvage anti-tank guns abandoned by the infantry, is one of a number of typical misuses. Thus, untried equipment, often thrown into action unsupported, suffered a scale of losses commensurate with the A.V.R.E.s.

From so small a Tactical H.Q., with limited communications, Hobart could not influence every battle and, as more units of 79th Armoured Division arrived, Nigel Duncan's H.Q. became increasingly overloaded. Although Montgomery and Hobart had foreseen the need to establish the complete 79th Divisional H.Q. in Normandy, their view was not universally shared, and some there were who heaved a sigh of relief at the thought of leaving the irrepressible Hobart behind in the United Kingdom. How-ever, as the number of specialised devices increased in response to their popularity, and suffered increasingly from misuse and mechanical failure, it became obvious that they could no longer be satisfactorily maintained without the organisation which had bred them. With the arrival of special workshops and the need for complete overhauls of battle-worn equipment, carefully phased programmes of work had to be prepared which could only be conducted with speed and efficiency if the tired machines were withdrawn to a plan related to future battle requirements.

The arrival of Main H.Q. 79th Armoured Division in Normandy coincided with the climax of a battle of attrition. The efforts of the British Army to draw the bulk of the German Panzer divisions on to its front before Caen culminated in a dramatic but costly thrust by 7th, 11th and Guards Armoured Divisions to the south of Caen on 18th July. Nevertheless Montgomery's aim had been achieved, for when the Americans broke out on the 25th July their armoured divisions presented a sight to gladden the heart of any armoured enthusiast and poured remorselessly south from St. Lo, through the last, paper-thin barrier of German resistance to Avranches, the gateway to Brittany in the west, and eventually the rest of France to the south and east.

14

THE LAST RIVERS

The two American armies which broke loose at the end of July 1944 were joined in the first week of August by General Dempsey's 2nd British Army acting in concert with the 1st Canadian Army attacking south from Caen. Under a rain of jabs and hooks the Germans, capable only of replying to the flurry of blows with a single desperate punch at Mortain, drew back in disarray. Elsewhere the frontiers of Hitler's Europe contracted upon the citadel of Germany itself. Rome had fallen in June as the Allies advanced steadily up the spine of Italy: the Axis armies were evacuating the Balkans and in Russia successive offensives had thrown the German armies back into Poland. In August 1944, when men began to think the war might be over by Christmas, it suddenly seemed too late to get killed and permissible, instead, to plan for peace in earnest.

Dorrie and Grizell Hobart certainly thought so and asked themselves, 'What shall we do with Pa after the war?' Almost as soon as the last shots were fired he would be returning to retirement, and the prospect of having such a dynamic personality loose at home, and lacking full employment, they viewed with respect. Tentatively his family suggested a number of occupations to appease him. Farming seemed a good idea—he might even write his Memoirs, but the response on the 7th August lacked encouragement.

Indeed it is a corking problem gnawing away at the back of my own mind whenever I'm not fully occupied.
I'm difficult. I have no hobbies. And no specialised knowledge outside soldiering. I'm not even fond of golf or bridge. In fact it would seem that I'm really not usable after 60 : I don't fit in. Farming is very attractive : in theory. . . . How many soldiers did I know who took to it after the last war. . . . Not one made good as far as I can remember. . . . I feel rather a worm. Throwing this bucketful of ice-water on your warm and enthusing letter. Especially as I have no alternative course to suggest. 'Pa is a problem' I'm afraid.

The war could not now be lost by the Allies, no matter how badly they arranged their affairs. Having left the close bocage of Normandy behind, the intense fighting gave way to the sort of open warfare Hobart had sponsored in the 1930's and to the optimists, in full chase after a running foe, it seemed that there might be no further use for deliberate assaults, and therefore only a limited future for 79th Armoured Division. In the break-out from Caen, during the annihilation of the German Army at Falaise and on the banks of the River Seine, specialised armour played important but nevertheless subsidiary roles. As the speed of the advance increased, elements fell behind, the first to suffer being the C.D.L.s whose arrival late in July came just too late for them to participate in the great drive at night towards Falaise. Indeed, for the C.D.L. Brigade this was the end, their next operational instruction detailing disbandment or conversion to new roles. Throughout the pursuit Hobart could best act only as an administrator and interested onlooker, concentrating on the inauguration of a vigorous overhaul of every available item of equipment and instituting a control system aimed at reducing the wear and tear on men and machines alike.

With the agreement of H.Q. 21st Army Group, it became a drill that no single part of 79th Armoured Division should be committed to battle unless its senior leaders had taken part in the planning at all stages and levels. No specialised armour remained under the command of another formation for a minute longer than operationally necessary, ensuring that the moment the battle ended, the 'Funnies' and their crews came out of the line for repair and rest. Above all the evolution of a system whereby Hobart and his H.Q. staff were consulted by Montgomery or his staff at the inception of each major operation, guaranteed the observance of 79th Armoured Division control: not very often were their respective headquarters far apart.

Once the nature and scope of an operation had been formulated, Hobart decided in person on the exact composition of the force to be employed before sending one of his brigadiers to live with the formation (usually Corps H.Q.) charged with the whole show. Nigel Duncan records that since, as often as not, the arrival of the senior adviser occurred before the formation commander had received orders from 21st Army Group, he became the harbinger of battle, and until the order appeared had to fend off the importunities of friends seeking news. Those of 79th Armoured Division indisputably had unique privileges. The senior adviser had power to ask Hobo for increased resources: those working at lower levels alongside divisional and brigade commanders were charged to ensure the maximum use without misuse of each 'Funny'. The system worked to the approval of tank crews whose confidence in the past had been shaken by occasional misemployment under commanders who misunderstood their limitations or felt no personal responsibility for the welfare of attached units. Now they felt they were being given a square deal.

In the midst of his division Hobo roamed the battlefields the better to know his men's problems, generally to ensure that his orders were being obeyed and, frankly, to appease his love of excitement and fortify his courage by challenging fear. If he believed the unit under investigation had something to hide, his visit could be pretty shattering. Beforehand he learnt by heart the name of every officer, connecting it with a photograph kept in a black book. Penetrating questions reinforced by an intense stare could throw all but the hardest man off balance. Often the tension became unbearable. During one inspection a rather lugubrious trooper, asked 'What do you do?' rolled forth, 'Mind

A.C.—X

my own business', and the staff, rooted to the ground, watching the back of Hobo's neck getting redder, waited horror-struck while one bystander gave vent to a pent-up wheeze as if a washer had burst. And then he surprised them all, bottling the explosion and gently elucidating that what the man said was true—he had in fact been the owner of a small shop.

In the forefront of the battlefield the behaviour of the G.O.C. at times conformed more to that of a junior officer, for he regarded the enemy as an agent to test his own courage. Nigel Duncan recalls a most difficult afternoon when he and Hobo were together, close to the front, after the Canadians had broken out towards Falaise. Despite repeated attacks (in error, of course) by the R.A.F., Hobo stayed quite unperturbed, and after the aircraft had been re-directed, decided to observe the German positions on the other side of the Laison River which the Canadians were trying to cross. Duncan writes:

I did induce him to leave the cars behind the crest of the hill. He and I walked on until we found a field quite bare of any cover . . . Hobo then sat down on the ground, produced a pair of binoculars, demanded a map and we stayed there with a large map flapping round us at a range of 3,000 yards from the Germans on the other side of the river while point by point identification between map and ground was made.

They then drove down to the battle to discover a tank stopped behind cover because a German Tiger tank just round the corner commanded all the approaches. This provoked Hobo who took the line that it just should not be allowed, and who was responsible? Getting no satisfactory answer to any of his questions and finding nobody prepared to attack the Tiger, he suggested, 'Let's go and stalk it ourselves! We can kill it all right! Go and get a Piat.' Duncan pointed out that he had no faith in the Piat as an anti-tank weapon and anyway did not know how to use one and 'if he thought I was going to take him crawling through ditches as my Number Two in order to fire a weapon of which neither of us had any experience, against a Tiger, he was entirely mistaken'. The Tiger continued at large.

It would appear that Hobart lost all interest in his personal safety once absorbed with the job on hand. His approach to battle started as a personal test of nerve but reverted to unconcern—not necessarily foolhardiness. However, that is not to suggest carelessness with other men's lives, for he hated suffering, and reviled the commanders whose bad plans had wasted men's lives in the past. The essence of every 79th Armoured Division drill was battlefield efficiency in the struggle to save waste—above all the wastage of lives.

*   *   *   *   *

The pursuit of the beaten enemy cleared the best part of France and Belgium of Germans in little more than a month before crossing the frontiers of Holland and Germany herself. Even so, by the beginning of September, the coalescence of a front revealed a new pattern. As the Germans fought harder in the approaches to their own country, the difficulty of maintaining a strong enough force to overcome greater resistance at the end of lengthening supply lines caused momentum to drop and the advance to falter. Isolated by the pursuit, the Germans had perforce to leave garrisons besieged in the Channel ports where they created a considerable nuisance value, for they not only posed the faint threat of a foray, but denied ports which had to be taken in order to shorten the Allied lines of communication. In any case, once the autumn gales began to reduce the capacity of the exposed artificial harbour in Normandy normal, sheltered harbours became indispensable. Brest, by the Americans, Le Havre, Boulogne and Calais by the 1st Canadian Army, and the approaches to the great port of Antwerp by Canadians and British, had all to be reduced. Antwerp Docks fell intact, in fact, to the 11th Armoured Division after a record-breaking three days advance from the River Seine, nothing giving Hobart greater pleasure than the knowledge that his old Black Bulls had carried all before them with the sort of dash of which he dreamed. Indeed, General Dempsey gave him permission to visit them in their moment of triumph, causing him to write to Dorrie in gratitude and also a certain pride in doing some

'liberating' on his own account close to where he had won the
M.C. in 1915:

> They were all, naturally, in great heart: and are highly praised
> by everyone. Pip Roberts[1] has really done splendidly. To catch them
> I had to drive through streets in Lens (a big mining etc town) that
> no Allied troops had been through—in fact they had more or less
> by-passed the town on both sides an hour or so previously—and
> saw real enthusiasm for the first time.
>   Women, children and men thronging into the roads waving hand-
> kerchiefs, little home-made flags, kissing their hands (they would
> have kissed me if I'd dared stop) cheering, and throwing flowers and
> hard little green apples, that hit you a smart rap on the head! they
> were happy and elated: even if it was only for an hour or two.

Then, after sharing some of the glory with his old division,
he hurried back to play his part in subduing the Channel ports.

To the Americans at Brest went a squadron of Crocodiles, to
work for General Simpson: the first time an American general
had specifically asked for one of the British specialised armoured
units, although the subsequent success of the Crocodiles did
much to encourage the Americans to ask again for Hobart's
devices whenever they had to attack fortresses in the future.

At Le Havre 1st British Corps under General Crocker faced
the task of prising open one of the most heavily fortified of all
the Channel ports. It was needed urgently, so overwhelming
forces, a mass of artillery, several hundred heavy bombers, two
infantry divisions, two brigades of tanks and the biggest assembly of specialised armour since D-Day congregated to do the
job.

Two flail regiments, a regiment of A.V.R.E.s carrying the
usual assortment of bridges and fascines, two squadrons of
Crocodile flame-throwers, and some Kangaroo armoured personnel carriers (obsolete tanks with their turrets removed), were
fitted by Brigadier Duncan into every phase of the assault. Hobart
stayed on hand but never interfered in the least. As Duncan says,
'He was always there ready to back you up if you wanted help,
but the planning you carried out yourself. Naturally one dis-

1. Major-General G. P. B. Roberts, Commander 11th Armoured Division.

cussed the operation with him, but provided that you were satisfied with your plan he never sought to alter it.'

Formidable defences guarded the plateau to the east of the
town and embraced the full range of concrete Atlantic Wall
fortifications guarding deep minefields and an anti-tank ditch.
After torrential rain the ground had become heavy, seriously
impeding the movement of tanks. Led by specialised armour,
the assault went in after a furious aerial and artillery bombardment, teams of Crabs and A.V.R.E.s, supported by tanks,
opening routes through the minefields and over the ditches
under almost constant fire; clearing the way for the Crocodiles
to flame the strongpoints beyond to help establish the infantry
on their objectives. By reducing the beating effect of the flail's
chains, the heavy state of the ground protected many mines from
detonation, with the result that they failed to explode until run
over by the Crabs themselves. Despite heavy losses most lanes
drove through exposing the strongpoints to envelopment by
flame.

Once a hole had been cut the momentum of the assault never
slackened, as Kangaroos, accompanied by A.V.R.E.s to bridge
each successive obstacle under fire, raced through the gaps to
deposit infantry in the precincts of the next line of strongpoints.
To the Germans watching, almost in impotence, it was a be-
wildering experience to see the strongest barriers and fortifications wilting in a matter of minutes, and the assault roll forward
unremittingly upon them. Rarely could they see men to fire at in
the open, for nearly always the targets were protected by armour,
and so their anti-tank guns alone had a critical part in the battle
and once these succumbed the whole defence collapsed.

The first breach, blasted through on the left of the plateau
on a beautiful Sunday evening, was duplicated at midnight on
the right under the light of searchlights shining above the lanes,
while bursts of tracer shells sailed overhead as direction-keeping
markers. By daylight both divisions were entering the outskirts of the town finding the German resistance on the verge of
collapse. A Scottish company commander, surprised to hear the
telephone ring in the dug-out he had just captured, answered
and invited the German at the other end to surrender. This re-

quest was refused, but it turned out that other subscribers had been listening in and they accepted the invitation with some alacrity. The battle guttered out while twelve thousand Germans surrendered in thirty-six hours for the loss of about fifty British dead, testimony to the fire power of aerial and artillery bombardment in support of armoured attack when concentrated on even the most modern fortifications.

A week later came the turn of Boulogne where ten thousand Germans had repulsed the first orthodox attack by the Canadian 3rd Division and now defied calls to surrender. Specialised armour, hurriedly sent by road to join the Canadians, found on arrival that their Divisional Commander and Brigadier G. S. Knight, deputed to plan the part to be played by 79th Armoured Division, had already concocted new variations on the old theme of assault. The fortifications here were even more massive than those at Le Havre, though divided in two by the River Liane running through the centre of the city. The Canadians envisaged breaking the crust of the defences with infantry and specialised armour prior to launching three armoured columns, commanded and almost entirely manned by 79th Armoured Division, to seize the bridges over the river in a *coup de main*. The historian of 79th Armoured Division remarks, with surprise, that the plan of assault was 'very original' since it involved infantry opening the way for the armour—an inversion of the normal method. The British Army had travelled a long way in thought since 1942.

Hobart's part in the planning at Boulogne took greater prominence than it had at Le Havre since he did not know Knight as well as Duncan and the new techniques demanded by the Canadians provoked his intellect and fancy. The follow through by three armoured columns after the orthodox breaching of the outer defences represent the kernel of his concept of armour in action. Each column comprised a troop of Crabs, two troops of Crocodiles, a half troop of A.V.R.E.s, a platoon of infantry carried in Kangaroos and were led by conventional gun tanks, and everybody in these columns sensed the enormous demand for speed while suffering acute misgivings at being pitchforked into the centre of a heavily defended area. Hobo came himself to speak to the crews shortly before H hour—his manner all fire that morning with at least one tank commander getting short shrift and drawing the conclusion that the Germans might be a safer proposition than his divisional commander. But Hobart seems to have sensed the need to inspire dash to overcome the meticulous psychology inherent in the more deliberate earlier actions: it was as if he willed those columns to justify his long-held armoured doctrine.

The Canadian plan partially miscarried. Infantry with only a thin supporting cast of tanks and specialised armour found it impossible to dominate the concrete forts. As fast as the Germans were driven down one hole they appeared to shoot from another. Only when, eventually, A.V.R.E.s and Crocodiles came up to blast and flame was success assured, but this unplanned effort temporarily disrupted the armoured columns. In any case, the columns could not be launched all at once; all were delayed to a certain extent by bomb craters, and the enemy, recognising their mission, blew all three bridges over the Liane. Nevertheless they effected an entry into the town and took a large share in clearing it of Germans at high speed, although four days had to be spent subjugating each and every one of the German forts by battering them into submission with A.V.R.E.s, Crocodiles and flails. The armoured columns, acting in too restricted an area, had enjoyed limited success, but it is worth recalling 1916 and the thousands who fell at Verdun trying to subdue forts of lesser calibre. At Boulogne the prize was won for the loss of only a few hundred men.

A similar tale could be told of Calais and of Cap Gris Nez, where lay the guns which had fired at England across the Straits of Dover for four years, in an area liberally dotted with forts surrounded by inundations. Against a determined enemy, the clearance of the stretch of coastline from Sandgatte to Cap Gris Nez could only be accomplished systematically from one strong-point to another, as at Boulogne. Armour ponderously led the way and the Canadian infantry moved into each concrete position after it had been battered and flamed. The cost in lives shrank remarkably small, the forecast dividend paid whenever the capital of specialised armour came to market.

                    *   *   *   *   *

As the advanced guards of the British and Canadian armies approached the waterways and inundations of Holland, measures to carry the fight through this intricate terrain entailed a reversion to the successful amphibious tactics of the 6th June. A new regiment of D.D. tanks had to be trained while some of the Crab and A.V.R.E. units recaptured the art of waterproofing and launching from L.C.T.s. Some engineer units swapped their A.V.R.E.s for a new tracked armoured amphibious vehicle propelled in the water by its own tracks and called the Buffalo.

Only by employing the facilities of the port of Antwerp could a full-blown campaign be supported logistically into the heart of Germany—and by the end of September it had become dismally apparent, in the light of failure at Arnhem and in the face of the Siegfried Line, that only by a large-scale offensive could Germany be conquered. Hopes of the war ending in the autumn or by Christmas withered. In their place a winter siege campaign to wear away the outer ramparts of Germany loomed up, but first of all strong enemy positions on both sides of the River Scheldt had to be cleared in order to free the approaches to Antwerp.

Starting early in October, each assault demanded variations on the old techniques while inevitably producing a crop of new problems for 79th Armoured Division. Much of the ground lay sodden below sea-level and under several feet of water. Only amphibious armour behaved efficiently under these conditions and upon it depended the whole success of operations, for infantry on their own, without cover in the wet flatlands, became exposed to fire whenever they moved. Because the Buffaloes could swim in the Scheldt, up the canals or across the inundations, they lived in constant demand, but these fragile vehicles, prone to constant trouble with their tracks, ran on a mechanical shoe-string. Indeed, after four days' work in their first operation, hardly one of the Buffaloes remained fit to move.

Three major areas of German resistance had to be overcome: the pocket on the south bank of the Scheldt centred on Breskens, and the islands of South Beveland and Walcheren on the north bank. The ability to mount one operation after another depended primarily on the availability of trained 79th Armoured Division units. At the hub was Hobo, and at the root of success the unswerving sense of urgency he imparted. An extract from his letter written to Dorrie on the 3rd October tells much between the lines: 'Am getting some new units and things: and hectically engaged in complicated movements and inspections, and the inevitable desperate race against time. NOT in the case of my own old units: they are all right'—but there were newcomers who needed indoctrination!

Deeply conscious that there need never be an end to improvements and that every important action in war should be analysed to find the lessons for application in the future, Hobart drove Duncan (in charge of a waterborne training wing) to examine wholesale improvisations. The assault on Breskens highlighted the mechanical unreliability of the Buffaloes demanding controlled use of the machines to preserve them for essential work. Against South Beveland D.D.s came up against an old problem in modern dress, for as they tried to climb up steep banks out of the water, their tracks lost sufficient tractive effort in conjunction with the drive from the propellers in the water, and the vehicles stuck, nose in the air. There was no quick solution to this and therefore there had to be a careful personal reconnaissance and search for suitable landing places before each landing to find a gently sloping exit.

Amongst the Scheldt defences Walcheren was the toughest nut, for where the ground rose above sea level the enemy held strong positions and where it sank below, the water lay deep and tidal after the R.A.F. bombed four gaps in the dyke. A naval assault mounted in L.C.T.s based on Ostend, and Buffaloes on Breskens attacked two beaches, one near Westkapelle and the other at Flushing on 1st November. Beset by the most awful adversities after the supporting bombardment failed to achieve its planned effect, the assault waves came ashore under heavy shell fire against an uncowed foe guarding unbroken obstacles amidst quicksands. Vehicles bogged, became jammed together, were often hit and burnt, but as had happened in these deadly breaches during many another assault, Hobart's men simply went on working their way forward in company with the Commandos, filling their losses from reserves, improvising here, battering aside obstacles there and turning their guns on the more troublesome enemy resistance when the opportunity presented itself. They were quite inexorable. In the skill of the drivers as by inspired use of throttle, gears and steering they persuaded their vehicles through appalling terrain, lay the key to success, for only when tanks advanced could the infantry be shot on to their objectives. It was done here and it was done at Flushing and Middelburg too. The mantle of the old-time 'Forlorn Hope' lay across the shoulders of 79th Armoured Division, although they would have been the last to claim it.

Until Flushing fell on 3rd November, after a hard fight, no direct progress could be made towards Middelburg in the centre of the island, since the best route along the strongly defended banks of a canal was impracticable. So Buffaloes, carrying a company of infantry, waded across the flooded fields to arrive unopposed after various adventures, in the centre of the town where the German commander refused to surrender to the subaltern in charge of the Buffaloes, and only consented to do so to an infantry major after the latter had promoted himself lieutenant-colonel on the spot.

The waterways to Antwerp were no longer closed by direct enemy fire and could be swept by the Navy unopposed. Nevertheless, many weeks would elapse before a flood of material could pour through the port to the waiting soldiers on the German frontier, and in the meantime a succession of battles had to be staged designed to establish a line on the River Maas, and close up to the Siegfried Line prior to eating through its outer crust. In these operations the full repertoire of 79th Armoured Division went on display as a matter of course, becoming so much in demand that a rapid expansion of the division established a vast organisation spread across Belgium and southern Holland.

The habit of passing special technical problems to Hobart remained practically in abeyance after D-Day, although there had been numerous minor practical experiments whenever a particular technical difficulty arose at short notice in connection with a specific operation. In Normandy brief investigations examined the firing of Crocodile flame-throwers at night and a series of trials, on and off the battlefield, looked into various radio direction-finding devices for keeping massed armoured columns on course through the enemy defences after dark, south of Caen. Now, early in December, General Dempsey, the commander of 2nd British Army, asked Hobart to investigate a whole series of projects including methods for detecting and clearing the highly effective German 'Schumine', an improved way of laying a quick local smoke-screen by means of a multi-barrelled smoke discharger, the fitting of a Bulldozer blade to a standard combat tank, and examples of more sophisticated tank bridges.

Although the trials carried out by 'F' Wing, located at Gheel in Belgium, had nothing like the scope enjoyed by its predecessors or its successors, its importance lay in the way the authorities turned instinctively to Hobart well knowing that he might achieve a quick, practical solution to a problem when the research and development organisation in England would take too long. From then on practically every piece of new specialised equipment went to him for testing, improvement, repair, and preparation for battle. By early February 1945 it had grown into the only all-armoured formation in the British Army, containing no less than seventeen regiments under command. Its strength of 21,430 all ranks and 1,566 tracked A.F.V.s, compared with the 14,400 men and 350 A.F.V.s in a normal armoured division, yet to run this enormous group the staff grew hardly at all, the appointment of a Chief of Staff in March 1944—a part filled by Colonel Alan Brown brought back specially for the task—representing the only significant change in the machinery of control. Hobo really commanded, the small staff was his agent: not for him a stifling proliferation of self-administering bureaucrats blurring the problem and emasculating his brain, the true source of power.

Divisional H.Q. set up first close to Antwerp, in the target area of a steady stream of German V1 and V2 rocket missiles. It was said that the danger of a hit became mitigated by the fascination of investigation of the parts recovered from the missiles, while the technical staff in the H.Q. used to test the intelligence of visiting officers on the score of their deductions when shown various bits and pieces of rocketry.

Between December when 'F' Wing started and mid-March, the scene on the Western Front became transformed. The Germans made their last great throw in the West through the Ardennes—and lost. The British Operation 'Veritable' started to clear the west bank of the Rhine from Nijmegen eastwards through Cleve in the direction of Wesel on 8th February 1945, leaving in its train memories of a battle fought in unutterably miserable conditions in cold, rain and flood, against a determined and well posted enemy.

With the exception of D.D.s, practically every 'Funny' in Hobart's armoury took part in 'Veritable' because the German defences and the appalling state of the ground challenged the assaulting infantry and tanks with nearly every variety of obstacle and opposition. Not that specialised equipment was flung in with the hope that the end of the war seemed in sight. Hobart's letters foretold a protracted German resistance to the bitter end, his meetings with Montgomery keeping him freely informed of the operations the Field Marshal planned to launch from the west bank of the Rhine. Ahead appeared a number of major water barriers, starting with the Rhine itself, which the Field Marshal assumed would be fiercely resisted. Each would be crossed methodically—speed and glory were not reasons for squandering lives.

In any case Hobart's instinctive hatred of waste cried out against misemployment of his machines under any circumstances and Operation 'Veritable' furnished a good example of the measure of protection his men received: for after some special teams had been allotted to one division, it came to light that the divisional commander, a very strong personality, intended to split them up contrary to accepted practice and the advice he had received. Nothing would change this general's mind and eventually the matter came to Hobart, who simply went straight to Montgomery with the result that the offending division was withdrawn and its place in the attack given to another.

This example is of great interest, for it is sometimes suggested that Hobart, with his propensity for experimentation off the battlefield during training, would have been inclined to experiment on it at appalling hazard. Yet he cannot be accused of this failing in practice: always ready to sacrifice himself, he did not willingly do the same to others. Indeed there is often a lot to be said for a commander of power who looks not over his shoulder at the sources of promotion.

'Veritable' churned forward for nearly a month, steadily drawing more and more German divisions into action at the expense of other fronts until, on the 23rd February, the 9th and 1st American Armies striking through the sectors to the south of the British, found comparatively light resistance because so many divisions, once opposite them, had gone north. A fortnight later and the west bank of the Rhine north of Cologne lay in Allied hands while to the south the pursuit of a beaten enemy raced headlong. In effect the German Army dropped, crippled by fighting west of the river: the remains watched in enfeebled state on the east bank while that which held back the Russians fought in a nightmare: there existed no central reserve.

*   *   *   *   *

Meanwhile three more 79th Armoured Division Wings assembled, lettered 'G', 'H' and 'J', sharing the work of trials and training in connection with the coming crossings of the Rhine, the teaching of crews to work heavy rafts and the development of navigational aids to help armoured vehicles keep on course through heavy smoke and in the dark.

The Rhine crossing, conceived in a different light to any other operation previously attempted by the British Army, marked the first occasion a British Army had ever tried to cross Europe's greatest water barrier against opposition. By now the training and equipment of the Army had reached a highly sophisticated state, enabling Montgomery to plan a range of operations which a year before might have stretched credulity. The successful experience with night actions with massed armoured formations in Normandy married to the knowledge acquired on D-Day and in the mouth of the River Scheldt, provided the essential ingredients for a massed river crossing at night in armoured vehicles.

Throughout February and the best part of March continuous trials and training covered stretches of the River Maas. Hobart raided his units for D.D., Buffalo and rafting experts. Two more British regiments, plus elements of an American tank battalion, had training on D.D.s, while two British regiments converted to operate Buffaloes, and the assault R.E.s spent long days learning how to assemble and steer heavy rafts. Even a squadron of C.D.L.s, re-formed from retirement, prepared to illuminate and protect bridges at night from underwater attack. As in Normandy, Montgomery intended to land a mass of armour in the van of the assault, but in the knowledge of the difficulty in getting D.D. tanks out of the water without assistance, the Buffalo, which could scale banks with relative ease because of the depth of its track grips, received promotion to assault leader. Therefore 79th Armoured Division invented a Buffalo to carry a chespale carpet (a simple development of the A.V.R.E. bobbin used on D-Day) and lay it up the bank to form a shallow, sloped causeway up which D.D.s could climb.

The final assault was to be launched in the dark after a smoke screen had obscured the west bank of the Rhine from enemy view during daylight for many days before. The need to find a way accurately through darkness and smoke created a requirement for navigational aids, inducing Hobart's technologists to explore a wide variety of devices. Basically an ordinary gyro-compass solved the problem best but, as a double check, they engineered a simple arrangement of existing radio equipments to act in the same way as the R.A.F. system of navigation on a beam. The movement of a needle to left or right of centre on a dial told the observer on which side of the correct course he was heading: quite often this rugged improvisation worked, though it exhibited alarming deviations when jammed by other nearby radio transmitters and more than one vehicle travelled in a circle across country pursued by an agitated trials staff.

Given sound directions and time, any practical engineer could dream up devices such as these. The real strength of Hobart's organisation lay in its ability to turn dreams into working, manufactured tools in a miraculously short space of time.

Experiments and the rehearsal of the troops allotted to the assault continued until only two days before the Rhine crossing, covering a period of unusual contentment in Hobart's association with the Army commanders, who in return, lavished practically unanimous praise upon the unstinted help given by 79th Armoured Division. He was absorbed in the technical work, but, once free of the intricate allocations of troops to tasks, his interest switched again to wider issues. Foremost in his thoughts grew a desire to shape the future of armour after the war and in the course of exchanges of letters with Montgomery, these thoughts became increasingly constructive and mellow. Their debate on armour will be described in the next chapter, although it even managed to intrude into his Christmas Day letter to Dorrie:

> Monty sent me, as an Xmas Card, a signed copy of his third pamphlet (on the Armoured Division in Battle) . . . Well—it's a good paper, perhaps the best paper on handling tanks I've ever actually seen. I differ from it in some matters—in some essential matters.[2] Profoundly.
>
> But—he is a successful man : who has achieved victories. And victories in which armour has been the principal arm.

Perhaps for the first time in twenty years a state of peace in mind can be detected, the need to struggle alone put aside in the knowledge that armour had triumphed, if not in quite the way he wished. No longer had he to fight for survival or even badger lower commanders on behalf of specialised armour, and with the new mood even greater latitude could be granted to his Chief of Staff and brigadiers—well content that they understood, and would do all he wished and, if anything went awry, Montgomery would step in to restore equanimity. Contentment cries

---

2. He was referring here to Montgomery's demand for a 'Universal' tank, capable of undertaking any task, whereas Hobart thought two types necessary— one medium and the other heavy.

forth in an unusual song of happiness on the 6th March when
he tells Dorrie:

Quite a day for me. Became a Commander of the U.S.A. Legion of
Merit. Had a good innings at the 21 A.Gp. HQ conference on the
next operation, where I got what I considered necessary. Got back
here in time to see Henry V film again.

Omar Bradley held the investiture. I found myself right of the
line. Apparently the order corresponds roughly to the Bath. And
Commander to 'K'. Two others got this rank: the Principal Administrative Officer and the Principal Signals Officer of 21. A.Gp.—
Graham and White. About 16 others got the Companion rank. I enclose my 'citation'. I'm pleased and gratified that the work and gallantry of the units of my Div. who've been helping the Americans
has been so handsomely recognised by them. But, as you will understand, it doesn't give me any personal 'Kick'—but I'm told that if
one visits the States and wears the 'Button' in one's buttonhole, one
has no trouble with the Customs!

*   *   *   *   *

Until the end of the war his letters reflect the true views and
spirit of the British Liberating Army, telling the tale of disaster
for Germany, struck down in the final act of Hitler's play by an
irresistible power. Indeed, so weak had the Rhine defences become that it can be argued that the crossings by the British and
Americans in the north were over-weighted, over prepared and,
consequently, later in delivery than necessary. Already the
Americans had 'bounced' two crossings further south. Nevertheless strong patches of local opposition flared up on the 24th
March when the British 2nd Army and the American 9th set
sail.

In quite perfect weather the operation of 21 A.Gp. crossing the
Rhine took place. I think the cost in casualties has been very light
indeed. Firstly because the Nazis decided to fight their battle for
W. Germany West of the Rhine: and in doing this they must have
lost between $\frac{1}{4}$ and $\frac{1}{2}$ million men in these $3\frac{1}{2}$ months. So they had
neither the men available nor the defences properly organised E of
the Rhine when the sweep started. Secondly—Air action. Not only

all the long-term interdiction of communications, destruction of rails, canals, roads etc. and vital industries, but the terrific softening-up of our immediate front these last 3 days and nights—culminating in today's airborne operation. It swept over our heads continuously for 2½ hours. We could not actually see the parachutists jump or the gliders land owing to the pall of smoke and dust that hung over the battlefield, but we could see the flak and the machines that were hit—very few really.

Thirdly of course our immense superiority in guns and ammunition.

Fourthly our special devices: and the technique of crossing a strongly fortified river line which is largely an adaption of our D-day landing (only much easier of course).

I went over in one of my amphibians—not in the assault, but later —and was relieved to find how small the casualties had been.

And on 26th March.

Had rather a valuable cargo in one of my Buffaloes crossing the Rhine today. The Bulldog,[3] Alan Brooke, Monty, Bimbo, Neil Ritchie.[4] The old man greeted me warmly but did not say much: it's difficult to talk against the noise of the craft. He was smoking a cigar of course and looked pretty well I thought, but worse—more than when I last saw him 18 months ago. He was in good spirits: always enjoys seeing the stuff and the chaps who've done it—and a few shells and things stimulate him. A grand man, indeed. Alan Brooke looked tired and not so fit as when I saw him a few months ago. He bid me to come and lunch with him when I come over—so perhaps I'll be able to ask if there's any chance of my further employment.

Next on the 27th March a mark of approval for the greatest of the American tank generals, George S. Patton.

. . . whilst the U.S. Armies are surging forward (against much weaker opposition) almost everywhere, and Georgie Patton is dashing well ahead. I'm told that he was directed, as his part of this Allied op to 'maintain in active defence and keep the enemy on his front occupied'! When he had made his breakthrough a few days later he is supposed to have wired to the Principal Administrative

3. Winston Churchill.
4. Lieutenant-General Ritchie, Commander 12th British Corps.

A.C.—Y

Officer responsible for his supply 'Get off your ass, send me some gas, and I'll be in Berlin in seven days.'

The advance rolled across Germany, sometimes unchecked though repeatedly hung up by fanatical resistance from diehard cadres. In between the skirmishes the satisfaction of living off a conquered country could be mixed with the pleasure of observing his nephew Pat[5] commanding the 1st Battalion Royal Tank Regiment in 7th Armoured Division, and wagering on the performance of his old Black Bulls against the Desert Rats.

20th April
I was up fairly close to Pat yesterday : as far as Div HQ, but they were forging ahead and the road was pretty full, so I didn't reach him. The Black Bulls just beat the Desert Rats to the Elbe, and so won me a small bet.

The Elbe, the last great river, as it came in sight, represented the last defended trench between Berlin and the Baltic, and it was here that 79th Armoured Division sang its swan song, leading the crossing with its Buffaloes, thus sounding the opening bars of the overture to 11th Armoured Division's last thrust to the Baltic coast.

Behind lay Germany—militarily prostrate and beginning to reveal the inner strength which had sustained her through nearly six years' conflict. On his journeys from front to front, Hobart pried into the sinews of Germany's war potential, examining at Meppen the hull of an experimental German tank designed to weigh 188 tons, seeing vast hidden factories in profusion making conventional munitions and, of most interest, gas and new secret weapons. The seeds of thickly sown research and development projects inspired one as educated as he. In Hamburg:

The U-boat slips at Blohm and Voss held twelve ocean-going submarines almost completed. Only one bomb had hit this great hangar : and had done in one submarine completely.

5. Charles Hobart's son, who fought with 7th Armoured Division for most of the war and today is Major-General P. R. C. Hobart—Director of Military Operations.

What was even more interesting was that on the quay alongside one of the big dry docks . . . were the remains of two smaller submarines. These were evidently practically complete : and had been thoroughly blown up after by the Huns themselves. The reason is said to be that they were propelled on a new principle that makes them faster under water than on the surface.

It seems to me more and more that we've only just won this war in time. If our invasion had been postponed even a few weeks; if Monty had been any slower over his break-out and great drive through France and Belgium . . .

What tremendous destruction was done to Hamburg in half a dozen bomber raids.

Yet in the outlying suburbs I found Pat's HQ ensconced in a block of working-men's flats with windows complete : also water running, electric light and gas. That was a remarkable effort on the part of the Huns to get those services going again—mains, pumps, power-plant etc.

Of the German Army :

It's late. I'm just back from the Baltic. Don't know how to begin to tell you. All surrealist. Columns and columns of sturdy German soldiers trudging steadily back along the road headed by their officers, with no weapons, and not a single British soldier bothering to look after them. And between the columns, the stragglers. Little knots of them, or single hobblers. Army, Navy, Luftwaffe, SS . . . Women among them. Some in uniform : some not. Most of the men looked well and fit and were of good military age. But there were some hundreds, in one batch, of boys of 14 or 15 in new uniforms. Mixed up with these were parties of ex P of W of all nationalities, of returning (or going?) evacuees, and of 'displaced persons' of all nations. Some in carts, some on bicycles, some wheeling prams or barrows, some pulling the absurd little hand carts common in this land. Some just carrying big bundles on their backs and a suitcase or two in their hands.

And of the German people on the 7th May :

I got a cipher this morning about 0930 saying that the Germans had signed unconditional surrender in Europe about 0150 G.M.T. this morning—i.e. about 6 hours previously.

I got all my Tac together at the flagstaff in the garden—for I had luckily been able to get hold of a Union Jack yesterday—and told them the war in Europe was over : and we had won. We saluted the flag : and had a minute's silence thinking of comrades who had gone.

What else to do to mark the day—?

It has been a perfectly glorious summer day. Everyone, except minimum guards and duties, day off.

I took John Borthwick and 3 clerks to see Hamburg. The streets were crowded (in the centre of the town). All the women anyway, in their best clothes—and hats (this very unusual). Evidently something had seeped out, something was expected. My unemotional driver Belston said 'The air is full of silver paper, Sir.' It was, like a silver snow storm thousands of feet up. As they fell slowly they danced and hovered and slid—it became apparent they were sheets of white paper in the strong sunlight. As the first ones reached earth the crowds rushed to pick them up and one heard the words *'Der Krieg bin ende'*. There was no cheering; but there was evident pleasure. No sign of grief on any woman's face (except *one* old woman I did see crying, but that may have been some private trouble). The men did not look so pleased, relieved.

But nowhere shame, contrition, or sorrow.

Finally I celebrated by having a haircut : a hot bath—and soaping all over; yes!

I used to say to you sometimes at Burdenshott 'I believe the next war will be won or lost, eventually and fundamentally, by the women —by the quality of the women of the nation'. I still believe that. Our women have worked flat-out, with courage, endurance, and above all fortitude. Especially in my opinion, the not-so-bloomin'-young ones.

It is abundantly obvious that these German fat fraus have not. There is none of the tired worn look in the faces of any—or hardly any—that is so widespread in England.

Of course, the ultimate finale had yet to come in the Far East and the implication that B.L.A. (British Liberation Army) stood for 'Burma Looms Ahead' embodied an ironic soldier's faith in the worst possible case. So victory in Europe could only be celebrated at half-cock with rejoicing in a minor key.

We're having a celebration dinner tonight. They've taken endless trouble over it—food and wine. And I don't feel a bit like it. They'll expect me to speechify—and I feel so much more like warning them of all the troubles I see ahead. All the sweat and tears and disappointments, if (a) we are to regain a leading place in the economic world, (b) we are to avoid another war.

They all, dear good chaps, think themselves such veterans : tough, experienced, cynical men of the world, bless 'em. They're all children. All except Cyril Edwards—about 30 years (or more) younger than me.

On 3rd July 1945 came thanks of the profusest and most sincere kind from Field Marshal Sir Alan Brooke, dotting the i's and crossing the t's on the last phase of twenty years' struggle :

My dear Hobo,

I have just received your letter of the 20th June and the pictorial record of your Division. I was *delighted* to receive both of them; the pictorial record is most interesting and very attractively put together giving an excellent bird's-eye view of the activities of your Division and of the part it took in the invasion.

It was your letter that I was specially pleased with, and I am so grateful for the kind things you said.

I cannot tell you what a relief it was to have you there to undertake the very difficult job of preparing the 79th Division for the all important role it had to play in the invasion.

I had full confidence that you would produce the vision, technical experience, organising ability, and above all the necessary drive, necessary to produce the type of formation we required. From the moment you took on the job I never had a moment's doubt that I had been right in my decision.

I think that perhaps one of the things that pleased me most about it all was to see you handling a job worthy of your abilities and one in which you were really happy. I felt you had well deserved something of that kind. . . .

Yours ever
Brookie

But already Hobo sat peering into the future, for he suffered the present and never lived in the past.

15

INTO HARBOUR

Towards the end of 1944, as the war in Europe moved into its last phase and thoughts began to turn more strongly to the problem of crushing Japan, it would not have been surprising if the preponderant motive in men's minds had been the study of peaceful schemes. In these circumstances a debate on the future of armour and the ideal type of tank needed in another war might appear beyond the bounds of reality. Yet, throughout the winter months of 1944–5, serious debate raged back stage, provoked in part by Montgomery, but largely by Hobart lighting bonfires all down the line by encouraging a large number of officers (unbeknown to each other) into putting their ideas on paper.

Montgomery, intent on a series of contemporary studies in the art of war, based on the successful armoured campaigns which had stalled on the approaches to the Rhine, had perforce to consider in detail on the manner in which Allied armour had compared with the Germans. The comparison only rarely showed to British advantage, since in armour and fire power the Germans far outclassed their rivals. It followed that Montgomery was led to consider tanks of the future and their place in the line of battle, and that the paper on armour had to be shown in draft to Hobart, asking not only for advice on the paragraphs dealing with specialised vehicles, but also for comments on the overriding philosophy. It transpired that the views of the brothers-in-law tallied to a marked degree, differing fundamentally only in respect of the design of a future tank. Montgomery, characteristically seeking a simplified solution to a battlefield problem, demanded a Universal Tank capable of operating in the far-ranging, deep-penetration role as well as in the rough and tumble of the close assault: Hobart, his original views hardened by experience and a closer consideration of the technical difficulties, saying that each kind of battle needed its own type of tank and therefore the original concept of a heavy and a cruiser tank had not altered.

They agreed to differ on this one aspect, though not unnaturally Montgomery's view prevailed and in course of time became enshrined in the policy around which many of Britain's post-war tanks have been designed.

However, from the heart of this debate flowed not only two decades of armoured development, but the inculcation of a doctrine dominating British armoured thought and practice. In addition, it contained the seeds of the start of Hobart's post-war employment.

On the day the war in Europe ended, but a month from his sixtieth birthday, and well and away the oldest major-general on active service of the British Army, Hobart summarily rejected immediate retirement. Concentrating his immediate efforts on selecting men and equipments for use against the Japanese in Asia, while presiding over the rapid dissolution of 79th Armoured Division, he focussed on the two post-war issues closest to his heart—the creation of a virile research and development organisation for the Army in peace and the construction of a stronger organisation governing the Royal Tank Regiment.

Everywhere shivered the shifting sands of a changing political situation, a General Election impending, the Prime Minister more concerned with the Hustings than the prosecution of the war. As the war atmosphere dispersed in Europe, the demand for administrators in the occupied territories overshadowed the need for fighting men, who could either take a well deserved rest or seek fresh laurels in South East Asia and perhaps in Japan itself. In any event, the commanders Hobart had served for the past two years were leaving their posts, and while Montgomery remained in Germany, Dempsey and de Guingand departed, the Americans moved into their own Sectors needing no further assistance from the British; and in London Weeks and Evetts ceased to manipulate Development and Supply. Soon, too, a successor would have to be found for the C.I.G.S., Brooke. Any help Hobart could acquire from his old powerful friends had to be taken now or not at all.

It was his wish to capitalise on the experience of 79th Armoured Division before its unique organisation became submerged in the military economies that must eventually follow the conclusion of Peace. So he approached the subject on the widest front possible, linking his suggestions with the sections on specialised armour he had written for Montgomery's armoured paper.

Only a week after VE-Day, Hobart sent detailed proposals to Montgomery's staff describing the patchwork growth of research bodies in the Ministries, declaring that whatever success had been achieved had been due more to the efforts of individuals than organisation, and in consequence, no legacy would survive so that a period of stagnation would soon again supervene. This dismal forecast he next contrasted with what he had seen of German long-term research, its thoroughness, energy, continuity and lavish implementation. The fruits of German labours ought to be seized by the British Army and integrated with future research, but should there be no organisation in existence to process the enemy records and material, even this initial boost would be lost.

It was not enough, he argued, to scratch about with improvisations such as 79th Armoured Division. Thought and direction had to come from the apex of power and should, therefore, be embodied in the person of an Army Council Member for Research and Development armed with full powers to consult with scientists, universities, industry and the Admiralty and Air Ministry. Within the Army he envisaged a Technical Intelligence Staff and an Expert Advisory Staff to guide thoughts along the right tactical, technical and economic lines, and, in immediate charge of all progress, a Commander of Research and Development with direct two-way access to field force commanders and immediate control over research, design, development, modifications and trials.

His plan embodied a reversion to the pre-war system whereby the Army developed its own equipment, but the introduction of research and development at every level, from the Army Council downwards, added immense power to the original arrangement. Fundamentally he aimed to remove the development of weapons from the field of Ministerial Committees by suggesting that responsibility and power should go hand-in-hand.

Hobart's views crystallised in a letter of hopes and fears to Dorrie on the 10th June:

You see what I feel very strongly is that it is essential in the national interest that we should establish Research and Development Organisations in the Defence Services that will
(a) keep abreast of modern scientific progress
(b) ensure that such progress is incorporated in our designs of equipment
(c) test out all such equipment.
The less the total amount of money we can afford to spend on armaments, the bigger the proportion of it that must be devoted to research and development.
I would like to see this new orientation of military hierarchy, which involves little less than a revolution in the orthodox soldier's mentality, started at the top—in the Army Council. But I can't directly influence that. So I must work at it from the bottom: from my little corner of Specialised Armour. Before I'm finally chucked out I want to be sure that for this at any rate, there is a proper establishment for research, design, development. Even this will take some doing: there are a lot of vested interests.

Through a round of negotiations supported at critical moments by Brooke and Montgomery, a rump of 79th Armoured Division survived under a new name. At the end of August 1945, the original formation died in Germany to be reincarnated (still bearing the birth-mark of a bull's head) at Woodbridge in

Suffolk and rechristened Specialised Armour Development Establishment (S.A.D.E.), its commander and staff the old firm of Hobart, Duncan, Brown and Jolly.

The memorial to the old division, *The Story of the 79th Armoured Division,* of which fifteen thousand copies were privately printed in Germany, appeared before the division disbanded. Hobart wrote: 'It is well done. The weakest part is the style. All the same it is a great credit to John Borthwick who has never done anything like that, and was after all, uneducated at Eton.' Another less lively document, *The Final Report of 79th Armoured Division,* passed up official channels to disseminate in detail the lessons of two years' labour and hard-taught experience, as well as to form the basic document for the work of S.A.D.E.

Nothing like the resources available in wartime could be acquired in peacetime, so the projects studied at S.A.D.E. and selected from a mass of ideas, became stunted in the arid desert of financial constriction. It must be admitted, however, that some of S.A.D.E.'s troubles came from over-stepping its terms of reference. Experiments in navigation, mine clearance and obstacle crossing fell neatly within legitimacy, so did the attachment of rockets to the corners of a Valentine tank to make it jump across a fifty yard gap. Developing a German Volkswagen car taken from the factory at Wolfsburg practised on marginal ground, and attempts to design a new light tank mounting a large gun fired by remote control from within by its crew, stepped well outside the charter and led to friction with the official tank design establishments.

Life at Woodbridge thrived on endless excitement, Hobart driving ahead with his old furious enthusiasm, not because a new war impended but because he reckoned that only results achieved in the short time left to him would convince those in power of the validity of his grand R. & D. Design. Anyway creative work of any kind satisfied him and it is never possible to switch away immediately from years of restless activity.

Simultaneously he tackled the post-war problems of the R.T.R. with customary vigour, although he held no official position in the regimental hierarchy. Impelled by a twin-pronged concern, first, for the future of mechanisation in the Army and, second,

for the welfare of the regiment as a whole, he found it impossible to stand aside. In his opinion the R.T.R. represented
the essential, progressive force in the Royal Armoured Corps
which, in turn, acted as the leading protagonist of mobile
mechanical warfare in the Army. While giving full marks to the
cavalry for their verve, courage and skill in battle, he had yet
to be convinced that their officers fully accepted the imperative
need to advance their thoughts in pace with the current rate of
technical progress. In Hobart's outspoken view, the cavalry
would remain technically backward so long as it recruited the
vast majority of its officers from their traditional source, the
public schools, but because the R.T.R. had drawn its leaders
from other sources as well as the public schools, they would
continue to lead the technical race in the R.A.C.

At the end of the war the three Colonel Commandants of the
R.T.R. were Generals Elles, Broad and Lindsay, although Elles
was a sick man who, in fact, died at the end of July 1945. Prior
to that, Hobart had taken soundings amongst the younger senior
members of the regiment to discover their wishes as to the future
higher organisation: from this came a charter and the founding
of the post-war organisation of the R.T.R. In course of time
changes of Colonels Commandant followed; Field Marshal
Montgomery, an infantryman of power, was invited to take the
place of Elles, and Lindsay's place was taken by Crocker, appointments entirely in accordance with Hobart's desires. Finally the
supreme moment arrived when on the 1st May 1947 he became
a Colonel Commandant himself in place of Broad.

Already the shape of his post-war activities assumed a recognisable form, a second retirement on the 31st March 1946 bringing about hardly a stutter in the eager roar of his life. Behind lay
S.A.D.E., well groomed in his ideas and expressions. In the
War Office the specifications for future armoured vehicles bore
the deeply ingrained influence from years of his indoctrination
upon the policy makers and technicians: one technical staff officer
states quite categorically that Hobart's philosophy predominated
because he had permeated the tank scene for so many years and
become irresistible. Quite instinctively, even after his retirement,

his old colleagues turned to consult him as he moved in their midst.

A first attempt to find direct employment failed. Sponsored by Viscounts Alanbrooke and Montgomery and the Right Honourable Winston S. Churchill, he sought the Chair of the Chichele Professorship of the History of War at the University of Oxford and, in competition with Captain Cyril Falls, failed. Perhaps it was well that this was so, and fortunate too that an idea of the new Prime Minister, Mr. Attlee, to give him employment in the political field came to naught. Hobo might have been too dynamic in the halls of Oxford: his impact on politics is more difficult to gauge.

Happily an invitation by Sir Miles Thomas to join the special section of the Nuffield Organisation devoted to making military vehicles and named Mechanisation and Aero Limited, called Hobart back to a world he understood well. Thomas wanted his specialised advice, to avoid Nuffields 'being asked to produce crazy curiosities', and says:

He knew everybody in the War Office, and the fact that he combined originality with honesty of thought and had an inbred liking for being concerned with the development and manufacture of armoured vehicles well fitted him for the post.

Knowing many of the factors conditioning everyday industrial life after delving deeply amongst factories during the war, Hobart approached weapon production in the spirit that nothing could be too good for the soldiers, expense a secondary consideration. In wartime he had abhorred the profit motive, particularly when he suspected it impinged on quality: the transition to peace did little to change this attitude. Above all he held the belief that British industry as a whole lagged far behind the leading industrial nations of the world. This opinion hardly changed after discussing with Lord Nuffield the possibility of manufacturing the Volkswagen car in Britain, and finding, to his surprise, that though the British motor-car industry as a whole had been offered the Volkswagen drawings and plant through the Custodian of Enemy Property, it had turned them down because the design was 'out of date'. Nuffield said he had a good car, its production line set up and therefore he saw no reason, economic or otherwise, to change. It is hard to disagree.

An indication of Hobart's transition to civilian life can be detected from his more ready acceptance of disappointment for, to Miles Thomas, he looked happy working for Nuffields having completely shed his army character. Nevertheless, his closest friends received an impression of unease. In fact he was probably as content as any man can be who finds himself bereft of an active environment, such as in the Services, when his faculties continue at full throb and are bulging with ideas.

In any case the period at Nuffields passed far from unhappily, for in addition to influencing several engineering projects, he became engrossed in the amassing of information from his friends, world-wide, and even turned his hands to assembling reminiscences of his early years and life in India before 1914. He cast his mind across the world scene and wrote copiously and penetratingly of what he perceived—the notes covering an enormous but uninterrelated field. 'Mine is a rag-bag of a mind', he said and refused to write his memoirs, seeing no sense in generals committing '*hara kiri*'.

In 1946 Field Marshal Montgomery took up the appointment of C.I.G.S. and shortly afterwards asked Hobart if he might like to be considered for the appointment of Lieutenant Governor and Secretary of the Royal Hospital, Chelsea.

The proposal contained a strong appeal because, besides re-binding him within the military circle in close contact with soldiers—the Chelsea Pensioners with their wealth of old associations—it offered residence in London amongst gracious surroundings when the duties of Representative Colonel Commandant of the R.T.R. began to generate an increasing volume of administrative work. Living close to the heart of the Commonwealth, where his many friends passing to and fro from one end of the world to another could call and be interrogated, resolved a host of problems. From October 1948 his apartments in the Royal Hospital became open house to a great circle of friends.

The Royal Hospital runs to a timeless routine, needing more

than an act of God to alter it much. Yet even here room could be found for changes and it is probably true that Hobo introduced as many as any other Lieutenant Governor.

Acting in the same forceful manner as had characterised his whole career, Hobo strode about the Hospital, looking into everything, talking at length with the Pensioners (whose names he learnt with great care), withall absorbing the atmosphere and history of an institution which fascinated and grew irresistibly upon him. Gradually the changes he wished to make came into operation, although not all reached fruition until the days of his successors.[1] Putting the welfare of the Pensioners first, he strove to improve their comfort and raise the standard of catering, but as projects of this sort implied a direct assault on somewhat ancient kitchens, progress did not take place overnight. Linked with schemes to establish a Pensioners' Club, run by themselves, and a thorough-going drive to organise occupational therapy, leather work, model-making and the like, the lot of the inmates improved.

Not every one of the innovations met with approval. Having arranged for the old regimental standards to be repaired (and in some cases renewed), Hobo proclaimed that the irreparable ones should be destroyed, an act of desecration abhorred by some old members, who promptly hid the original standards until the day Hobo left. But in addition to encouraging the writing of a history of the Hospital, Hobo did much else to preserve the fabric of the place which, in the course of time, met with unstinted approval. Quite the most touching memorial lives in the memories of the Pensioners who knew him best and whose eyes light up at the mention of his name.

So there were times when, in a minor key, he struggled against his own generation for improvements to the Royal Hospital just as he had struggled throughout the whole of his army career to promote more weighty affairs. Automatically, in the search for receptive minds which cared for the future and were not bound by the past, his thoughts reached across to the next generations, gathering young people round him in the same manner

1. There was inbuilt resistance to change—Hobart once remarking that the Pensioners were even more reactionary than the old Army Council.

as he had once selected a young staff. To the Royal Hospital came the medical student friends of his daughter, herself an aspiring doctor. Amidst the cobwebs of venerable tradition gusts of unfledged ideas took wing, the students finding in the general's mentality and outlook the image of a man twenty years his junior, while Grizell began to suspect that her boy friends found the attraction of her father greater than her own.

Clearly he abided by Dean Swift's Resolutions:

Not to keep young company unless they reely desire it.

Not to be peevish or morose, or suspicious.

Not to scorn present Ways, or Wits, or Fashions, or Men, or War, etc.

Not to tell the same story over and over to the same people.

Not to neglect decency, or cleenliness, for fear of falling into Nastyness.

Not to talk much, nor of myself.

Not to be over severe with young People, but give allowances for their youthfull follyes and weeknesses.

Not to be influenced by or give ear to knavish tatling servants or others.

Not to be too free of advice, nor trouble any but those that desire it.

Not to boast of my former beauty or strength, or favour with Ladyes, etc.

Not to be positive or opiniative.

Not to set up for observing all these Rules, for fear I should observe none.

remarking to Sir John Evetts: 'If I can keep any of these Resolutions (except the last) I'll be glad.'

For the Royal Tank Regiment he toiled endlessly, every spare moment given to it, and its welfare. The affairs of the Royal Armoured Corps Benevolent Fund received exhaustive attention, no application for help being dismissed until every aspect had been investigated in full; but if the day-to-day tasks absorbed abundant energy, so too did the future. Throughout his career he had pestered his staff, rewarding their diligence and loyalty by guiding their steps thereafter, and they now repaid his perspicacity by attaining heights which had eluded their mentor. For

Crocker, a one-time brigade major, became Adjutant General in 1950; Birks finished the war as a major-general; Duncan became Director of the R.A.C.; and of the wartime principal staff officers Brown rose to brigadier before retiring for reasons of health, Rory O'Connor rose to lieutenant-general, and Jolly became Quarter-Master-General of the Army. Casting around after the war, Hobart judged, amongst others, his own nephew, Patrick, and Michael Carver as candidates for high rank, having acted often as a sort of foster-father to the former in Charles Hobart's absences from England. To both Patrick Hobart and Carver he extended advice and encouragement, seeking to widen their already wide horizons by protracted discussion on almost every subject under the sun—always, as Carver says, looking to the present and the future in relation to the past, but never falling into idle reminiscence, except to appeal to them to lead and provoke, but not to fall into his own errors by fighting so hard against authority that they erected a wall of resistance to every move. Once again his selection has proved well. Patrick Hobart became a Major-General and Director of Military Operations in the Army Department; Carver a Field Marshal and Chief of the Defence Staff.

Only in one matter did he search diligently in the past, continuing the task commenced by Broad in sponsoring the production of an R.T.R. history in conjunction with its author, Liddell Hart. His eyes would light up when talk turned to it, for he dreamed of a work far outranging the scope of a conventional regimental chronicle of heroic acts set amidst a succession of events. To him this history aimed at being more than just a study in the art of war and the story of the R.T.R.; but above all the story of tanks and the evolution of the Armoured Idea. Times there were when his resolution wavered in the face of financial conflicts and as the years passed, a closer inclination to the need for regimental reminiscence at the expense of pure study and led to more rows with Liddell Hart than had ever arisen earlier. History usually won, but at times his remorseless search for perfection tried the patience of those he co-opted to rewrite various episodes and stretched goodwill to the limit. The work went forward slowly and painstakingly, and it is sad that he did not live to see published what grew to be a classic amongst regimental histories—*The Tanks*.

As a man enters the evening of his life he will as often as not seek tranquillity and examine the beliefs which are the heritage of civilisation, seeking peace of mind in religious salvation. Hobart never relinquished his grip on life and only temporised when his health allowed no other course. He respected those for whom religion gave a true faith, understanding the need that men have for this comfort, but for himself he had evolved a faith of his own. Duncan remembers many a discussion while engaged on the sort of perambulation Hobart habitually took round a garden.

> It was always difficult arguing with him. For one thing, he was infinitely better read on the subject than I, for another he wasn't prepared to accept faith as a reasonable end to an argument. He demanded proof—the one thing which one cannot give.

In rejecting the traditional solution to any problem if reason moved against it, he stayed true to himself while accepting tradition if it gave positive assistance in furthering an end. In his opinion the English public school system had failed to keep pace with the needs of a technological age—it schooled youth for the past and did not educate them in the new values of the present. But he conceded that possession of a public school 'ticket' gave a child a start in life's race since it opened gates to so many careers which might otherwise be closed.

Politically his views coalesced slightly left of centre, but here too he had reservations. He respected the ability of the post-war Labour leaders and mistrusted the Conservatives in no small part because under their rule so many of his own misfortunes had been manifest. But the Socialist ideology failed to possess him in full, for as he wrote:

> All our lives we've been told 'It is more difficult for a rich man to enter the Kingdom . . .'. But it is one of the things that mankind can't realise. Especially when he sees the wretchedness of poverty and unemployment: and the continual uncertainty and lack of security, and fear, fear of destitution.

And yet I am still convinced that that fear—that sharp insistent necessity to keep tuned up, that struggle—is an essential of life.

And if we achieve Security without Effort we may be thrusting our fellows down an invisible slope of degeneracy.

Written in 1945, that is a solemn thought today.

*   *   *   *   *

Very rarely did Hobart ruminate on his accomplishments, and if he did it was only to savour some hard fought battle for an improvement which still smouldered from lack of fulfilment and the need for further attack. Failure was not a cause for complaint because, to him, it was transient, not brought about by hard luck but acting only as a spur to redoubled efforts.

The test of greatness in a General in 99 per cent of cases is gauged by triumph or defeat in battle, the measure of his success shown in the matching of wits against foes of comparable finesse and ability. Very few win laurels from radically altering the 'normal' in their own lifetime without at the same time leaving an indelible mark on history's battle pages.

Victory came to Cromwell through a prolonged course in the organisation, training and leadership of men, yet the fame of the professional martial strength of the Ironsides might be forgotten were it not for Cromwell's victories in battle. Defeat at Corunna in no way robs Moore of his greatest glory—the revitalisation of the training of British soldiers by new humanitarian, intelligent methods in direct contrast with those of the rest of the Army in his day. The perpetual influence of these two great men, making full and improved use of new weapons and a higher intelligence, is sealed on the battlefield. Apart from being men of striking personal originality, they had the wit, personality and drive to convert new ideas into action despite the reaction of conservatives.

The Tank Idea was no more Hobart's than the idea of All-Armoured formations. As part of a team he took a place amongst the leaders of the Armoured Idea and as one after another of his colleagues drifted, or were pushed aside, he found himself practically alone and exposed in a silent fight, where his greatness became marked by persistence. His personality drove men, often against their better judgement and natural inclinations, to adopt new positions contrary to the easier doctrines of the majority. So compelling his enthusiasm, so logical his arguments and so sincere were his beliefs that a permanent impression marked all who served with him. This was the pattern dreamed of and etched by Fuller, Liddell Hart, Lindsay, Broad and Martel but converted into mass produced hardware by Hobart. Desert Rats and Black Bulls owed their skills to Hobart: the success of every assault by specialised armour was Hobart's battlefield victory, even though the public credit goes to others. That much is visible—what cannot be seen or calculated is his influence on the minds of the men who conducted the last campaigns, on Brooke, Eisenhower, Bradley, Montgomery and many another who became exposed to his advice. Who can measure the whole extent of Hobart's contribution to final victory?

To this day his valediction is quoted by every unit of the Royal Armoured Corps and in many of the other armies of the world which frankly copies the British example. It can be observed in the reality of all-armoured tracked formations; it can be heard on the radio in the slick, often vituperative conversations, officer to officer (a technique still not practised by every army); it can be measured by the accuracy and reliability in movement of British armoured forces and the image of tank officers working alongside their men in their efforts to achieve the highest possible standard of maintenance.

There can be no discussion of the development of tanks without consideration of Hobart and, because of this, his ability as strategist and tactician has passed from view. There are some who hold that, because Hobart spent so much time immersed in experimentation, he would have continued to experiment in the face of the enemy with an incommensurate loss of lives. It is suggested that he might at best have been capable of Commanding a Corps, and that above that his judgement would not have been as cool and detached as demanded at rarified heights. Such is the opinion of no less a person than Field Marshal Montgomery—and it is probable that on this subject Hobart would have agreed with his brother-in-law. Yet Hobart never consciously displayed carelessness of men's lives, and thereby he demonstrates that essential humanism which generated the principal part of his charm. Personally ambitious he certainly was—and he could be selfish—but when it came to a choice between his career and a cause, the career went to hazard and, if necessary, eventual sacrifice. He was unique and unforgettable and has left an indelible mark on history. For these reasons Hobart was great.

*   *   *   *   *

In 1955 they found he was suffering from cancer, not a fatal outbreak in itself, but the side-effects, when added together, engineered a decline which could not be arrested. In the midst of physical failure he hung to every shred of life, striving for as long as he could to serve the community, acting as Treasurer of the Red Cross Society at Farnham, where he had moved in 1953 after leaving the Royal Hospital, and as a highly active Governor of Reed's School. To his delight Grizell married and gave birth to her first child, enabling him to savour the delights of being a grandparent in the shadow of his last days.

In August 1956 plans were afoot at the British Broadcasting Corporation for General Sir Brian Horrocks to present a television programme about D-Day in which Hobart was to speak for four minutes on the part played by specialised armour, but his part had to be described by another for the rate at which he sank proved too fast for the programme planners.

Not by one inch did he give ground to pain unless pain wrested it from him by brute strength. His letters are written in the firm compact hand of old, exhibiting their customary startling clarity of thought and observation of detail. In letters to Grizell he discusses his disease with composed objectivity, studying its effects on him as if he were a machine under trial, comments on the political scene with caustic wit and revels in lambasting the Television which, in fact, gave him more pleasure than he admitted.

We had begun to wonder, [he wrote in January 1957] whether our flagging interest in TV was due to our senile impatience : waning of novelty : or—could it possibly be the extremely poor quality of the programmes. . . . I don't know whether you had time to read the Lords debate on TV, but was amused by Lord Lucas'. 'It isn't advertisements I object to, but the frightful items in between'

Towards the end Hobart's mind turned strongly to contemplate those objects of beauty which had inspired in him the greatest tranquillity throughout his life; concerning the meaning of modern art, he reduced his thoughts to a final, all-embracing definition. Alas, the original document is lost, but we can be sure that it represented the writer's catholic taste and everlasting appreciation of interpretation and the most deep-seated emotion. Indeed, the approach had such impact that a friend copied and sent it to Bernard Berenson, the world-famous authority on art. And to Hobart, in response, Berenson wrote :

There is not a word in this paper that I would not be proud to sign. It expresses exactly what I have to say on the subject and does it, I feel, ever so much better than I could.

a letter to be treasured for ever, he demanded, because it meant more to Hobart than any of his other honours.

Picture Hobo living fiercely combative at Bull Lodge in Farnham until the end came on the 19th February 1957, always a step ahead of his countrymen, mentally, if in no other way, fighting to the last, and then like any other tank man, coming to harbour at night to make ready for the next battle.

BIBLIOGRAPHY

The Indian Sappers and Miners. Lieutenant-Colonel E. W. C. Sands

Operations against the Mohmands 1908. (Indian Government)

The Royal Visit to India, 1911–12. Hon. John Fortescue (Macmillan)

Queen Mary. James Pope-Hennessy (Allen & Unwin)

'Report on the Survey and Emarcation of the Delhi Durbar and the Fire Precaution Arrangements. Lieutenant P. C. S. Hobart (*The Royal Engineers Journal,* February 1914)

Sheila. P. C. S. Hobart (Blackwoods)

The Escape. P. C. S. Hobart (Blackwoods)

In the Clouds above Baghdad. Lieutenant-Colonel J. E. Tennant (Published by Cecil Palmer)

Official History of the War, Mesopotamian Campaign, Vols. I to IV. (H.M.S.O.)

Critical Study of the Campaign in Mesopotamia up to April 1917. By officers of the Staff College, Quetta, General Staff H.Q., India

Operations in Waziristan, 1919–20. (H.M.S.O.)

Official History of Operations on the NW Frontier of India, 1920–35. (Government of India Press)

General Lord Rawlinson's despatch covering operations in Waziristan, 1st April to 31st December 1921. (*London Gazette,* 1st December, 1922)

Vickers—A History. J. D. Scott (Weidenfeld & Nicolson)

Wavell, Scholar and Soldier. J. Connell (Collins)

Auchinleck. J. Connell (Cassell)

An Outspoken Soldier. Giffard le Q. Martel (Praed)

Eight Years Overseas. H. Maitland Wilson (Hutchinson)

The Tanks, Vol. I and II. B. H. Liddell Hart (Cassell)

History of the Second World War: Design and Development of Weapons. M. M. Postan, D. Hay, J. D. Scott (H.M.S.O.)

Memoirs, Vol. I and II. B. H. Liddell Hart (Cassell)

Panzer Leader. H. Guderian (Michael Joseph)

The Other Side of the Hill. B. H. Liddell Hart (Cassell)

Armour. Richard Ogerkiewicz (Stevens)

Montgomery. A Moorehead (Hamish Hamilton)

The Desert Rats. H. L. Verney (Hutchinson)

The Ironside Diaries, 1937–40. Edited R. Macleod (Constable)

History of the 79th Armoured Division. (Private)

Taurus Pursuant. (Private)

The First and the Last. J. P. D. Stirling (Art and Edn Publishers Ltd.)

The Turn of the Tide. A. Bryant (Collins)

Triumph in the West. A. Bryant (Collins)

Operation Victory. F. de Guingand (Hodder & Stoughton)

Three Years with Eisenhower. Harry C. Butcher (Heinemann)

Organisation and Equipment for War. Ronald Weeks (Cambridge University Press)

Crusade in Europe. D. D. Eisenhower (Heinemann)

Memoirs. B. L. Montgomery (Collins)

The Struggle for Europe. C. Wilmot (Collins)

The Second World War. W. S. Churchill (Cassell)

Omaha Beachhead. (U.S. War Department)

Utah Beachhead to Cherbourg. (U.S. War Department)

Flame over Britain. Donald Banks (Low)

History of the 13th/18th Royal Hussars (1922–47). Charles Miller (Chisman Bradshaw)

History of the 70th Tank Battalion. Chester Hall (Private)

INDEX